An Odyssey

An Odyssey

A Father, a Son,
and an Epic

DANIEL MENDELSOHN

ALFRED A. KNOPF
New York
2017

THIS IS A BORZOI BOOK
PUBLISHED BY ALFRED A. KNOPF

Copyright © 2017 by Daniel Mendelsohn

All rights reserved. Published in the United States by Alfred A. Knopf,
a division of Penguin Random House LLC, New York.
Simultaneously published in hardcover in Canada by Signal,
an imprint of McClelland & Stewart, a division of Penguin
Random House Canada Limited, Toronto.

www.aaknopf.com

Knopf, Borzoi Books, and the colophon are registered trademarks
of Penguin Random House LLC.

Permission to reprint previously published material may be found
following the acknowledgments.

Library of Congress Cataloging-in-Publication Data
Names: Mendelsohn, Daniel Adam, 1960– author. |
Mendelsohn, Jay, 1929–2012.
Title: An odyssey : a father, a son, and an epic / Daniel Mendelsohn.
Description: First edition. | New York : Alfred A. Knopf, 2017.
Identifiers: LCCN 2017011844 | ISBN 9780385350594 (hardcover : alk. paper) |
ISBN 9780385350600 (ebook)
Subjects: LCSH: Mendelsohn, Daniel Adam, 1960– | Fathers and sons—
United States—Biography. | Odysseus, King of Ithaca (Mythological
character)—Influence. | Homer. Odyssey—Influence. |
Mendelsohn, Daniel Adam, 1960–Travel—Mediterranean Region. |
Mendelsohn, Jay, 1929–2012–Travel—Mediterranean Region. |
Fathers—United States—Death.
Classification: LCC CT275.M46919 A3 2017 | DDC 306.874/2—dc23
LC record available at https://lccn.loc.gov/2017011844

Jacket art: (waves) Markovka, (meander pattern) spline_x,
(boat) Malysh Falko, all Shutterstock.com
Jacket photographs courtesy of the author

Manufactured in the United States of America
First Edition

For my mother

Author's Note

For the purposes of narrative coherence and in consideration of the privacy of the students in my *Odyssey* seminar and the passengers aboard the "Retracing the *Odyssey*" cruise, names have been changed and a number of details relating to events and characters have been modified.

All translations from Greek and Latin are my own.

PROEM

(Invocation)

———— ⟫⊶⊷⟪ ————

1964–2011

The plot of the *Odyssey* is not long in the telling. A man has been away from home for many years; Poseidon is always on the watch for him; he is all alone. As for the situation at home, his goods are being laid waste by the Suitors, who plot against his son. After a storm-tossed journey, he returns home, where he reveals himself, destroys his enemies, and is saved.

—ARISTOTLE, *Poetics*

One January evening a few years ago, just before the beginning of the spring term in which I was going to be teaching an undergraduate seminar on the *Odyssey*, my father, a retired research scientist who was then aged eighty-one, asked me, for reasons I thought I understood at the time, if he might sit in on the course, and I said yes. Once a week for the next sixteen weeks he would make the trip between the house in the Long Island suburbs where I grew up, a modest split-level in which he still lived with my mother, to the riverside campus of the small college where I teach, which is called Bard. At ten past ten each Friday morning, he would take a seat among the freshmen who were enrolled in the course, seventeen- or eighteen-year-olds not even a quarter his age, and join in the discussion of this old poem, an epic about long journeys and long marriages and what it means to yearn for home.

It was deep winter when that term began, and when my father wasn't trying to persuade me that the poem's hero, Odysseus, wasn't in fact a "real" hero (because, he would say, *he's a liar and he cheated on his wife!*), he was worrying a great deal about the weather: the snow on the windshield, the sleet on the roads, the ice on the walkways. He was afraid of falling, he said, his vowels still marked by his Bronx childhood: *fawling*. Because of his fear of falling, we would make our way gingerly along the narrow asphalt paths that led to the building where the class met, a brick box as studiedly inoffensive as a Marriott, or up the little walkway to the steep-gabled house at the edge of campus that for a few days each week was my home. To avoid having to make the three-hour trip twice in one day, he would often spend the night in that house, sleeping in the extra bedroom that serves as my study, stretched out on a narrow daybed that had been my childhood bed—a low wooden bed that my father built for me with his own hands when I was old enough to leave my crib. Now there was something about this bed that only my father and I knew: it was made out of a door, a cheap hollow door to which he'd screwed four sturdy wooden legs, securing them with metal brackets that are as solidly attached today as they were fifty years ago when he first joined the steel to the wood. This bed, with its amusing little secret, unknowable unless you hauled off the mattress and saw the paneled door beneath, was the bed on which my father would sleep that spring semester of the *Odyssey* seminar, not long before he became ill and my brothers and sister and I had to start fathering my father, anxiously watching him as he slept fitfully in a series of enormous, elaborately mechanized contraptions that hardly seemed like beds at all, whirring noisily as they inclined and declined, like cranes. But that came later.

It used to amuse my father that for a long time I divided my time among so many different places: this house on the rural campus; the mellow old home in New Jersey where my boys and their mother lived and where I would spend long weekends; my apartment in New York City, which, as time passed and my life expanded, first to include a family and then to teach, had become little more than a pit stop between train trips. You're always on the road, my father would sometimes say at the end of a phone conversation, and as he said the word "road" I could picture him shaking his head from side to side in gentle bewilderment. For nearly all of his life my father lived in one house: the one he moved into a month before I was born, and which he left for the last time one January day in 2012, a year to the day after he started my class on the *Odyssey*.

The *Odyssey* course ran from late January to early May. A week or so after it ended, I happened to be on the phone with my friend Froma, a Classics scholar who had been my mentor in graduate school and had lately enjoyed hearing my periodic reports about Daddy's progress over the course of the *Odyssey* seminar. At some point in the conversation she mentioned a Mediterranean cruise that she'd taken a couple of years before, called "Retracing the *Odyssey*." You should do it! Froma exclaimed. After this semester, after teaching the *Odyssey* to your father, how could you *not* go? Not everyone agreed: when I e-mailed a travel agent friend of mine, a brisk blond Ukrainian called Yelena, to ask her what she thought, her response came back within a minute: "AVOID THEME CRUISES AT ALL COSTS!" But Froma had been my teacher, and I was still in the habit of obeying her. The next morning, when I called my father and told him about my conversation with her, he made a noncommittal noise and said, Let's see.

We went online to look at the cruise line's website. As I slumped on the sofa in my apartment in New York, a little worn out by another week of traveling up and down Amtrak's Northeast Corridor, staring at my laptop, I could picture him sitting in the crowded home office that had once been the bedroom I shared with my older brother, Andrew: the simple low beds that he'd built and the plain oak desk long since replaced by particle-board desks from Staples whose slick black surfaces were already bowed by the weight of the computer equipment on top, the desktops and monitors and laptops and printers and scanners, the looping cables and swags of cords and winking lights giving it all the air of a hospital room. The cruise, we read, would follow the mythic hero's convoluted, decade-long itinerary as he made his way home from the Trojan War, plagued by shipwrecks and monsters. It would begin at Troy, the site of which is located in what is now Turkey, and end on Itháki, a small island in the western Greek sea that purports to be Ithaca, the place Odysseus called home. "Retracing the *Odyssey*" was an "educational" cruise, and although he was contemptuous of anything that struck him as a needless luxury—cruises and sightseeing and vacations—my father was a great believer in education. And so a few weeks later, in June, fresh from our recent immersion in the text of the Homeric epic, we took the cruise, which lasted ten days in all, one day for each year of Odysseus' long journey home.

During our voyage we saw nearly everything we'd hoped to see, the strange new landscapes and the debris of the various civilizations that had occupied them. We saw Troy, which to our untrained eye looked like nothing so much as a sand castle that's been kicked in by a malicious child, its legendary heights reduced by now to a random agglomeration of columns and huge stones blindly facing the sea below. We saw the Neolithic monoliths on the island of Gozo, off Malta, where there is also a cave that is said to have been the home of Calypso, the beautiful nymph on whose island Odysseus was stranded for seven years during his travels, and who offered him immortality if only he would forsake his wife for her, but he refused. We saw the elegantly severe columns of a Doric temple left unfinished, for reasons impossible to know, by some Greeks of the classical era in Segesta, on Sicily— the island where, toward the end of their homeward voyage, Odysseus' crew ate the forbidden meat of the cattle that belong to the sun god Hyperion, a sin for which they all died. We visited the desolate spot on the Campanian coast near Naples that, the ancients believed, was the entrance to Hades, the Land of the Dead—that being another, unexpected stop on Odysseus' journey toward home, but perhaps not so unexpected because, after all, we must settle our accounts with the dead before we can get on with our living. We saw fat Venetian forts, squatting on parched Peloponnesian meadows like frogs on a heath after a fire, near Pílos in southern Greece, Homer's *Pylos*, a town where, according to the poet, a kindly if somewhat long-winded old king named Nestor is said to have reigned and where he once entertained the young son of Odysseus, who had come there in search of information about his long-lost father: which is how the *Odyssey* begins, a son gone in search of an absent parent. And of course we saw the sea, too, with its many faces, glass smooth and stone rough, at certain times blithely open and at others tightly inscrutable, sometimes of a weak blue so clear that you could see straight down to the sea urchins at the bottom, as spiked and expectant as mines left over from some war whose causes and combatants no one any longer remembers, and sometimes of an impenetrable purple that is the color of the wine that we refer to as red but the Greeks call *black*.

We saw all those things during our travels, all those places, and learned a great deal about the peoples who had lived there. My father, in whom a crabbed cautiousness about the dangers of going pretty much anywhere had given rise to certain notorious sayings that his five children loved to mock (*the most dangerous place in the world is a parking lot, people drive like maniacs!*), came to relish his stint as a Mediterranean tourist. But in the end, as the result of a string of irritating events beyond the control of the captain or his crew, which I will describe presently, we were unable to make the last stop on the itinerary. And so we never saw Ithaca, the place to which Odysseus strove so famously to return; never reached what may be the best-known destination in literature. But then, the *Odyssey* itself, filled as it is with sudden mishaps and surprising detours, schools its hero in disappointment, and teaches its audience to expect the unexpected. For this reason, our not reaching Ithaca may have been the most Odyssean aspect of our educational cruise.

Expect the unexpected. Late in the autumn that same year, a few months after my father and I returned home from our trip—which, I would sometimes joke with Daddy, because we had never reached our goal, could still be considered to be incomplete, could be thought of as ongoing—my father fell.

There is a term that comes up when you study ancient Greek literature, occurring equally in both imaginative and historical works, used to describe the remote origins of some disaster: *arkhê kakôn*, "the beginning of the bad things." Most often the "bad things" in question are wars. The historian Herodotus, for instance, trying to determine the cause of a great war between the Greeks and the Persians that took place in the 480s B.C., says that a decision taken by the Athenians to send ships to some allies many years before the actual opening of hostilities was

the *arkhê kakôn* of that conflict. (Herodotus was writing in the late 400s
B.C., approximately three and a half centuries after Homer composed
his poems about the Trojan War—which, according to some ancient
scholars, had taken place three centuries before Homer lived.) But *arkhê
kakôn* can be used to describe the origins of other kinds of events, too.
The tragic playwright Euripides, for instance, uses it in one of his dramas
to describe an unhappy marriage, an ill-fated union that set in motion
a sequence of events whose disastrous outcome furnishes the climax of
his play.

Both war and bad marriages come together in the most famous *arkhê
kakôn* of them all: the moment when a prince of Troy called Paris stole
away with a Greek queen called Helen, another man's wife. So, according to the myth, began the Trojan War, the decade-long conflict waged
by the Greeks to win back the wayward Helen and punish the inhabitants
of Troy. (One of the reasons the war took so long to prosecute was that
Troy was surrounded by impregnable walls; these finally yielded, after a
ten-year siege, only because of a trick—the Trojan Horse—devised by the
Odyssey's notoriously crafty hero.) Whatever its basis in remote history
may have been—there had indeed been an ancient city located on the
Turkish site that my father and I visited, and it was destroyed violently,
but beyond that we can only guess—the mythic cataclysm that resulted
from Helen's adultery with Paris has furnished poets and playwrights and
novelists with material for the past three and a half millennia: countless
deaths on both sides, the shocking sack of the great city, the enslave-
ments and humiliations and infanticides and suicides, and then, finally,
the wretchedly prolonged homecomings of those Greeks clever or lucky
enough to survive the war itself.

Arkhê kakôn. The second word in that phrase is a form of the
Greek *kakos*, "bad," which survives in the English "*caco*phony," a "bad
sound"—a reasonable way to describe the noise made by women as their
young children are thrown over the walls of a defeated city, which is one
of the bad things that happened after Troy fell. The first word in the
phrase, *arkhê*, which means "beginning"—sometimes it has the sense

of "early" or "ancient"—also makes its presence felt in certain English words, for instance "archetype," which literally means "first model." An archetype is the earliest instance of a thing, so ancient in its authority that it sets an example for all time. Anything can be an archetype: a weapon, a building, a poem.

For my father, the *arkhê kakôn* was a minor accident, a single false step that he took in the parking lot of a California supermarket where he and my brother Andrew had gone to get groceries for a long-awaited family reunion. All five of his children were coming with their families to join him and Mother for a long weekend at Andrew and Ginny's place in the Bay Area; all were traveling great distances to get there. My parenting partner, Lily, and our two boys and I were flying in from New Jersey, my younger brother Matt and his wife and daughter were coming from DC, my youngest brother, Eric, from New York City, our sister, Jennifer, and her husband and small sons from Baltimore. But before any of us got there, my father fell. Like some unlucky character in a myth, he had unwittingly fulfilled his own glum warnings in a way no one could have guessed: for him, a parking lot had turned out to be the most dangerous place of all, but not because of the cars, the people who drive like maniacs. He and Andrew had finished loading the car with groceries, and as Daddy was returning the empty cart he tripped on a metal stanchion and fell. *He couldn't get up*, Andrew told me later, *he just sat there looking dazed.* By the time we all arrived my father was confined to a wheelchair. He'd fractured a bone in his pelvis, an injury from which it would take him months to recover; but of course we knew he would recover, since, as everyone used to say, *Jay is tough!*

And he was indeed tough, mastering first the wheelchair and then the walker and then the cane. But the fall he'd feared for so long set in motion a series of complications whose outcome was grossly disproportionate to the mishap that had triggered them, the hairline fracture leading to a small blood clot, the blood clot requiring blood thinners, the blood thinners causing, ultimately, a massive stroke that left my father helpless, unrecognizable: unable to breathe on his own, to open his eyes, to move, to speak. At a certain point we were told it would soon be over, but he fought his way back yet again. He was *tough*, after all, and for a brief period he was well enough to converse about ball games and Mother and a certain Bach piece that he was eager to practice on his electronic keyboard although, he said, he knew it was too hard for him. This last period was one in which (as we would say later on, retelling the remarkable story over and over as if to convince ourselves that it was all real) "his old self" had reappeared: a term that raises questions first posed, as it happens, in the *Odyssey*, a work whose hero must, at the end of his decades-long absence from home, prove to those who once knew him that he is still "his old self."

But which is the true self? the *Odyssey* asks, and how many selves might a man have? As I learned the year my father took my *Odyssey* course and we retraced the journeys of its hero, the answers can be surprising.

All classical epics begin with what scholars call a *proem*: the introductory lines that announce to the audience what the epic is about—what will be the scope of its action, the identities of its characters, the nature of its themes. These proems, while formal in tone, perhaps a bit stiffer than the stories that follow, are never very long. Some are almost disingenuously terse, such as the proem of the *Iliad*, an epic poem of fifteen thousand six hundred and ninety-three lines devoted to a single episode that takes place in the final year of the Trojan War: a bitter quarrel between two Greek warriors—the commander-in-chief, Agamemnon, son of Atreus, and his greatest warrior, Achilles, son of Peleus—that threatened the mission to destroy Troy and avenge the abduction of Helen. (For Agamemnon, the king of Mycenae, the war is personal: Helen's cuckolded husband, Menelaus, the king of Sparta, is his younger brother. Achilles, for his part, fights only for glory. "The Trojans never did any harm to *me*," he bitterly remarks.) In the end, the two warriors reconcile and their mission is successful—although it should be said that the destruction of Troy, the ruse of the Trojan Horse, the nighttime ambush, the slaughter of the city's warriors and enslavement of its women and children, the razing of its once-impregnable walls, an outcome familiar to the Greek audiences of the epic from their real-life wars and made famous through many literary and artistic representations of the Fall of Troy, is not actually narrated in the course of the *Iliad*'s fifteen-thousand-some-odd lines. Epics, despite their great length, are in fact tightly focused on whatever theme is announced in their proems. The proem of the *Iliad* is concerned simply with the quarrel between the two Greek warriors, its causes and effects, and what it reveals about the characters' understanding of honor and heroism and duty and death. But because epic has a sophisticated array of narrative devices—because it can hint, and foreshadow, and even flash forward into the future—the *Iliad* leaves us in no doubt as to how things will end.

The proem of the *Iliad* consists of seven lines:

Rage! Sing the rage, O goddess, of Peleus' son, Achilles—
devastating rage, which put countless pains upon the Greeks
and hurled to Hades many sturdy souls of
heroes, while making their bodies into pickings for dogs
and all manner of birds, as Zeus' plan was achieving its fulfillment—
from the moment when first the two stood forth in strife,
Atreus' son, the lord of men, and Achilles, a man like a god.

In themselves, these seven lines tell us fairly little about the plot of the epic. We know simply that there is rage, death, and a divine plan; Agamemnon and Achilles. The reference to Zeus' plan is arrestingly coy: what exactly is it? How are the rage and the pain and the dogs and birds helping to fulfill it? We aren't told right away, and there's no doubt that part of the reason the poet hints without explaining is to make us keep listening—to make us find out what this plan is. But it's also hard not to feel that the reference to a "plan" is slyly pointed: for it implies that the poet, at least, has a plan, even though at this early point we have only the dimmest idea of what it might be. In epic, we need the proem because it reassures us, at the very moment we set out upon what might look like a vast ocean of words, that this expanse is not a "formless void" (like the one with which another great story, Genesis, begins) but a *route*, a path that will take us someplace worth going.

"Someplace worth going" is a good way to summarize the great preoccupation of the *Odyssey*, which in certain ways is a sequel to the *Iliad*. A poem of twelve thousand one hundred and ten lines, it takes as its subject the convoluted and adventure-filled return home of one of the Greeks who took part in the war against Troy. This particular Greek is Odysseus, the ruler of a small island kingdom called Ithaca; he is a trickster about whose ruses and ploys, some successful, others not, the Greeks loved to tell tales. One of the most popular of these legends concerns the run-up to the Trojan War. We are told that when the Greeks came asking Odysseus to join their coalition in the war against Troy, Odysseus—"a clever man," as an ancient commentator on the *Odyssey* drily observed, "who perceived how vast the conflict would be"—tried to avoid conscription by pretending to be crazy: in the presence of the Greek scout he yoked an ass and an ox together and began to plow salt into his fields. Familiar with his reputation, the scout took Telemachus, Odysseus' infant son, and placed the baby on the soil in front of the plow; when Odysseus swerved to avoid his child, the scout concluded that he couldn't be all that crazy, and took him away to the war.

The conflict was indeed vast—but so are Odysseus' trials during his protracted homeward voyage. For he is continually harassed and delayed, shipwrecked and castaway, by the machinations of the angry sea god, Poseidon, whom Odysseus has offended (for reasons we learn later in the poem) and whom the hero will learn to appease only after he finally gets home. Odysseus' far-flung wanderings over ten years as he struggles to return to his wife, Penelope, and their son—to get back to his family and home—stand in stark contrast to the immobility of the Greeks as they sat before the walls of Troy during the ten years of their war. So, too, does the mutual devotion of the couple at the heart of the *Odyssey*—Odysseus, whose allegiance to the wife he hasn't seen in twenty years withstands the seductive attentions of various goddesses and nymphs whom he encounters on his way home, and Penelope, who remains true to him in the face of the aggressive attentions of the Suitors, the dozens of young men who have taken up residence in her palace, intent on marrying her—stand in sharply ironic contrast to the adulterous affair between Paris and Helen that was the cause of the war in the first place: the *arkhê kakôn*.

Most classicists agree that the proem of the *Odyssey* consists of its first ten lines:

> *A man—track his tale for me, Muse, the twisty one who*
> *wandered widely, once he'd sacked Troy's holy citadel;*
> *he saw the cities of many men and knew their minds,*
> *and suffered deeply in his soul upon the sea*
> *try as he might to protect his life and the day of his men's return;*
> *but he could not save his men, although he longed to;*
> *for they perished through their wanton recklessness,*
> *fools who ate of the cattle of Hyperion,*
> *the Sun; and so they lost the day of their return.*
> *From some point or another, Daughter of Zeus, tell us the tale.*

It is an odd way to begin. After modestly introducing his subject as, simply, "a man"—Odysseus' name isn't mentioned—the poet seems to wander away from this "man" to other men: that is, the men whom he had commanded and who, this proem tells us, died through their own recklessness. Just as the man himself had widely wandered, so does the proem.

Perhaps inevitably, in the case of this meandering work about a meandering and unexpectedly prolonged homecoming, some scholars have argued that the proem of the *Odyssey* itself strays: that, in fact, it runs for the first *twenty-one* lines of the poem. The eleven additional lines describe the circumstances in which Odysseus' divine patroness, Athena, the goddess of wisdom, urges her father, Zeus, king of the gods, to bring Odysseus home at last despite the implacable opposition of the enraged sea god:

> *. . . tell us the tale.*
> *Now all the others—those who'd fled steep death—*
> *were home at last, safe from war and sea;*
> *but he alone, yearning for home and wife,*
> *was detained—by the Lady Calypso, most heavenly of goddesses,*
> *in her hollow caves: she longed to marry him.*
> *But then the time came in the course of the whirling years*
> *when the gods devised a way to bring him home*
> *to Ithaca; but even there he was hardly free of woe,*
> *even when he was back among his people. All the gods felt pity*
> *for him except Poseidon, who raged hotly against*
> *Odysseus, that godlike man, until he reached his homeland.*

And so, again very much like Odysseus, the proem not only wanders, but may wander on longer than it had intended to.

The *Iliad* and the *Odyssey* are the most famous epics in the Western tradition, but they are far from being the only ones to come down to us from Greek and Roman days. The landscape of classical Greek and Roman literature, from the two Homeric poems in the eighth century B.C. to Christian verse epics composed in the fifth century A.D., was dotted with epic poems, which reared up from those landscapes much the way that Troy must have risen from its smooth plain above the sea, seemingly unassailable and permanent. Even when the poems themselves were lost over the millennia, as many of them were, the proems often survived, precisely because of their gripping succinctness.

A proem could memorialize other poems. Take, for example, the proem of Virgil's *Aeneid*, which knowingly alludes to the opening lines of both the *Iliad* and *Odyssey*:

Wars and a man I sing: the first who came
from Troy to Italy and to Latium's shores,
exiled by Fate: tossed about on land and sea
by the violence of the gods above, all because
of the ever-wakeful wrath of savage Juno;
he suffered greatly too in war, so he could found
his city and bring his gods to Latium, whence arose
the Latin people, the Alban fathers, and the walls of lofty Rome.

The *Aeneid* revisits the world of Homer's poems but radically shifts their point of view to that of the losers: it retails the adventures of Aeneas, one of the few Trojans to survive the Greek obliteration of Troy. After escaping the burning wreckage of his city with (this is one of the epic's most famous and touching details) his father strapped to his back and his young son in tow, Aeneas first undergoes a series of elaborate wanderings (meanderings that remind us of the *Odyssey*) before he settles in Italy, the land that has been promised to him as the homeland of the new state that he will found, where he must then fight a series of grim battles against the locals (warfare that reminds us of the *Iliad*) in order to establish himself and his people forever. While he lacks the cruel glamour of the *Iliad*'s Achilles or the seductive slyness of Odysseus, Aeneas does embody a dogged sense of filial obligation, a quality much prized in Roman culture and signaled by the Latin adjective most often used of Virgil's hero: *pius*, which means not "pious," as might seem natural to an English-speaker's eye, but "dutiful." The proem of the *Aeneid* is seven lines long; the first of these, in which the poet announces that he will sing of "wars and a man," *arma virumque*, is itself a nod to both the *Iliad*, which is above all about "wars" or "arms," *arma*, and to the *Odyssey*, whose own first line, as we know, announces that it is about "a man."

A proem, therefore, can not only summarize its own action, look into its own future, and forecast, in miniature, what is to come, but can nod gratefully backward in time at the earlier epics, the *archetypes*, to which it is indebted.

When I was growing up, there was a story my father liked to tell about a long journey he and I once made, a story that hinged on a riddle. *How*, my father would inevitably ask at some point as he told this story, not quite looking you in the eye while he talked—a habit my mother disliked and about which she would sometimes scold him because, she would say, *it makes you look like a liar*, a reproof that amused us children because one thing that everyone knew about my father was that he never lied— *How*, my father would ask when he told this story, *can you travel great distances without getting anywhere?* Because I was a character in this story, I knew the answer, and because I was only a child when my father started telling this story, I naturally enjoyed spoiling his telling of it by giving the answer away before he reached the end of his tale. But my father was a patient man, and although he could be severe, he rarely scolded me.

The answer to the riddle was this: *If you travel in circles*. My father, who was trained as a mathematician, knew all about circles, and I suppose that if I had cared to ask him he would have shared with me what he knew about them; but because I have always been made nervous by arithmetic and geometries and quadratics, unforgiving systems that allow for no shadings or embellishments, no evasions or lies, I had an aversion even then to math. Anyway, his esteem for circles was not the reason he liked to tell this story. The reason he liked to tell it was that it showed what kind of boy I had once been; although now that I am grown up and have children of my own, I think that it is a story about him.

A *long journey he and I once made*. In the interests of precision, a quality my father much admired, I should say that the trip we made together was a homecoming. The story starts with a son who goes to rescue his father, but, as sometimes happens when travel is involved, the journey home ended up eclipsing the drama that had set it in motion.

The son in question was my father. It was the mid-1960s, and so he would have been in his mid-thirties; his father, in his mid-seventies. I must have been four or so; at any rate, I know that I wasn't yet old enough to go to school, because that's why I was the one chosen to accompany my father. It was January: Andrew, four years older than I, was in the second grade, and Matt, two years younger, was still in diapers, and my mother stayed home with them. *Why don't I take Daniel, Marlene?* I remember my father saying, a remark that made an impression because until then I don't think I'd ever done anything alone with him. Andrew was the one who went places with Daddy and did things with him, handed him tools as he lay on the concrete floor of the garage under the big black Chevy, stood next to him in front of the workbench in the basement as they pored over model airplane instructions. I thought of myself, then, as wholly my mother's child. But Andrew was in school, and so I went with Daddy down to Florida when my grandmother called and said, Come quickly.

In those days my father's parents lived on the ninth floor of a high-rise apartment building in Miami Beach overlooking the water—a building, as it happened, that was located next door to the one in which my mother's father and his wife lived. I doubt that the two couples spent a lot of time with each other. My mother's father, *Grandpa*, was garrulous and funny, a great storyteller and wheedler; vain and domineering, he devoted a good deal of thought each day to the selection of the clothes that he was going to wear and to the state of his gastrointestinal tract. Although he had only one child, my mother, he'd had four wives—and, as my father once hissed at me, a *mistress*. The average length of these marriages was eleven years.

My father's father, by contrast—Poppy, the object of our traveling that January when I was four—barely spoke at all. Unlike my mother's father, Poppy wasn't given to displays of, or demands for, affection. A small man—at five foot three he was dwarfed by my tall grandmother, Nanny Kay—he always seemed vaguely surprised, on those occasions when we drove to Kennedy Airport to pick up the two of them, when you gave him a welcoming hug. He liked being alone and didn't approve of loud noises. He'd been a union electrician. *You'll hurt the wiring!* he would cry out in his high, slightly hollow voice when we ran around the living room; we would tiptoe for the next fifteen minutes, giggling. He took his modest enjoyments, listening to comedy shows on the radio or fishing in silence off the pier in back of his building, with quiet care—as if he thought that, by being cautious even in his pleasures, he might not draw the attention of the tragic Fury that, we knew, had devastated his youth: the poverty so dire that his father had had to put his seven brothers and sisters in an orphanage, his mother and all those siblings and his first wife, too, all dead by the time he was a young man. These losses were so catastrophic that they'd left him "shell-shocked"—the word I once over-heard Nanny Kay whisper as she gossiped with my mother and aunts under a willow tree one summer afternoon when I was fourteen or so and was eavesdropping nearby. *He was shell-shocked,* Nanny had said as she exhaled the smoke from one of her long cigarettes, explaining to her daughters-in-law why her husband was so quiet, why he didn't like to talk much to his wife, to his sons, to his grandchildren; a habit of silence that, as I knew well, could be passed from generation to generation, like DNA.

For my father, too, liked peace and quiet, liked to find a spot where he could read or watch the ball game without interruption. And no wonder. I'd heard from my mother about how tiny his family's apartment in the Bronx had been, and I'd always imagined that his yearning for peace and quiet was a reaction to that cramped existence: sharing a foldout bed in the living room with his older brother Bobby, who'd been crippled by polio (*I remember the sound as he leaned his iron leg braces against the radiator before we got into bed,* he told me years later, shaking his head), his parents just yards away in the one small bedroom, Poppy listening to Jack Benny on the radio, Nanny smoking and playing solitaire. How had they managed before his oldest brother, Howard, went off and joined the army in 1938? I couldn't imagine . . . And yet since he himself had gone on to have five children, I had to believe that my father also, para-doxically, craved activity and noise and life in his own house. Why else, I sometimes asked myself, would he have had so many kids? Once, when I was talking about all this with Lily—the boys were small, Peter maybe five or six, Thomas, never a good sleeper, tossing restlessly in his crib, muttering little cries as he slept, not yet two—I asked this question about my father out loud. Lily looked at me and said, Well, *you* grew up in a crowded house with lots of siblings, and you wanted to have kids, didn't you? And it was a lot more complicated for you! I grinned, thinking of how it had all begun and how far we'd come: her shy request, when she'd first started thinking of having a child, whether I might want to be some kind of father figure to the baby; how nervous I'd been at first and yet how mesmerized, too, once Peter was born, how increasingly reluctant I'd grown to return to Manhattan after a few days visiting with them in New Jersey; the gradual easing, over months and then years, into a new schedule, half a week in Manhattan, half in New Jersey; and then Thomas' arrival somehow cementing it all. *Your first kid, it feels like a miracle, almost like a surprise,* my father had said when I told him about Thomas. *After that, it's your life.* All that had been five years earlier; now, as I wondered aloud why my father had had so many children, Lily cocked her head to one side. I thought she was listening for Thomas, but she was thinking. It's funny, she said slowly, that you ended up doing just what your father did.

For this reason—because the men in that family didn't talk much to others, didn't share their feelings and dramas the way my mother's relatives did—it seemed strange to me that one day we had to rush down to Florida to be with Poppy, my small, silent grandfather. Only gradually did I perceive the reasons for Nanny's frantic phone call: he was gravely ill. So we went to the airport and got on a plane and then spent a week or so in Florida in the hospital room, waiting, I supposed, for him to die. The hospital bed was screened by a curtain with a pattern of pink and green fish, and the thought that Poppy had to be hidden filled me with terror. I dared not look beyond it. Instead, I sat on an orange plastic chair and I read, or played with my toys. I have no memory of what my father did during all those days at the hospital. Even when his father was well, I knew, they didn't talk much; the point, I somehow understood, was that Daddy was there, that he had come. *Your father is your father,* he told me a decade later when Poppy was really dying, this time in a hospital near

our house on Long Island. Many of my father's pronouncements took this
x is x form, always with the implication that to think otherwise, to admit
that *x* could be anything other than *x*, was to abandon the strict codes
that governed his thinking and held the world in place: *Excellence is
excellence, period;* or *Smart is smart, there's no such thing as being a "bad
test taker."* Your father is your father. Every day during Poppy's quiet final
decline in the summer of 1975, my father would drive to this hospital on
his lunch break, a drive of fifteen minutes or so, and sit eating a sandwich
in silence next to the high bed on which his father lay, seeming to grow
smaller each day, as desiccated and immobile as a mummy, oblivious,
dreaming perhaps of his dead wife and many dead siblings. *Your father is
your father,* Daddy replied when I was fifteen and asked him why, if his
father didn't even know he was there, he kept coming to the hospital.
But that would come later. Now, in Miami Beach in 1964, he was sitting
in the tiny space behind the curtain with the fish, talking quietly with
his mother and waiting. And then the tiny old man who was my father's
father, who had had a heart attack, did not die; and the drama was over.

It was when we flew home that the strange return, the circling, began.

Who wandered widely.

The English language has several nouns for the act of moving
through geographical space from one point to another. The provenances
of these words, the places they came from, can be interesting; can tell us
something about what we have thought, over the centuries and millennia, about just what this act consists of and what it means.

"Voyage," for instance, derives from the Old French *voiage,* a word
that comes into English (as so many do) from Latin, in this case the word
viaticum, "provisions for a journey." Lurking within *viaticum* itself is the
feminine noun *via,* "road." So you might say that "voyage" is saturated
in the material: what you bring along when you move through space
("provisions for a journey"), and indeed what you tread upon as you do
so: the road.

"Journey," on the other hand—another word for the same activity—is rooted in the temporal, derived as it is from the Old French *jornée*, a word that traces its ancestry to the Latin *diurnum*, "the portion for a day," which stems ultimately from *dies*, "day." It is not hard to imagine how "the portion for the day" became the word for "trip": long ago, when a journey might take months and even years—say, from Troy, now a crumbling ruin in Turkey, to Ithaca, a rocky island in the Ionian Sea, a place undistinguished by any significant remains—long ago it was safer and more comfortable to speak not of the "voyage," the *viaticum*, what you needed to survive your movement through space, but of a single day's progress. Over time, the part came to stand for the whole, one day's movement for however long it takes to get where you're going—which could be a week, a month, a year, even (as we know) ten years. What is touching about the word "journey" is the thought that in those olden days, when the word was newborn, just one day's worth of movement was a significant enough activity, an arduous enough enterprise, to warrant a name of its own: *journey*.

This talk of arduousness brings me to a third way of referring to the activity we are considering here: "travel." Today, when we hear the word, we think of pleasure, something you do in your spare time, the name of a section of the paper that you linger over on a Sunday. What is the connection to arduousness? "Travel," as it happens, is a first cousin of "travail," which the chunky Merriam-Webster dictionary that my father bought for me almost forty years ago, when I was on the eve of the first significant journey I myself ever made—from our New York suburb to the University of Virginia, North to South, high school to college— defines as "painful or laborious effort." Pain can indeed be glimpsed, like a palimpsest, dimly floating behind the letters that spell TRAVAIL, thanks to the word's odd etymology: it comes to us, via Middle English and after a restful stop in Old French, from the medieval Latin *trepalium*, "instrument of torture." So "travel" suggests the emotional dimension of traveling: not its material accessories, or how long it may last, but how it feels. For in the days when these words took their shape and meaning, travel was above all difficult, painful, arduous, something strenuously avoided by most people.

The one word in the English language that combines all of the various resonances that belong severally to "voyage" and "journey" and "travel"—the distance but also the time, the time but also the emotion, the arduousness and the danger—comes not from Latin but from Greek. That word is "odyssey."

We owe this word to two proper nouns. Most recently, it derives from the classical Greek *odysseia*: the name of an epic poem about a hero called Odysseus. Now many people know that Odysseus' story is about voyages: he traveled far by sea, after all, and (ironically) lost not only everything that he started out with but everything he accumulated on the way. (So much for "provisions for a journey.") People also know that he traveled through time, too: the decade he and the Greeks were besieging Troy, the ten arduous years he spent trying to return home, where sensible people stay put.

So we know about the voyages and the journey, the space and the time. What very few people know, unless they know Greek, is that the magical third element—emotion—is built into the name of this curious hero. A story that is told within the *Odyssey* describes the day on which the infant Odysseus got his name; the story, to which I shall return, conveniently provides the etymology for that name. Just as you can see the Latin word *via* lurking in *viaticum* (and, thus, in *voiage* and "voyage" as well), people who know Greek can see, just below the surface of the name "Odysseus," the word *odynê*. You may think you don't recognize it, but think again. Think, for instance, of the word "anodyne," which the dictionary my father gave me defines as "a painkilling drug or medicine; not likely to provoke offense." "Anodyne" is actually a compound of two Greek words which together mean "without pain"; the *an-* is the "without," and so the *-odynê* has to be "pain." This is the root of Odysseus' name, and of his poem's name, too. The hero of this vast epic of voyaging, journeying, and travel is, literally, "the man of pain." He is the one who travels; he is the one who suffers.

And how not? For a tale of travel is, necessarily, also a tale of separation, of being sundered from the ones you are leaving behind. Even people who have not read the *Odyssey* are likely to have heard the legend of a man who spent ten years trying to get home to his wife; and yet, as you learn in the epic's opening scenes, when Odysseus left home for Troy he also abandoned an infant son and a thriving father. The structure of the poem underscores the importance of these two characters: it begins with the now-grown son setting out in search of his lost parent (four whole books, as its chapters are called, are dedicated to the son's journeys before we even meet his father); and it ends not with the triumphant reunion of the hero and his wife, but with a tearstained reunion between him and his father, by now an old and broken man.

As much as it is a tale of husbands and wives, then, this story is just as much—perhaps even more—about fathers and sons.

And knew the minds of many men.

From Miami we flew home to New York. It was night. As we settled into our seats, the stewardess mentioned that there was "bad weather" waiting at home. Daddy briefly looked up from the book that he was reading, registered the information, and then went back to the book. Soon after we were in the air, however, the pilot announced that, because of the weather, there would be a lengthy delay before we could land; we would have to "circle." The plane started to bank gently, and for a long time we went round and round. Up where we were, there was no weather at all: the night was as dense and matte as the piece of velvet a jeweler might use to display his stones—like the jeweler from whom, my mother once whispered to me, her own father had bought her engagement ring, haggling in a narrow back room on Forty-Seventh Street with an old Jewish man, one of Grandpa's many, many friends, who rolled some uncut brilliants onto the black cloth as he and my grandfather argued in Yiddish, all because my father didn't have enough money to buy the kind of stone her father thought she should have—the sky was like a piece of black velvet and the stars were like those brilliant winking stones. I knew that we were going in circles because the moon, as round and smoothly luminescent as an opal, kept disappearing and then reappearing in my window. I had a book of my own that night but ignored it when the circling first began, happily looking at the moon instead as it went past once, twice, three, four times, I eventually stopped counting how many times it showed its bland face to me.

My father wasn't looking at the moon. He was reading.

But then he always seemed to be reading. My father, whose parents never got beyond high school, once told me a story about how he became a great reader. Having been misdiagnosed with rheumatic fever in the seventh grade, he'd had to stay in bed for months, and during that period he became attached to books. *There's nothing you can't do if you have the right book*, he liked to tell his five children, and he, at least, lived by his own rule. He was never happier than when puzzling over his latest haul from the public library, some volume about how to play jazz guitar, how to play drums and recorder, violin and piano, how to write pop lyrics, how to construct a built-in wet bar, how to build an accelerator for the barbecue coals, how to make a compost heap, Colonial furniture, a harpsichord. At the end of Book 5 of the *Odyssey*, when the love-mad nymph Calypso finally allows Odysseus to leave her island and make his way toward home, she fetches a set of tools that she had hitherto kept locked away and gives them to the shipwrecked man; it is with these few tools, and whatever trees and plants there are to hand, that the hero builds himself the raft on which he begins the final legs of his journey home. Whenever I read this passage, I think of my father.

In part because he seemed always to be coiled over a book, always to be using his own mind and absorbing the contents of others', when I was a child I thought of my father as being all head. The impression that his head was the greater part of him was enhanced by the fact that he went bald when he was still quite young, certainly by the time I was a small child, and the impression I had was that the massive brain beneath his skull had expanded to the point where it had, somehow, forced the hair from his scalp. Many of my memories of him start with an image not of his face—the sallow oval with its arced brows and narrowly set dark brown eyes, the long broken nose with the rubbery swerve at the end, the thin-lipped mouth that tended to be set in a tight frown—but of his head, which, devoid of hair, seemed almost touchingly exposed, available to injury. A fringe of residual hair made a U around the base of his head, this U being dark throughout my childhood, gray later on, then shaved, and then, bizarrely, a little fuzzy again because of the drugs he had to take. And then there was the forehead, nearly always wrinkled in concentration as he thought his way through a problem, an equation, my mother, one of us.

This was the head that was bent, that night of the long and circling plane ride, over a book.

What was my father reading? It isn't impossible that it was a Latin grammar, or maybe Virgil's *Aeneid*, the Roman epic that nods so elegantly to its Greek archetypes. Although my father spent his working life among scientists and equations and figures—first in his job at Grumman, an aerospace corporation, where whatever he did was unknown and unknowable to us, since the facility he worked in was top secret, and besides, as he later pointed out to me, I wouldn't understand; and then, after he retired in the 1990s, during a second, decade-long career teaching computer science at a local university—he took pride in the fact that he had once, long ago, been a Latin student. *Oh,* he would say sometimes, when I was in college and majoring in Classics, *Oh, in high school I read Ovid in <u>Latin</u>, you know!* And I, instead of being impressed, as he hoped I would be, by this early feat of scholarship, noticed only that he'd pronounced the poet's name with a long *o: Oh-vid.* My father's mispronunciations, which embarrassed me a great deal at one point in my life, were the inevitable result of him having been the bookish child of parents who had no education to speak of; I suspect a good many of the proper names and words he had encountered, by the time I was old enough to disdain his errors, were words he'd never heard uttered aloud. Only now do I see how greatly to his credit it was that he himself would be the first to joke about these gaffes. *I was in the army before I realized there was no such thing as "battle fa-ti-gyoo"!* he'd say with a tight little grin, and if I happened to be there when he was telling this joke on himself I would wait, with a complicated pleasure, for the person he was telling it to to realize that the word in question was "fatigue."

So my father liked to boast that he had been good enough in Latin to read *Oh-vid* in the original, although I came, in time, to know that a great regret of his was that he had stopped studying Latin before he had a chance to read Virgil. The knowledge that my father had never finished Latin, had never read the *Aeneid*, gave me a faintly cruel satisfaction, since I myself pursued and eventually completed my classical studies and had, therefore, read Virgil in Latin; and Virgil's Latin, as I would sometimes take pleasure in pointing out to my father, was denser, more complicated, and more difficult than was Ovid's.

Throughout the years I was growing up, my father would occasionally make a stab at recouping what he had lost all those years ago, back in the late 1940s. I would sometimes come home to Long Island on spring or fall break to find his copies of *Latina pro populo* (*"Latin for People"*) and *Winnie ille Pu* lying next to the black leather recliner downstairs in the den where he would try, and often fail, to find the solitude he craved. Already when I was a child of seven or eight or nine, I was reading books about the Greeks and their mythologies, drawn, no doubt, by the allure of naked bodies and of lascivious acts, by the heroes and the armor and the gods, the ruined temples and lost treasures, and although I never suspected it at the time, I now realize that my father liked the idea that I had an antiquarian bent.

Years later—long after I had failed, in high school, to master the math courses that would have allowed me to go on to study calculus—my father would occasionally remark that it was too bad, because it's impossible to see the world clearly if you don't know calculus. He said this not to hurt me but from, I believe, genuine regret. It was *too bad*, he would say; just as, at other times, he would say that it was *too bad* that I couldn't appreciate the "aesthetic dimension" of math, a phrase that made no sense to me whatsoever because I associated mathematics with being forced to perform fruitless exercises that had no purpose, and only much later did I realize that they only seemed to have no purpose because I wasn't working hard enough, or maybe wasn't being taught well enough (*Why isn't your teacher explaining these things better?* he would exclaim, shaking his shiny head in dismay, although when I asked him to explain the same things he would shake his head again, confounded by my inability to grasp what was so clear to him), and so I went on cluelessly through junior high school and high school, uncomprehendingly copying out diagrams and geometric shapes and quadratic equations, having no idea what they were supposed to be leading to, like someone forced to practice scales on a guitar or piano or harpsichord without guessing that there was something called a concerto. Much later, when I was a freshman in college learning Greek, I sat in a classroom with three other students every weekday morning at nine o'clock, and we would recite, precisely the way you might play scales, the paradigms of nouns and verbs, each noun with its five possible incarnations depending on its function in the sentence, each verb with its scarily metastasizing forms, the tenses and moods that don't exist in English, the active and passive voices, yes, those I knew about from high-school French, but also the strange "middle" voice, a mode in which the subject is also the object, a strange folding over or doubling, the way a person could be a father but also a son. And yet I happily endured these rigorous exercises because I had a clear idea of where they were leading me. I was going to read Greek, the *Iliad* and the *Odyssey*, the elaborately unspooling *Histories* of Herodotus, the tragedies constructed as beautifully as clocks, as implacably as traps . . . Years after all this, whenever my father made this comment about how you couldn't see the world clearly without calculus, I'd invariably reply by saying that you couldn't really see the world clearly without having read the *Aeneid* in Latin, either. And then he'd make that little grimace that we all knew, half a smile, half a frown, twisting his face, and we'd laugh a sour little laugh, and retreat to our corners.

So he might have been studying his Latin, perhaps even taking a stab at Virgil, that night when we circled for hours in the airplane bringing us back from Florida, where my dutiful father had hurried to be with his silent parent. Years later, when he said he wanted to take my course on the *Odyssey*, it occurred to me that you might devote yourself to a text out of a sense of guilt, a sense that you have unfinished business, the way you might have a feeling of obligation to a person. My father was a man who felt his responsibilities deeply, which I suppose is why, when I asked him a certain question years later, he replied, simply, *Because a man doesn't leave.*

That night when I was four years old I sat there, quiet next to my quiet father, as the plane leaned heavily on one wing so that it could spin its vast arcing circle, not unlike the way in which, in Homer's epics, a giant eagle will wheel high in the sky above the heads of an anxious army or a solitary man at a moment of great danger, the eagle being an omen of what is to come, victory or defeat for the army, rescue or death for the man; I sat as the plane went round and my father read. I don't remember how long we circled, but my father later insisted that it was "for hours." Now if this were a story told by my mother's father, I'd be inclined to doubt this. But my father loathed exaggeration, as indeed he disliked excess of all kinds, and so I imagine that we did, in fact, circle for hours. Two? Three? I'll never know. Eventually I fell asleep. We stopped circling and began our descent and landed and then drove the thirty minutes or so through the cold and were safely home.

When my father told this story, he abbreviated what, to me, was the interesting part—the heart attack, the (as I saw it) poignant rush to my grandfather's side, the *drama*—and lingered on what, to me at the time, had been the boring part: the circling. He liked to tell this story because, to his mind, it showed what a good child I had been: how uncomplainingly I had borne the tedium of all that circling, all that distance without progress. *He never made a fuss*, my father, who disliked fusses, would say, and even then, young as I was, I dimly understood that the gentle but citrusy emphasis on the word "fuss" was directed, somehow, at my mother and her family. *He never made a fuss*, Daddy would say with an approving nod. *He just sat there, reading, not saying a word.*

Long voyages, no fuss. Many years have passed since our long and circuitous return home, and during those years I myself have traveled on planes with small children, which is why, when I now think back on my father's story, two things strike me. The first is that it is really a story about how good my father was. How well he had handled it all, I think now: downplaying the situation, pretending there was nothing unusual, setting an example by sitting quietly himself, and resisting—as I myself would not have done, since in many ways I am, indeed, more my mother's child, and Grandpa's grandchild—the impulse to sensationalize or complain.

The second thing I am struck by when I think about this story now is that in all that time we had together on the plane, it never occurred to either one of us to talk to the other.

We were happy to have our books.

Twists and turns.

It is not for nothing that, in the original Greek, the first word in the first line of the twelve thousand one hundred and ten that make up the *Odyssey* is *andra*: "man." The epic begins with the story of Odysseus' son, a youth in search of his long-lost father, the hero of this poem; it then focuses on the hero himself, first as he recalls the fabulous adventures he has experienced after leaving Troy, then as he struggles to return home, where he will reclaim his identity as father, husband, and king, taking terrible vengeance on the Suitors who tried to woo his wife and usurp his home and realm; then, in its final book, it gives us a vision of what "a man" might look like once his life's adventures are over: the hero's elderly father, the last person with whom Odysseus is reunited, now a decrepit old man alone in his orchard, tired of life. The boy, the man, the ancient: the three ages of man. Which is to say that, among the journeys that this poem charts, there is, too, a man's journey through life, from birth to death. How do you get there? What is the journey like? And how do you tell the story of it?

The answers are deeply connected with Odysseus' own nature. The first adjective used to describe the man with whom the proem begins— the first modifier in the entire *Odyssey*—is a peculiar Greek word, *polytropos*. The literal meaning of this word is "of many turns": *poly* means "many," and a *tropos* is a "turning." English words containing the element *-trope* are derived, ultimately, from *tropos*. "Heliotrope," for instance, is a flower that turns toward the sun. "Apotropaic," to take a less cheery example, is an adjective that means "turning away evil": it is used of superstitious rites that are intended to avert bad luck—such as the custom, common among Eastern European Jews of my grandparents' era, of tying a red ribbon around the wrist of an infant in order to keep the Evil Eye away. *Oh, my mother loved you so much,* my mother will occasionally say to me, even now, *when she took you to the park she would tie a red ribbon around your wrist!* And then she'll cluck her tongue sadly, *tskkk,* and sigh. The anecdote, I am aware, is not just about my grandmother's great devotion to me: her deep emotion in this story is meant to stand in contrast to the relative lack of interest in me shown by my father's parents, who didn't meet me until I was two years old as the result of one of the grim silences that occasionally arose between my father and his brothers and his parents.

It is difficult to resist the notion that there is something suggestive, programmatic, about making this particular adjective, "of many turns," the first modifier in the first line of a twelve-thousand-line poem about a journey home. Odysseus, we know, is a tricky character, famed for his shady dealings and evasions and lies and above all his sly way with words; he is, after all, the man who dreamed up the Trojan Horse, a disguise that was also an ambush. So in one sense *polytropos* is figurative: this is a poem about someone whose mind has many turns, many twists, not all of them strictly legitimate. And yet there is a plainer sense of *polytropos*. For "of many turns" also refers to the shape of the hero's motion through space: he is the man who gets where he is going by traveling in circles. In more than one of his adventures, he leaves a place only to return to it, sometimes inadvertently. And then of course there is the biggest circle of all, the one that brings him back to Ithaca, the place he left so long ago that when he finally comes home he and his loved ones are unrecognizable to one another.

The *Odyssey* narrative itself moves through time in the same convoluted way that Odysseus himself moves through space. The epic begins in a present in which Odysseus' son, grown to manhood in his father's absence, goes searching for news of his long-lost parent (Books 1 through 4); it then abandons the son for the father, zooming in on Odysseus at the moment when the gods, having decided that he has wandered enough and should be allowed to go home, free him at long last from the clutches of Calypso and bring him to the island kingdom of a hospitable people called the Phaeacians (Books 5 through 8); then, in a flashback that lasts four full books (9 through 12), Odysseus himself relates to the Phaeacians all of the adventures he has had since leaving Troy. The narrative then comes back to the son in the present, briefly picking up the tale of the youth's adventures only to turn once more to Odysseus himself as he finally reaches home; then, at last, it brings the father and the son together as they work to reestablish mastery of their home and punish the Suitors and their accomplices (Books 13 through 22). Only after this does the poem reunite the husband and his wife (Book 23) and conclude, finally, with a vision of the men of the family, the son, the father, the grandfather, standing together after vanquishing the Suitors and their families (Book 24): the future and the present and the past juxtaposed in a single climactic moment as the epic draws to its close.

These elaborate circlings in space and time are mirrored in a certain technique found in many works of Greek literature, called *ring composition*. In ring composition, the narrator will start to tell a story only to pause and loop back to some earlier moment that helps explain an

aspect of the story he's telling—a bit of personal or family history, say—
and afterward might even loop back to some earlier moment or object or
incident that will help account for that slightly less early moment, there-
after gradually winding his way back to the present, the moment in the
narrative that he left in order to provide all this background. Herodotus,
for instance, often relies on the technique in his *Histories*, that sprawling
account of the great war between the Greeks and the Persian Empire (a
conflict that Herodotus himself saw as a latter-day successor to the Trojan
War). At one point, for example, the historian digresses from his military
saga to give a book-long history of Egypt, its government, culture, religion, and customs, because Egypt was part of the Persian Empire, whose
invasion of Greece in 490 B.C. and the conflicts that ensued from it are
the ostensible subjects of the *Histories*. The vast length of his Egyptian
digression suggests that the ancients might have had a very different idea
from our own about what it means for a book to be "about" something.

But ring composition undoubtedly arose much earlier than Herodotus and his *Histories*, clearly before writing was even invented. The most
famous example of the technique is, in fact, to be found in the *Odyssey:* a passage in Book 19, which I shall discuss in greater detail later
on, that begins with someone noticing a telltale scar on Odysseus' leg,
at a moment when he is trying to remain incognito. But when the scar
is noticed, Homer pauses to tell us how Odysseus, as a youth, got the
wound that would become the scar; then goes back even further in time
to provide details about an episode in the hero's infancy (featuring his
mother's father, a notorious trickster); then returns to the incident during
which Odysseus got the wound; and finally circles all the way back to the
moment when the scar is noticed. Only then, after all the history, does
he describe the reaction of the character who noticed it to begin with. As
complex as it is to describe this technique, the associative spirals that are
its hallmark in fact re-create the way we tell stories in everyday life, looping from one tale to another as we seek to clarify and explain the story
with which we started, which is the story to which, eventually, we will
return—even if it is sometimes the case that we need to be nudged, to

be reminded to get back to our starting point. For this reason, ring composition might remind you of nothing so much as a leisurely homeward journey, interrupted by detours and attractions so alluring that you might forget to stay your homeward course.

And so ring composition, which might at first glance appear to be a digression, reveals itself as an efficient means for a story to embrace the past and the present and sometimes even the future—since some "rings" can loop forward, anticipating events that take place *after* the conclusion of the main story. In this way a single narrative, even a single moment, can contain a character's entire biography.

Hence the occurrence of the word *polytropos*, "of many turns," "many circled," in the first line of the *Odyssey* is a hint as to the nature not only of the poem's hero but of the poem itself, suggesting as it does that the best way to tell a certain kind of story is to move not straight ahead but in wide and history-laden circles.

In twists and turns.

Fools!

The silence in which my father and I sat all those years ago, on the plane coming home from Miami Beach, was to become typical of what went on between us for a long time. For the first half of my life—until I was in my late twenties—there was a long quiet between us. Perhaps because I had once thought of him as all head, all cranium, the word that came to mind when I thought of him was "hard," and this hardness made me afraid of him when I was a child and teenager and, indeed, a young man in my twenties. He could be *hard on people*, certain members of my family would say. He did, indeed, have exacting standards for virtually everything. Grades, certainly, where we children were concerned; but there were other things, too. As I was growing up, I came to understand that everything, for him, was part of a great, almost cosmic struggle between the qualities he would invoke when explaining why a certain piece of music we liked or a movie that was popular at the moment wasn't really "great," wasn't really worth the time we were lavishing on it—those qualities being hardness and durability and, as I think he really meant, *authenticity*—and the weaker, mushier qualities that most other people settled for, whether in songs or cars or novels or spouses. The lyrics of the pop music we secretly listened to, for instance, were "soft." *A rhyme is a rhyme, you can't approximate!* For him, the more difficult something was to achieve or to appreciate, the more unpleasant to do or to understand, the more likely it was to possess this quality that for him was the hallmark of worthiness.

X *is x.* His sense that there is a deep and inscrutable essence to things, an irreducible hardness that he had intuited but which many if not most other people had failed to discern, informed his dealings with people, too. Because he had these hard standards—or, rather, because so few people ever met them—there were certain holes in his life, holes that had once been occupied by people: his parents, at one point, during those first two years of my life when he and my mother stopped speaking to his mother and father; each of his three brothers, too, for varying amounts of time, from weeks to years to decades, periods when he would simply not speak to this or that wayward sibling. I was in my thirties before I had a real conversation with Uncle Bobby, with whom some violent quarrel with my father (so we imagined: Daddy never discussed it) had exiled from our lives until the two of them reconciled in the 1990s, when they were in their seventies. And we didn't even know that he had another older brother, the product of Poppy's brief first marriage, until my grandfather lay dying and this strange new half-uncle, Milton, showed up in the hospital one day. *Milton, Milton, where have you been?* Poppy croaked from the high hospital bed as my father looked away in disgust.

So used was I to my father's habit of silence that it didn't occur to me until fairly recently to ask why, for him, the obvious way to deal with people who had disappointed his expectations was to act as if they no longer existed.

Hence I was afraid of him for a long time. When I was in grade school and middle school and was having trouble understanding my math homework, I would stand nervously in the doorway to his bedroom, where he would sit at the little teak desk going through bills or reading papers for work, getting up the nerve to ask for his help; once I did, his incredulity in the face of my inability to understand something as obvious to him as the math problem that I couldn't solve would fill me with shame. This shamed feeling colored my dealings with him through much of the early part of my life, making me want to hide from him. It's true that I was hiding from many things in those days: I was a gay teenager, it was the 1970s, and we were in the suburbs. I lived cautiously. But the fact is that my anguished, furtive grappling with my sexuality was the least part of my fear of my father back then. I knew well that he and Mother were open-minded and without prejudices on that subject. When I was in high school and a succession of charismatic gay teachers became mentors to me, my parents made efforts to demonstrate that they knew what these men were and had no problem with it. Indeed, my father reacted with surprising gentleness when, as a college junior, I finally came out to my parents. (*Let me talk to him, I know something about this*, he told my mother, although it would be many years—not until we were on the *Odyssey* cruise, in fact—before he explained himself.) No: it wasn't that I was gay. I simply felt that everything about me was hopelessly mushy and imprecise, doomed to fail the *x is x* test. I didn't even know what *x was*—didn't know what I was or what I wanted, couldn't account for the turbulent feelings, the heated enthusiasms and clotted fears to which I was prone. And so I hid—from many things, but above all from him, who knew so clearly what was what.

This was the reason, at least on my part, for the long period of quiet between us. What his reasons might be, I never asked.

My resentment of my father's hardness, of his insistence that difficulty was a hallmark of quality, that pleasure was suspect and toil was worthy, strikes me as ironic now, since I suspect it was those very qualities that attracted me to the study of the Classics in the first place. Even when I was fairly young and first absorbed in books of Greek and Roman myths, I had an idea that beneath the flesh of the lush tales I was reading, with their lascivious couplings and unexpected transformations, there was a hard skeleton that represented some quality fundamental to both the culture that produced the myths and the study of that culture. When I was fourteen, my high-school English teacher instructed us to memorize a passage from a play. Among the austere boxed sets of books on the bookshelves downstairs near the black-upholstered oak rocking chair in which my father liked to read was one called *The Complete Greek Tragedies*; most of the others were collections of papers about mathematics. I opened one of the volumes in the four-volume set at random and read a speech that turned out to be from Sophocles' *Antigone*, a play about a conflict between a headstrong young woman and her uncle, the king, who has issued a harsh new edict that she intends to defy. The speech to which I had randomly turned was one in which Antigone protests that the laws that she obeys are not those made by mortals but the eternal laws of the gods; she declares that she will follow those divine laws even though it means her death. *"For me it was not Zeus who made that order, / nor did that Justice who dwells with the gods below / mark out such laws to stand among mankind."* When I read those words, I remember thinking that here at last was the bone beneath the flesh: a play in which x was x, a drama whose action revolves around stark choices between which there was no middle ground. Nothing soft *here*. When, a few years later, I began to study Greek, I found an equally satisfying flintiness not only in the myths or dramas themselves but in their own bones, the language itself: a syntax that was as stark as Antigone's choices, that allowed for no messiness or approximation. The paradigms of nouns and adjectives that ran across the pages of the slim black textbook we used in Greek 101 were as crisp and unforgiving as theorems.

Much later I was pleased to learn that my instinct about the "hardness" of Classics itself had been right. The discipline traces its roots back to the late eighteenth century, when a German scholar named Friedrich August Wolf decided that the interpretation of literary texts—an undertaking that many people, among them my father, casually think of as subjective, impressionistic, a matter of opinion—should, in fact, be treated as a rigorous branch of science. For Wolf, many of the theories about education that were circulating at the time were deplorably sentimental and soft—for instance, those being promoted by John Locke in England and Jean-Jacques Rousseau in France, which emphasized the practical aims of education, its role in preparing students for "real life." What, these philosophers were wondering, could studying the ancient classics possibly teach students in the present day? Locke, like many parents today, derisively wondered why a working person would need to know Latin. Wolf's answer was, Human nature. For him, the object of his new literary "science"—"philology," from the Greek for "love of language"—was nothing less than a means to a profound understanding of the "intellectual, sensual, and moral powers of man." But to study the ancient texts and cultures properly, one had to approach them as scientifically as one did when studying the physical universe. As with mathematics or physics, Wolf argued, meaningful study of classical civilization could arise only from mastery of many essential and interlinked disciplines: immersion not only in Ancient Greek and Latin (and, often, in Hebrew and Sanskrit), in their vocabularies and grammars and syntaxes and prosody, but in the history, religion, philosophy, and art of the cultures that spoke and wrote those languages. To this immersion, he went on, there had to be added the mastery of specialized skills, such as those needed to decipher ancient papyri, manuscripts, and inscriptions, such mastery being as necessary, ultimately, to the study of ancient literature as the mastery of plane and solid geometry, of arithmetic and algebra, and, indeed, of calculus is to proper study of the field we call mathematics.

And so classical philology was born. When I learned about this in graduate school, I shared it with my father. He winced and shook his head and said, *Only science is science.*

The silence between my father and me started to thaw when I began my graduate study in Classics, when I was twenty-six. Yes, only science was science; but as time went by, it was as if the arduousness of the course of

study to which I was devoting myself were eroding his resistance. Whatever he might think of the mushy, subjective business of literary interpretation, he had a grim respect for the classical languages themselves, their
grammars as impervious to emotion or subjectivity as any mathematical
proof; through mastering them, I had become worthier in his eyes. He
started to ask me, with real interest, about the progress of my studies,
about what I was reading and how the seminars were conducted. It was at
this time, in fact, that he reminisced about his own Latin studies so many
years before and shared with me the story of how he'd read Ovid in high
school but quit before he'd been able to read Virgil.

During my first year of graduate school I took a seminar on the *Aeneid.*
My father asked me to xerox some pages from Book 2 and send them to
him; he wanted to have a go at them, he said. Now as it happens Book 2
is the part of the epic in which the Fall of Troy is recounted in harrowing
detail: the awful climax to which the *Iliad* and *Odyssey* allude but never
fully describe, the one peering into the future toward the devastating
event, the other gazing backward at it. It is Virgil, the Roman, who gives
us the whole story at last: the Greeks hidden within the gigantic Trojan
Horse, which the Trojans have taken inside their city's walls; then the
ambush in the dark, the smoke from the burning city, the panic and the
flames; the image of the headless trunk of the murdered Trojan king,
Priam, a pitiable old man, the quintessential epic father, who is slain
before the altar at which he desperately prays for the safety of his city by
Neoptolemus, the son of the now-dead Achilles—a youth who, by killing
the elderly king, seeks to outdo his own father in cruel bravery. My father
wanted to see some pages from Book 2 because, he said, he was curious
to know whether he'd be able to follow the Latin. But too much time
had passed since those days decades earlier when he had read *Oh-vid* so
fluently.

It's no good, he told me over the phone one night, with that tight
rueful tone he could sometimes have, a tone of voice that was the vocal
equivalent of someone frowning and waving a hand dismissively, as if to
say, *Why bother?*

It's no use. I'm just no good at this anymore, he said after he'd had a go at Priam and Neoptolemus. It's too late.

Oh, well, I said. It was so long ago. Nobody could remember all that.

To which my father replied, It's okay. Now you'll read it for me.

A sweet comment. Although my father was hard, was *tough*, every now and then he would say things or let slip a remark that was so unexpectedly tender or generous or poetic that you'd be confounded—would find yourself in a state of what Greeks called *aporia*, "helplessness." (The word literally means "without a path"; "a feeling of being stranded" would be one way of translating it.) But then, this was the parent who, for all his hardness, despite the severity that had etched itself into his very flesh—the stern horizontal lines running across his forehead like the rulings of the black-and-white-marbled composition books we dutifully took notes in, the sunken vertical planes of his cheeks beneath the ridged cheekbones and the high symmetrical arcs of his eye sockets shadowing the spheres beneath like illustrations in a geometry textbook—had somehow acquired the comically incongruous nickname "Daddy Loopy." *Daddy Loopy!* we would cry on the rare occasions when he'd tickle or tease us, *Who's your Daddy Loooooopy?!* he would say, slightly self-conscious but also obscurely pleased, as he tucked me in tightly, *a super-duper-tucker-inner, like a mummy!* which is the way I preferred it when I was four or five and he'd come into my bedroom, sitting carefully on the edge of the narrow bed he had built for me, would read me *Winnie-the-Pooh.*

That's okay, you'll read it for me, I heard him say, this sweet thing he said one autumn evening half a lifetime ago, and I thought, not for the first time, *Who is this man?*

And so my father and I started talking again, thanks to Virgil. I would call him throughout the term and recap the seminar discussions, and sometimes he would take out the pages I sent to him and we would make our laborious way through a passage over the phone, and every now and then there would be a pleased little swagger in his voice as he recognized some grammatical principle he had learned sixty-five years earlier and then forgotten, as for instance when we were reading some lines from

Book 2, the book with the dreadful descriptions of the Fall of Troy, lines from a scene in which the aged king Priam feebly dons his old battle gear in hopes that he might defend his beloved city one last time. Oh, sure, I see, *sumptis armis* is an ablative absolute there, my father said, and I said, Yes, that's right!; and we talked about how, in the line *ipsum autem sumptis Priamum iuvenalibus armis*, "Priam himself, having taken up the arms he bore in his youth," the detail that the arms that the old king struggles to wield—because he yearned to protect his palace from the Greeks who had sprung from the belly of the wooden horse, the notorious ruse dreamed up by Odysseus—were the very ones he had borne when he was young and strong, added a special poignancy to the scene. And my father said yes, he could see that. We had many such conversations in the autumn of my first year at graduate school, which were not like any conversations we had had before.

It is for this reason that I can say that I didn't really feel that I got to know my father until I began to study the Classics in earnest.

From some point or another.

Unlike the tightly focused proem of the *Iliad*, the proem of the *Odyssey* rambles, is filled with ambiguity. In the first line of the *Iliad* the poet calls on the Muse to sing his great theme, which is summed up in the first word of that first line: "rage." Whose rage? The rage of Achilles, the son of Peleus. Compare with this the opening of the *Odyssey*, which begins by asking the Muse to follow the story of "a man" but doesn't give his name: it could be anyone. As the line proceeds, of course, we get more information from the subordinate clauses that start piling up: the man *who* wandered widely, *after* he sacked Troy's sacred citadel, *who* was a great sufferer, *who* tried and failed to save his men. But the proem's attention proceeds to slither away from "the man" to those men, delving in curiously elaborate detail into a specific episode that apparently doomed them: the eating of the forbidden flesh of the Cattle of the Sun. By the time you reach the end of the proem, you're acutely aware of the discrepancy between the wealth and specificity of certain information you've received about this man and the gaps that remain, not the least of which, of course, is his name: a glaring omission, to say the least, in a passage whose purpose is to introduce him. Of course we know that "the man" is Odysseus; so why doesn't Homer just say so? One possible answer to that question is that, by drawing attention to the tension between what he allows himself to say ("the man") and what he knows and we know (Odysseus), the poet introduces an important theme that will continue to grow throughout his poem, which is: What is the difference between who we are and what others know about us? This tension between anonymity and identity will be a major element of the *Odyssey*'s plot. For its hero's life will depend on his ability to conceal his identity from enemies—and to reveal it, when the proper time comes, to friends, to those by whom he wants to be recognized: first his son, then his wife, and finally his father.

The proem's sly refusal to commit itself to a name is mirrored in another bizarre evasion. The *Iliad* begins with a precisely worded request to the Muse to start singing from a specific moment in the story—*from the moment when first the two stood forth in strife, / Atreus' son, the lord of men, and Achilles, a man like a god*. The poet of the *Odyssey*, by contrast, doesn't seem to care particularly about where his epic ought to begin. He asks the Muse to begin telling her story at "some point or another," *hamothen*—anywhere in Odysseus' journey that suits her. But *hamothen* also has a temporal overtone: "from some point *in time* or another," "at any random moment in the narrative." In the *Odyssey*'s opening lines, space and time are themselves suggestively vague, indistinct from each other.

This strangely tentative careering between concrete specifics and unhelpful generalities gives you a familiar feeling: the feeling of what it's like to be lost. Sometimes it's as if you're on familiar territory; sometimes you feel at sea, adrift in a featureless liquid void with no landmarks in sight. In this way, the opening of this poem about being lost and finding a way home precisely replicates the surf-like oscillations between drifting and purposefulness that characterize its hero's journey.

The proem's re-creation of a feeling of movement, of *travel*, brings you back to the deepest roots of the word "proem" itself. The word literally means "before the song": *pro-*, "before," plus *oimê*, "song." This makes sense: the proem is the part that comes before the song proper, the "song" being the epic itself. And yet *oimê* has a suggestive provenance. It comes from an older word, *oimos*, which means "path" or "way"—because, possibly, some ancient stock phrase like "the way of song" was eventually reduced, simply, to "the way" and in time came to mean just "song." That "song" should come from "path" makes a kind of natural sense: any kind of song, from a ballad to an epic of fifteen thousand lines, leads you from the beginning to the end, winds its way through a story to a climax, a conclusion. It is a "way" toward something.

And yet if we travel even further into the heart of the history of these words, more is made clear. For *oimos*, "path," is linked ultimately to *oima*, a word that suggests something like our "impetus"—a rush, a forward spring, a purposeful movement forward.

I've always found this etymology of the word "proem" interesting because it takes you down a road from introductions to songs to the elemental idea of movement itself: the idea of, quite simply, "going." For the Greeks, poetry was motion.

In every sense, it is supposed to move you.

Tell us the tale.

On a Wednesday night in a January half a century after the tediously circling homecoming about which my father, *Daddy Loopy*, liked to tell his story, I was thinking about long journeys again, and about long silences.

Once again I found myself sitting next to my father without speaking. This time, we were not in an airplane. My father was lying, as imperturbable as a dead pharaoh in his bandages, in a complicated bed in the neurological intensive care unit of a hospital fifteen miles or so from the house that he had moved into fifty-two years earlier, the house he'd continued to live in as it filled with five children and then was emptied of them, leaving him and my mother alone to live their lives, which were, on the whole, quiet and circumspect, at least in part because she never liked to travel, really.

Expect the unexpected. My father had fallen, and it was clear there would be no more educational trips. But we had had our odyssey—had journeyed together, so to speak, through this text over the course of a semester, a text that to me, as I sat there looking at the motionless figure of my father, seemed more and more to be about the present than about the past. It is a story, after all, about strange and complicated families, indeed about two grandfathers—the maternal one eccentric, garrulous, a trickster without peer, the other, the father of the father, taciturn and stubborn; about a long marriage and short dalliances, about a husband who travels far and a wife who stays behind, as rooted to her house as a tree is to the earth; about a son who for a long time is unrecognized by and unrecognizable to his father, until late, very late, when they join together for a great adventure; a story, in its final moments, about a man in the middle of his life, a man who is, we must remember, a son as well as a father, and who at the end of this story falls down and weeps because he has confronted the spectacle of his father's old age, the specter of his inevitable passing, a sight so overwhelming that this man, who is himself an expert storyteller, adept at bending the truth and at outright lying, too, a manipulator of words and hence of other people as well—this man is so undone by the sight of his failing father that he can bring himself no longer to tell his lies and weave his tales, and has, in the end, to tell the truth.

Such is the *Odyssey*, which my father decided he wanted to study with me a few years ago; such is Odysseus, the hero in whose footsteps we once traveled.

TELEMACHY

(Education)

———◦◦◦———

. . . the pretext for Telemachus' journey is the inquiry about his father; but for Athena, who advises it, the aim is education. The son would not have become worthy of his father had he not heard from his father's companions about his deeds; he knows how to behave toward his father on the basis of the stories that he has heard about him.

—Ancient commentator on *Odyssey*, 1.284
("Go first to Pylos and question godlike Nestor")

I. PAIDEUSIS

(Fathers and Sons)

One of the rare stories that my father liked to tell about his youth—rare, that is, while we were growing up, since as he got older he became increasingly talkative about his past, although it must be said that his stock of anecdotes could never really compete with the funny and dramatic tales that my mother and her father told—was the one about how his classical education had come to an end.

One day, he would begin, one spring day toward the end of the war (my father always referred to World War II simply as "the war," the way that some ancient bard might say the word "war" and mean "Troy"), it must have been the end of my junior year in high school, my Latin teacher, who was a very natty guy, a European refugee—a German, I remember, he got away just in time—my Latin teacher asked a bunch of us what we were planning to do the next year. We were fourth-year students, we'd been taking Latin since the seventh grade, and that year we'd been reading selections from Ovid.

Oh-vid.

My father might, at this point, clear his throat. He was a German guy, he repeated. I remember he always tried to dress well, although you could see his clothes had been washed a lot, the collar was frayed and the elbows of his suit were shiny. So that day, he asked us who was planning to continue with the Latin language into our senior year. See, senior-year Latin was the climax of Latin study, when you finally got to read Virgil. The *Aeneid*.

During more recent retellings of this story I would note the way in which he would linger on the details of the teacher's clothes: the frayed collar, the shiny elbows. The fact that he'd even noticed such things would have struck me, earlier on, as odd, since my father was notorious for his indifference to clothes; he had as an unerring a sense for wearing the wrong thing as certain people do for wearing the right thing. On the first night of the "Retracing the *Odyssey*" cruise, as we were dressing for the captain's cocktail party, he started to button himself into a shiny brown shirt, and I said, Daddy, we're on a Mediterranean cruise, you can't wear brown polyester, and I took the shirt and walked to the balcony and threw it into the sea. *Whaaat!?!* he cried, that was an expensive shirt! He strode across the stateroom to the balcony and looked forlornly down as the shirt, which on contact with the water had taken on a dense animal gleam, like the skin of a seal, briefly bobbed along until it finally sank under its own weight. Only when he was entering his late, nostalgic phase—I must have been in my mid-thirties at the time—did he surprise me with an anecdote that explained his fastidious attention to his long-ago teacher's dress. While he was studying as an undergraduate at NYU, he said one day (a university, he liked to remind us, that he'd been able to attend because of the GI Bill; which, in turn, he had been able to take advantage of because he had joined the army at the age of seventeen, precisely for the purpose of being able to go to college, to get an education)— while he was in college he had worked at Brooks Brothers. He gave his tight little grin when he saw me reacting to this news. *Well,* he said, *it was only in the packing room, but I learned something!* As he said this I could feel the presence of a shy, stubborn pride just beneath the surface of his self-deprecation, a slight vainglory about his brief entrée into the rarefied world of patrician American taste: as if to say, *See where I got? Not bad for a boy from the Bronx.* When he said, *but I learned something,* I had a sudden vision of him as a youth of twenty, impossibly slender as he was then, his trousers awkwardly crimped around the narrow waist, held in place by a belt, tiptoeing through the vast mahogany-paneled sales floors on Madison Avenue, clutching some paper-wrapped package as he loped beneath the coffered ceilings and the chandeliers, gawking at the gleaming paneling with its sleek brass fittings—not at all very different, I like to think, from the way in which, in the fourth book of the *Odyssey*, Odysseus' young son goggles at the rich decor of the palace of the Spartan king Menelaus, the long-suffering husband of Helen of Troy, when Telemachus visits him as part of his fact-finding mission about his missing father. "Zeus' court on Olympus must be like this!" exclaims the naïve youth, who in the poem is twenty, the age my father was when he worked at Brooks Brothers.

So, my father would repeat as he recalled his German-refugee Latin teacher, the one who'd tried to dress with flair even though his clothes were so poor, *so he asked us who was going to go on into the fifth year, to read Virgil.*

Here my father would pause. He was re-creating the silence that had fallen in the classroom in the Bronx all those years ago.

Nobody said anything, he would then say, not quite meeting my eye. *The teacher asked the question once, and then he asked again, and no one said a word.*

Sixty-five years after this event took place, long after the teacher and his frayed collars and dashed hopes had disappeared, long after many of the boys who had squirmed in that embarrassed Bronx silence had become men and then fathers and then grandfathers and then, like my father, old men who had become, suddenly and improbably, nostalgic about old and unredeemable mistakes—sixty-five years later, my father shook his head and pursed his narrow lips into the tight familiar line.

I still remember the room, he said, *because it was so quiet. We were too embarrassed to talk. And the teacher suddenly looked at us and pointed his finger at each of us like this—*(here my father put on a stagy German accent) *and said, "You refuse de riches of Fergil! Diss, you vill regret!"* And then he closed his briefcase and walked out of the room.

After a moment my father said, As I remember it, that was the end of Latin instruction in that school.

Remember, he added, it wasn't the *best* high school, but still it was a good school.

I did remember, dimly: some story that someone had once told us, my mother, my aunt, I can't recall who, maybe one of my uncles. Daddy had been *the smartest kid in junior high school*, a math whiz, but for some reason he hadn't gone on to the most competitive high school, a place called Bronx Science, which is where math and science whizzes went. But I couldn't remember the rest of the story, and didn't know why he hadn't gone to the best school.

So it was a very good school, my father was saying. There weren't many of us who were taking Latin, so the program depended on us! But we didn't go the distance. And I think that a couple of years after that spring, Latin just petered out and died.

You could see that it still bothered my father, after all those years— the way he and his classmates had rejected the teaching of the mild-mannered German Jew who'd come so far with only this rarefied knowledge to give. You could see, when he told this story, that he was still angry with himself for the way in which, having come so far himself in his study of the ancient language, he'd failed to travel the final leg of his classical journey and read the greatest work in that language—a work about a man who rescues his aged father from the burning ruins of his vanquished city and then travels far to a new and unknown land, care-fully keeping both his father and his young son in tow, in order to make a new life with them there. *Aeneas*, that paragon of filial dutifulness; which quality, as my father knew well, is no trivial thing.

When I was a child and first heard the story of my father's failure to pursue Latin—and, even later, when I was in college and then graduate school and the subject of higher education or advanced degrees or Clas-sics would come up, which would occasion his telling this tale again, speaking in the slightly musing way that he had, almost as if by telling

it over and over he might finally understand why the rest of his life had
come out the way it had—when I was young and used to hear this story,
I was so taken with the drama and the poignancy of it, the poor German
Jew and his narrow escape, the heedless teenagers looking longingly out
the windows on a warm day in New York City just after the end of the
war, indifferent to the riches of the past, above all the almost unbearable
image of a teacher filled with knowledge that no one wanted, that it never
occurred to me to ask why my father would have given up studying a subject at which he had excelled, had been a star; just as it hadn't occurred
to me to ask why such a star had ended up in the second-best school.

A lonely boy sits off to the side of a crowded room, dreaming of his absent
father.

   The boy is Odysseus' son, Telemachus. Two decades have passed
since his father left for Troy, never to be heard from again. Since then,
the palace has been overrun by dozens of young men from Ithaca and
the islands beyond who, assuming that Odysseus is long since dead, are
courting the still-beautiful Penelope, hoping to become her husband
and assume the kingship of Ithaca. But their presence there constitutes
a grotesque violation of the laws both of courtship and of marriage: for
instead of observing custom, instead of bringing offerings and bride gifts
to Penelope, they have made themselves at home in her palace, drain-
ing its stores of food and wine, carousing day and night, seducing the
servant girls. The social fabric of the island kingdom has frayed, too, its
government ground to a standstill. Some citizens are still loyal to the
absent king, but others have chosen to throw their lot in with the Suitors; meanwhile, no assembly of the island's citizens has been held since
Odysseus left.

   The missing king's family is falling apart. The dejected queen has
withdrawn to her chambers above the banquet hall, having long since
exhausted her repertoire of tricks designed to keep the Suitors at bay:

as the pressure mounts daily for her to make a choice, she swoons and weeps. As for Odysseus' careworn father, Laertes, he is so disgusted by the mayhem in the palace that he

> *no longer comes down into town,*
> *but toils alone in the countryside, far from men;*
> *an old woman-servant is there to serve him food and drink*
> *when his arms and legs are gripped by weariness*
> *from scrabbling up and down the vineyard's slopes.*

So not only is Telemachus' father gone, but his father's father has vanished, too. The melancholy youth now teeters at the brink of manhood with no one to show him the way.

This is how the *Odyssey* begins: the hero himself nowhere in sight, the crises precipitated by his absence taking center stage. However long the proem of the *Odyssey* actually is—ten lines, twenty-one lines—it turns out to be misleading: despite its promise to tell us about "a man," the fact is that this man appears at first only as a memory, a ghost about whom we hear stories, reminiscences, rumors. He's on his way home, someone says; someone else recalls having glimpsed him back in Troy, disguised as a beggar on a spying mission. Another, rather unsavory story surfaces: Ah yes, Odysseus, he once came looking for some poisoned arrows. (These, we understand, are not at all the weapons that noble warriors are supposed to use.) The rumors whirl and eddy, but the hero himself—"the man"—is nowhere to be seen, either on Ithaca or in Homer's narrative. And all the while, the wife weeps, the populace seethes, the son daydreams hopelessly. It's as if the Muse had mischievously decided to take the words of the proem literally—to begin at random, at "some point or another," and that starting point turns out to be a different one altogether from the one we had expected.

It is hard not to feel that Homer's decision to obscure and blur and postpone our view of the epic's main character is designed to pique our curiosity about this shadowy figure, who, in these crucial first pages, seems to lurk at the far edges of his own story, curiously small and difficult to make out, like one of those tiny figures in a Dutch painting that you risk not noticing at all because your eye is drawn to the painting's ostensible subject, the figure in the foreground, and only when you peer at the picture more closely do you realize that this smaller, more distant, even partial shape is of deeper interest after all, is the element that will reward the closest study—is, perhaps, the painting's true subject. The most famous example of this visual sleight of hand is a painting called *Landscape with the Fall of Icarus*, by the Netherlandish master Pieter Brueghel, which hangs in a museum in Brussels and takes as its subject another of antiquity's many father-son dramas: the myth of the great inventor Daedalus and his son Icarus, who sought to fly on artificial wings made of feathers bound by wax. In the best-known version of the myth, which appears in a poem by Ovid, Daedalus warns his son not to fly too high, since the sun's warmth will melt the wax; but the heedless son, giddy with excitement, disobeys his father, soars too high, loses his wings, and crashes into the sea. With poignant irony, Brueghel's canvas illustrates the split second in time just after Icarus has fallen: the painting is almost entirely taken up by the shore and the sea and, especially, by three peasants who go about their business, plowing, herding, and fishing, utterly unaware of the catastrophe—the only sign of which is a tiny detail off in the corner, which turns out to be poor Icarus' legs waggling pathetically just above the waterline. In Brueghel's hands, Ovid's tale of a son's willful rejection of his father's wisdom becomes a story about the need for a kind of humility—for, you might say, perspective; an admonition about what we miss when we are intent on our own narratives, about the dangers of mistaking the foreground for the whole picture.

The character who stands front and center as the *Odyssey* begins, and who remains the center of our attention during its first four books, is the person who slowly gathers all the rumors, gossip, and stories: Odysseus' son. When we meet him, a little after the proem ends, Telemachus cuts a melancholy figure. He is, Homer says, "sorrowing in his heart" as he sits forlornly in the great hall of the royal palace at Ithaca, watching powerlessly as the Suitors laugh and feast uproariously around him. Having no idea how to assert himself, Odysseus' only child is reduced to helpless fantasies,

> picturing his noble father in his mind, wishing that
> he'd come and sweep the Suitors from the house!

The problem is not simply that no one knows for sure just where his noble father is; the greater dilemma is that nobody knows if he's even alive. This uncertainty triggers further questions: whether Penelope is a wife or a widow, still married or now marriageable; whether the hero's son can, if necessary, be the king and man his father had been. At present, the answer to this last question is clearly no.

The agonizing suspense in which the royal family, the Suitors, and the populace have been languishing is vividly evoked by means of a story we hear during these first few books of the *Odyssey,* the books from which Odysseus himself is absent. The tale, which concerns the best known of the ruses that Penelope has employed to keep the Suitors at bay, has an obvious symbolic meaning. The queen, one of the Suitors angrily complains, had once promised to marry one of them at last, but only after she finished weaving a funeral shroud for her father-in-law, Laertes, the decrepit old man who now glumly tends his farmstead far from the scene of his absent son's humiliation. The Suitors agreed to her plan; but every night, in secret, the cunning queen would unravel what she had woven during the day, thereby indefinitely postponing the completion of her handiwork. This deceit worked for several years, until one of Penelope's maids, a faithless girl who's been sleeping with one of the Suitors, exposed the ruse. The Suitors confronted the queen, who was then forced to complete the shroud. Since then—all this, we learn, took place three years before the *Odyssey* begins, three years before the moment when the prince sits helpless and forlorn in his hall, wishing his father could miraculously appear—the queen has disappeared into her chambers.

This story tells us a great deal about Penelope's desperation—and about her cunning, which is every bit a match for her husband's well-known wiles. But even more, the weaving and unweaving, knotting and then loosening, speeding and then delaying, beautifully capture the torpor, the lack of forward motion, that characterizes life on Ithaca during Odysseus' long absence. This seesawing, the surf-like back-and-forth, is, too, the rhythm of the *Odyssey* itself: the forward push of the plot, the backward pull of the flashbacks, of the backstories and digressions without which the main narrative would seem thin, insubstantial.

So the great epic of travel, of voyages, of journeying, begins with its characters frozen in place. The unwholesome sense of stalemate that characterizes that state of affairs on Ithaca also raises a number of questions that are, in essence, literary. How to start the poem? Where does a story begin? How do you put an end to the past and turn it into the present?

One answer to that question is, By an act of will. After the proem ends, the action moves to the lofty peaks of Mount Olympus, the heavenly home of the gods, where Athena, moved by pity for her favorite mortal, prods her father, Zeus, to break the ten-year-long deadlock. Recalling his affection for the wily mortal, the king of the gods agrees. The divine plan to get Odysseus home will have two parts. First, Hermes, the messenger god, will hasten to the island where the lovesick nymph Calypso has been holding Odysseus captive for the past seven years, and there he will order her to let her prisoner go. But this scene is, in fact, postponed until Book 5—the book in which the action will finally pick up Odysseus' story. Until then, the poem is preoccupied with the other part of the divine plan, which unfolds on Ithaca and involves the hero's son.

After flying down to the island kingdom, Athena infiltrates the palace disguised as an old friend of Odysseus' called Mentes; slipping into the banquet hall where the Suitors are feasting and dancing, she contrives to meet Prince Telemachus. (The youth's name means "the far-off warrior":

the son who defines himself by the absence of his father has a name that recalls both the absence and the reason for it.) As he politely converses with the disguised Athena, Telemachus bitterly betrays his insecurities, which run very deep indeed: at one point, he sulks that although his mother, Penelope, has always insisted that Odysseus is his father, he can't know for sure. After pausing to remark on the "outrageous arrogance" of the Suitors' insulting behavior, Athena seeks to assuage the young man's anxieties. She assures him, first, that Odysseus is not at all dead but in fact alive on an island, being held captive by "savage men" (with amusing delicacy, she edits out the lovely nymph Calypso); she comments, too, on the young man's strong physical resemblance to his father: the head, those fine eyes . . .

But the best medicine for him, she knows, would be to act, and so she takes him in hand. First, she says, he should call a council of Ithaca's citizens and "speak his mind" to them: "command the Suitors to scurry back home!" Then she tells him to get hold of a ship and travel to the homes of two of his father's wartime companions, Nestor, the elderly king of Pylos, and Menelaus, husband of Helen and king of Sparta:

> *If you hear your father lives and is returning home,*
> *then have the patience to wait out one full year:*
> *but if you hear that he has died and is no more*
> *then come you home to your beloved fatherland*
> *and build a tomb for him and heap it high*
> *with grave-goods, as befits him, and marry off your mother.*

This passage, in fact, lays out the plots of the *Odyssey*'s next three books. In Book 2, Telemachus will call the long-overdue assembly of the citizens of Ithaca and confront the Suitors in the presence of the people. In Book 3 he leaves home for the first time in his life, sailing to Pylos, where he meets Nestor and learns a little about his father's wartime activities; in Book 4 he travels from Pylos to Sparta, where he finds Menelaus and Helen living in great splendor, both of them full of reminiscences about Odysseus' cleverness and gumption.

All of which is to say that during the first four books of the epic, Odysseus' son will have his own adventures at last. These travels will allow him to share in the experiences that, according to the proem, Odysseus has had: "to see the cities and know the minds of men." In this way, the poem ingeniously reassures Telemachus that he is, indeed, his father's son.

To this unexpected but suggestive opening section, as to certain other episodes of the *Odyssey*, tradition has assigned a name. Just as *Ilias*, the *Iliad*, is a song about Ilion (another name for Troy), just as *Odysseia*, the *Odyssey*, is a song about Odysseus, so *Telemakheia*, the Telemachy— the title of the epic's first major section—is a song about Telemachus. As the trajectory of these four books suggests, they tell the story of how an absent father's child starts to learn about his parent, and about the world.

It is the story of a son's education.

I just don't see why he's supposed to be such a great hero!

It was eleven-fifteen on the morning of January 28, 2011, about an hour into the first meeting of Classics 125: The *Odyssey* of Homer. Since we'd sat down, my father hadn't stopped complaining about Odysseus.

He'd gotten to my house at nine. Although the weather was bad, he'd insisted on driving. It would be easier to drive than to take two trains, he'd said over the phone a few days earlier, which of course wasn't true; but then, my father had never liked being a passenger. Earlier that morning, as I waited for him to arrive, I'd pictured him moving cautiously through the heavy snow in his big white car, wearing one of the baggy white sweaters that he favored. In order to get to campus with a little time to spare before class started, at ten past ten, he would have had to leave his house on Long Island well before seven; and although he didn't say so, I was aware that this added element of hardship, of discomfort, made the idea of driving more attractive to him. *If it isn't hard, it's not worth doing.* I could already hear the boastful complaint that he'd be making the following week to his buddies at Town Bagel, Ralph and Milton and Lenny and the others, as they sat at the bright orange Formica tables, the giant Styrofoam cups of coffee steaming in front of them while they talked, as they had done every morning for many years, about the usual things: their wives and children and divorces and grandchildren, the Mets and the Giants, the arthritis and the prostates. *I had to get up at five-thirty! Jesus!* Daddy would be telling them.

In his own way, my father, too, was a man of pain.

I could picture him, scowling as he drove, talking to himself silently, his thin lips moving over narrow teeth that were grayish yellow after years of smoking, a habit he had quit all at once one day in 1970, I suspect because "going cold turkey" was the severest way to stop, the most painful. I'd watched my father drive many thousands of times over the years: nosing the car along the hushed streets of the neighborhood we lived in, shaded by maples and pin oaks, the houses seeming to peer out suspiciously through their shuttered windows; grinding along on exhaust-choked interstates and turnpikes to summer barbecues and holiday parties, to the apartment buildings in Brooklyn or Queens where mysterious relations of my mother lived, elderly people whom we could faintly hear, after we rang the doorbell, as they shuffled to answer the brown-painted steel doors, with their many clanking locks and the peepholes through which they would cautiously peer after we rang, one eye looming gigantically, comically, through the convex glass, like the single eye of some mythic monster. I would watch him drive to the school concerts, orchestra, band, choir, chorale, madrigals, autumn, winter, and spring; drive us to summer camp, to piano and cello and guitar lessons, drive us to bar mitzvahs and weddings and, as the years passed and my grandparents and the parents of Mother and Daddy's friends started dying (and then, later, as their own friends themselves started dying), would drive in funeral processions, too, during which he liked to complain bitterly about motorists who

failed to yield to the slow-moving cortège, because as much as he hated
ceremony of any kind, which he vehemently did, he had a great regard
for the dead, even those he hadn't much liked while they were alive—
out of respect, I suppose, for their having finally done the hardest, most
painful thing of all.

As my father drove he would often, spontaneously, hunch his narrow
left shoulder, as bony as the wing of a chicken, toward his ear, as if in a
spasm, and as he did this his lips would curl into a grimace, the uncon-
scious gesture you might make if you're carrying on an argument with
yourself about something, maybe something to do with your numerous
children, their frequently delayed travel plans, or the money they say
they need to make the long trip to see you; maybe it is yet another replay
of some ancient debate with your wife, perhaps about her reluctance to
travel (which is the reason you yourself, who are curious about the world,
eager to see it, never go anywhere); perhaps about something else, something even older, the exchanges so familiar by this point that you can
play both parts equally well as you drive your big white car, which is one
of the few luxuries you permit yourself—a kind of compensation, maybe,
for all the places you didn't go.

> *It doesn't matter what you said, it was* how *you said it.*
> *Oh, stop writing scripts for me already!*
> *Well, Daddy would never have let them talk to me that way.*
> *Oh, your father, your father! Trust me, he wasn't such a hero. I know*
> *   things . . .*

My father's thin frame would tense as he replayed these ancient conversations in his mind, the left shoulder twisting upward, his right hand
at the twelve o'clock mark on the wheel, his lips moving soundlessly.

I supposed his lips were moving in just that way as he pulled into my
driveway that January day, maneuvering the comically large vehicle with
exaggerated caution, as if to say, *It wasn't easy to get here.* And the first
thing he said, in fact, as he swung both legs out the driver's-side door and

reached for the inside handle above the window to hoist himself out of the soft bucket seat—a thing I had never seen him do until recently—was, as I knew it would be, "You can't believe the traffic!"

He loved to complain about how difficult it was to get places. *You can't believe the traffic!* was the refrain that ran through our childhood, our adolescence, even our adulthood, long after we'd left the neat white house and the trim white car and the baggy white sweaters behind; the sentence would explode out of his mouth as soon as he arrived somewhere, as unvarying and formulaic as the stock phrases that Homer resorts to when describing certain kinds of typical scenes or actions, sunrises or banqueting or arguments, "When Dawn the child of morning appeared with her fingertips of rose" or "When they had put away desire for food and drink" or "What speech has escaped the barrier of your teeth?!" So, too, with my father and driving. *The parkway was a nightmare!* he would say as he walked through someone's door, or *The Long Island Expressway is one giant parking lot!* he would cry as we arrived, late as usual, at some function, and we would all nod, even though, in certain cases, we knew that this wasn't quite true, wasn't entirely the reason we were late. (For instance, if our destination was a religious service of any kind, he would leave the house at the precise time the service was supposed to begin, and then pretend, when we got there an hour late, that we'd hit traffic on the way.) Even when he wanted to get somewhere on time—to his friend Nino's, for instance, with whom he'd worked when they were both young men pursuing graduate degrees in mathematics, or to play tennis on Tuesday evenings with his work buddy Bob McGill—it seemed that some implacable traffic god was against him. We would pile into the car, all seven of us, Andrew in the front passenger seat because he got "car sickness" if he sat in back, Matt and Eric and Jennifer in the deck, me in the backseat next to Mother (who liked to sit in the back so she could put her right leg, purpled with the varicose veins her many pregnancies had left her with, up on the front seat between my father's right shoulder and Andrew's left shoulder, *because this way I can rest my bad leg*), and pull away from the curbside with plenty of time to spare, and yet even then the traffic would be somehow bad, the expressway like a parking lot, and we'd be late.

You can't believe the traffic! my father exclaimed as he pulled himself out of the car that January morning, stomping both feet into the white powder, his footprints like angry exclamation marks in the snow. As I stood on the porch awaiting him, I could see how gingerly he made his way up the steps, because of his great fear of falling. As he gripped the handrail, he looked up at me and asked me what we'd be covering in the first day of class, and I said, The beginning.

Now, an hour into the first session of the class, it was clear he didn't think much of Odysseus.

One week before the start of classes, I'd sent an e-mail to the students enrolled in the course, asking them to read Book 1 in advance of the first class session and to come prepared to share their thoughts about why the epic begins the way it does. The class would be meeting every Friday for just under two and a half hours, from 10:10 in the morning to 12:30, with a short coffee break around 11:15. On this first day of the semester, I wrote to them, we'd spend the first half of the session talking about Book 1. After the break I'd be lecturing about the basics of Homeric poetry: the history of the debate about how Homer's poems were originally composed, the nature of oral poetry, elements of epic technique, and my expectations for the course.

I also mentioned that my father would be sitting in on the course. Better to warn them, I thought, so his presence on the first day of class wouldn't be a distraction.

So, I declared, looking down the length of the seminar table at 10:15, I've asked you to think about how the *Odyssey* begins. We can't have a full discussion of Book 1 today—next week we'll be talking about 1 and 2 in detail—but we can at least get the ball rolling. What strikes you right away about the opening of our poem—anything strange, anything worth noticing?

A boy who was sitting at the far end of the table grinned and said, It's long! He had deep dimples that undercut whatever cool his carefully groomed scruff was meant to convey. As I rolled my eyes, the slender, dark-eyed girl sitting next to him elbowed him sharply. Girlfriend and boyfriend. Her eyes were so black that you couldn't tell the irises from the pupils.

Try harder, I said drily. What's your name?

The scruffy boy said, Jack. The girl said, Nina.

On the table in front of me lay the printout of the class roster that the registrar's office had sent. I scanned it for their names. Next to his I wrote "Jack of the Dimples." Next to hers I wrote "Nina Dark-Eyes."

I'd gotten into this habit twenty years earlier, when I was a graduate student instructor. On the first day of class, as the students identified them-selves, I'd jot down some memorable physical characteristic next to their names on the roster in order to be able to remember who they were. As a result of these jottings it would often be the case that, even after I knew the students well, I would continue to think of them reflexively as Zack of the Tiny Wire-Rimmed Glasses or Maureen Green-Eyes, as if those physical appurtenances and traits, rather than being superficial, were in fact evidence of some inalienable inner essence, a taste for precision or an irrepressible impishness. This isn't all that different from the way that, in Homer's epics, certain characters are identified by stock epithets that refer to a physical characteristic or attribute ("swift-footed Achilles" or "gray-eyed Athena") or by a particular stance or gesture. For instance, every time Penelope comes downstairs from her bedchamber to the great hall of the palace where the Suitors are feasting, the scene is described in exactly the same way, starting with the first such moment, which occurs in Book 1:

> *She came down the lofty stairway of the house,*
> *nor was she alone: two maidservants came along.*
> *When this goddess among women reached the Suitors*
> *she stood beside the door-post of the well-built hall,*
> *and held the gleaming veil before her cheeks,*
> *a maidservant standing by on either side.*

Some modern readers find the verbatim repetitions of phrases, the oddly mechanical recurrence of gestures and stances, off-putting. But certain scholars have argued that, apart from whatever technical function these prefabricated lines and phrases may have served, they provide insight into the mind-set of the archaic poets—not least, their belief in the underlying consistency of nature and people and objects, whatever the distortions of history and violence and time—a belief in such constancy being of particular importance in this poem, whose characters are striving to recognize one another after decades of separation and trauma. This view of the epithets' function is rather comforting; and indeed, their recurrence comes to feel reassuring. Like pitons stuck into the vast face of the epic, they give the audience a safe hold as they make their way through the sprawling text.

I looked around the room and repeated my question about what they might have found interesting about the opening of the poem.

After an awkward silence a tall boy with a big Adam's apple and lots of dark hair, who seemed to be outgrowing his clothes as I stood looking at him—on that late-January morning his wrists were poking out far beyond the cuffs of his sweater—said, I think it's interesting that Odysseus is barely even present in Book 1.

A cartoonist might do this kid as a dark splotch atop a single vertical stroke. He looked, in fact, just like the Don Quixote in a Picasso drawing my parents had in the house somewhere, one of the reproductions from the Metropolitan Museum that my mother liked to have framed.

Good, I said. Yes. The focus is somewhere else at first.

I asked him for his name.

Tom, he said.

Next to his name I wrote "Don Quixote Tom."

Good, I repeated. Odysseus is a kind of ghost in Book 1. What's the book actually focused on?

A gray-eyed girl sitting next to me looked up and said, nodding, I'm Trisha. A mass of fairish curls quivered when she spoke.

I made a mark on the roster. "Trisha of the Botticelli Hair."

The book's focused on the situation in Ithaca, she said.

Yes, I said, good. And what exactly is the situation?

It's like there's this . . . stagnation at the beginning, she went on.

Good, I said. So why do you think Homer focuses on the stagnation in Ithaca in Book 1 instead of getting right to Odysseus?

I looked around the table with an encouraging expression, but nobody said anything.

Every now and then when you're a teacher—not often, but sometimes—you get a group with whom you have no chemistry. You talk and talk, you ask leading questions and feed them half-lines to get them going, but they just sit there, politely taking notes and occasionally venturing a muttered comment with the unconfident, upward intonation of a question. The interactions are inert, one-sided, lacking the fizzy back-and-forth that is the hallmark of a really good seminar. It was too early to tell, but I was worried that this group seemed a little reticent. *Oh God*, I thought, *of course this would be the class that Daddy is observing.*

Finally, a large blond kid with a round face and sharp blue eyes behind wide-rimmed glasses raised his hand.

I'm also Tom, he said.

On the printout I wrote "Sancho Panza Tom." Then I crossed it out and wrote "Blond Tom."

Is it a kind of setup? He wants to show you how bad things are at home, so when Odysseus finally gets back it feels like a climax?

Nice idea, I said. But let me ask you this: based on our glimpse of Odysseus in Book 1, how likely does that climax seem?

A slender girl down on the right lifted a pale hand about three inches off the surface of the table and gave it a little wiggle, like someone trying to signal to a friend during a church service. Her hair was remarkable: dark red, almost henna-colored, falling straight to her shoulders in a shimmering sheet.

Not very likely! she said. I thought he was kind of mopey, actually—

Excuse me, I said. What's your name?

She blushed and said, Sorry.

Nothing to be sorry about! Go on.

I'm Madeline?

I found her name on the roster. "Madeline of the Shining Red Hair."

Okay, Madeline. How, "mopey"?

He's just very *depressed*, she went on. When Athena is talking to Zeus at the beginning, when they're deciding what to do about Odysseus and how he's stuck on the island with Calypso, she describes him as just mop- ing around the island, crying.

Trisha's curls bobbled as she wrote in her notebook. Looking up at me, she said, I think the first book is meant to be a kind of surprise. So here we are at the beginning of this big epic about this great hero, and the first reference to him is that he's a kind of *loser*. He's a castaway, he's a prisoner, he has no power and no way of getting home. He's hidden from everything he cares for. So it's as if he can't go any lower, it can only go uphill from there.

Great, I said. Yes. It provides a baseline for the hero's narrative arc.

It was at this point that my father raised his head and said, "Hero"? *I* don't think he's a hero at all.

In unison, the students' heads swiveled in his direction. Instead of sitting with the rest of the students at the seminar table, he'd taken a seat in a corner of the room off to my left and a little behind me, at my eight o'clock, in a blocky wooden chair beneath a window that looked out onto a depressing expanse of gravelly plowed snow. He would sit in this same chair every Friday for the next fifteen weeks.

I'll tell you what I think is interesting about Odysseus!

I turned and stared at him. When we'd first talked about the pos- sibility of his sitting in on the course, he'd promised me that he wasn't going to talk in class. *Nahh,* he'd said at some point not long after the November day in 2010 when he'd called and said, I've been reading the *Odyssey* on my iPad, but there's a lot of stuff I just don't *get.* Didn't you say you were going to be teaching it next term?—which is how all this began. At first I'd hesitated. Did he really want to come up every week,

two and a half hours each way, and sit there for two and a half hours more
with a bunch of freshmen? Sure, he'd said. Why not? Don't forget, I was
a professor, too. I know how to deal with college kids! I'd reflected for a
moment. Okay, I finally said. But remember, it's a seminar, not a lecture
class—it's going to be a bunch of kids sitting around a table talking about
the text. There's nowhere to hide. Would you be uncomfortable in that
kind of setting? Nahh, my father had replied, I'm just gonna sit there and
listen.

Now, on the first day of the class, he was talking. *I'll* tell you what I
think is interesting, he repeated.

He sat at the desk holding his hand up in the air. A curious effect of
his being in the room with these very young people was that now, for the
first time, he suddenly looked very old to me, smaller than I remembered
him being, paler. The shock of perceiving my father as an old man wasn't
entirely new to me by that point, but sometimes his appearance, because
of the light or the circumstances, still had the power to startle me. A few
months earlier, in September, I'd taken the train from Manhattan out to
the suburbs in order to spend a few days with my parents for my father's
eighty-first birthday. No, he had said, when I called to tell him which
train I was going to be on, don't take a cab from the station, I'll pick you
up myself. When I got out onto the platform at Bethpage I scrutinized
the mass of cars in the parking lot below and wondered why a desiccated-
looking man in too-large clothes was waving at me and then suddenly I
thought, *Daddy.* With some embarrassment, I went down the steps that
led from the platform to the parking lot, and he puckered his mouth in
the way he sometimes did when he was exasperated by someone's inex-
plicable stupidity—a driver who had cut him off, the checkout girl who
made the wrong change—and said, *I was standing right there, waving!*
and I said, Sorry, the sun was in my eyes.

Okay, I was saying to my father now. What do you think is so interesting? Why don't you think he's a "hero"?

My father cleared his throat and motioned to Trisha. First, I agree
with her that he's a loser—but not only because he's a helpless prisoner!

The students looked amused.

Am I the only one, my father went on, who's bothered by the fact that Odysseus is *alone* when the poem begins?

What do you mean, "alone"?

I couldn't see where he was going with this.

Well, he said, he went off twenty years earlier to fight in the Trojan War, right? And he was presumably the leader of his kingdom's forces?

Yes, I said. In the second book of the *Iliad* there's a list of all the Greek forces that went to fight at Troy. It says that Odysseus sailed with a contingent of twelve ships.

My father's voice was loud with triumph. Right! That's hundreds of men. So my question is, What happened to the twelve ships and their crews? Why is he the only person coming home alive?

Some students looked around the room at one another. Others ruffled the pages of their copies of the *Odyssey* and stared intently at the print, as if by doing so they could force an answer from the paper.

I said, Actually that's a good question. Anyone want to try to answer it?

They watched silently as I scanned the room, wildly hoping that some youngster would handily respond to my father's question.

After a moment or two I said, Well, I think there are actually two ways of answering that question. The first has to do with the plot. If you read the proem carefully, you'll recall that it calls his men "fools"—it says they died "through their own recklessness." As we go through the poem we'll get to the incidents during which his men perished, different groups at different times. And then you'll tell me whether you think it was through their own recklessness.

My father made a face, as if he could have done better than Odysseus, could have brought the twelve ships and their crews home safely. He said, So you admit that he lost all his men?

Yep, I said, a little defiantly. I felt like I was eleven years old again, and Odysseus was a naughty schoolmate whom I'd decided I was going to stand by even if it meant being punished along with him.

He was clearly not convinced.

Nina, the dark-eyed girl, looked across the table. You said there were two ways of answering the question about why he comes back all alone. What's the other way?

Well, I said, that answer has to do with "narrative," really. When you think of it, he *has* to be the only one to make it home.

I looked around the room.

Think about it, I went on after a moment. If he's the only one still standing, then—what?

Trisha looked up from her notebook. Then he gets to be the hero of the story.

Right, I said; and thought, *This* one is a live wire.

Think, I said to the whole class, think of what the *Odyssey* would be like if he'd returned with twelve men, or five—even just one other ship-mate. It would never work. To be the hero of an epic, you have to get rid of the competition, so to speak.

Again my father said, Well, *I* don't think he's such a great hero!

He looked around the table. What kind of leader loses all his men? You call that a hero?!

The students laughed out loud. Then, as if fearful that they'd over-stepped some boundary, they peered inquisitively down the length of the seminar table at me. Since I wanted to show them I was a good sport, I smiled broadly.

But what I was thinking was, *This is going to be a nightmare.*

They came back from the campus cafeteria a little before half past eleven, clutching their coffee cups and stomping the snow off their shoes. After they'd settled back into their seats, I launched into my lecture. I ended up talking for most of the remaining hour.

This is the last time I'm going to talk so much in this course, I began. The point of a seminar is for you to do the talking. They don't pay me enough to talk so much!

There were a few nervous giggles.

I started with the controversy known as the Homeric Question, a centuries-old debate about how Homer's epics had come into being— whether they had started as written texts or as oral compositions. It was important for the students to grasp the fundamentals of the debate, since significant questions of interpretation hang on which theory you sub- scribe to.

The Greeks themselves tended to think that there had been a poet called Homer who wrote down his poems. Herodotus thought that Homer must have lived around 800 B.C., four hundred years before his own time; several centuries after Herodotus, Aristarchus, the head of the Library of Alexandria (the greatest scholarly institution of the ancient world) and a renowned authority on Homer's texts, surmised that the poet had lived about 1050 B.C., a century and a half after the Trojan War itself was supposed to have taken place. It was generally believed that Homer wrote both the *Iliad* and the *Odyssey*; but some ancient scholars, called the Separatists, thought the poems were written by two different people. No fewer than seven cities in ancient times claimed Homer as a son.

That was the received wisdom until, in the late 1700s, a French scholar called Villoisin discovered a tenth-century manuscript of the *Iliad* moldering away in a library in Venice. This manuscript was unlike others that had circulated over the centuries: along with the Greek text of the epic it included transcriptions of the marginal notes of ancient commentators, from Byzantine sages back to the Librarians of Alex- andria themselves, writing in the 200s and 100s B.C. The notes made it clear that those earlier commentators had had access to different and sometimes competing versions of the poem. Seizing upon this rev- elation, a German scholar who was reviewing Villoisin's work—none other than Friedrich August Wolf, as it happens, the great advocate of philology, the scientific study of literature—arrived at a revolutionary insight: the texts of the *Iliad* and *Odyssey* that we possess could not have been fixed in writing until relatively late in their history. Wolf argued—shockingly, to many of his contemporaries—that Homer himself must have been illiterate. Rather than writing his poems down, as had previously been thought, he had instead composed a series of ballads (known as lays) that were short enough to be memorized and which were transmitted orally for generations, perhaps by guilds of professional reciters. At some point later on, these discrete lays were assembled into the immensely long and complex poems we have today by a sophisticated editor/compiler who, unlike his predecessors, did know how to write.

Wolf's hypothesis ultimately paved the way for what is now known as the oral theory of Homeric composition, to which most classicists today adhere. According to this theory, there was no single Homer: rather, the bards who performed the epics, itinerant singer-performers who were repositories of a centuries-old tradition, at once reproduced material that earlier poets had composed while refining it and adding new material of their own, sometimes improvising as they performed. (For convenience's sake, most classicists refer to the corporate author of the epics as "Homer," as I do here.) This composition-in-performance, as those who took up Wolf's ideas argued later, was made possible by certain conventional features of Homeric poetry. Take those prefabricated stock epithets, for instance—"Agamemnon, the Lord of Men" or "Dawn with the Fingertips of Rose." Imagine that you're improvising as you tell a story in verse; if you know that the next line you're going to sing will end with ". . . said Agamemnon, the Lord of Men," you can focus on how you're going to fill the beginning of that line—the part where your creative energy needs to go.

One advantage of the oral theory was that it explained a number of inconsistencies and oddities in the texts of the *Iliad* and *Odyssey*. Some of these are rather technical: for instance, the poems will sometimes juxtapose in a single scene tools and objects and even techniques of warfare that date from wildly disparate periods of Greek history. (Others are less abstruse: a few characters die twice.) Further apparent anomalies are present in the epics' structures. One example, seized upon both by the followers of Wolf and by those who insisted that there was one Homer who wrote the epics, was, in fact, the Telemachy. For those who wanted to see the epics as the layered products of many poets over many generations, the apparent lack of continuity between the first four books of the *Odyssey*, with their intent focus on Telemachus and his attempt to gather information about his long-lost father, and the story of Odysseus himself and his homecoming, which begins in Book 5, was proof that Books 1 through 4 had once been a separate lay, eventually tacked onto the larger story by a later editor, leaving the "obvious and imperfectly fitted joints" (as Wolf put it) between the two sections still showing. By contrast, those who wanted to see the poems as the product of one creative genius called attention to what they argued was an obvious series of continuities between the Telemachy and the rest of the poem. For them, the prince's voyages by sea in Books 3 and 4, his meetings with fascinating strangers who have interesting histories, are miniaturized versions of his father's adventures in the later books. These scholars emphasized, too, that the descriptions of the dire situation on Ithaca in Books 1 through 4 are necessary for setting the stage for Odysseus' return later on. All this, they argued, had to have been part of a single artistic vision that worked its way through the epic's many themes and episodes.

Whatever else it may mean, the fact that both of these hostile camps could make use of the same examples to prove diametrically opposed interpretations suggests a truth about how all of us read and interpret literary texts—one that is, possibly, rooted in the mysteries of human nature itself. Where some people see chaos and incoherence, others will find sense and symmetry and wholeness.

Is all this clear? I asked at the end of my long disquisition about the Homeric Question on the first day of Classics 125: The *Odyssey* of Homer. I know it's a lot to absorb, but it's important to have a sense of how these poems probably came together as you go through the *Odyssey*, since you should be looking out for the kinds of inconsistencies and unities that these scholars have been arguing about.

They nodded dutifully.

Uh-huh, I said, and they laughed nervously.

You know, I said, this improvising-while-you-perform thing sounds impossible, but we all do it, to various extents.

Then I told them a story.

When my boys were little, their favorite part of the *Odyssey* was the episode involving a witchlike nymph called Circe, on whose island Odysseus lands during his travels and who, at one point, transforms his men into pigs. Perhaps because of this comical transformation, Peter and Thomas loved this part and would insist on hearing it over and over. This would have been when Peter was seven or so; Thomas was still in pre-kindergarten. On weekday mornings after Lily went to work, I'd bundle the boys into my car and, as I drove along the twisting country roads that led to their school, I'd spin out some version of the Circe story for them: the arrival on the island, the transformation of the men into swine, how a helpful god gives Odysseus a rare herb that foils the witch's magic. (The episode ends with Odysseus and Circe sleeping together, but I left that part out.) They were going through a finicky phase just then; in a desperate attempt to give their lunch some allure, I'd work the items in their lunchboxes into the version of the story that I was rattling off. *And when Odysseus and his men landed on the island of Aiaia, what should he see in the forest clearing but some delicious applesauce!!* As I rambled on, calculating how much time I would need to bring the story to its end—*And when she knew she had been beaten she let Odysseus and all of his men stay in her palace for a year and they became very good friends, everyone cooperating with everyone else!*—I could almost feel the force of their attention on the back of my neck, their fervent wish that I'd find a way to wind up the story just as we pulled up in front of the school, which of course I always did.

Hurry, Nano, hurry! Peter would be whispering as we crunched along the gravel driveway, using the nickname he'd given me when he first began to talk and couldn't pronounce "Daniel" . . . Years later, when he was in high school, he took a mythology course, which of course pleased me—although when we mentioned it to our friends I was quick to say that I hadn't "pressured" him to like the Classics. One night he called me, laughing. *Nano!* That story you used to tell us, with Circe and the tangerines and the peanut butter sandwiches, it's *nothing* like the way it is in the book! I grinned. Hey, I'm just doing what Homer did. What's that? Peter asked, and I said, Improvising!

I told the smiling students this story and said, You see? You'd be surprised how often we make things up as we go along in front of an audience.

Even as I said the words, I was thinking, *like teaching*.

I went on to catalog the special features of Homer's poetry, starting with the long, six-beat, oom-pah-pah meter, called dactylic hexameter, to which every one of the *Odyssey*'s twelve thousand one hundred and ten lines dances:

BUM-buh-buh BUM-buh-buh BUM; buh-buh BUM-buh-buh BUM-buh buh BUM BUM

I talked about the stock epithets, so useful for quick identification of the characters, so crucial for oral composition. I told them to look out for "epic similes": passages in which the poet pauses to compare a character or an action in his fabulous tale, sometimes at considerable length, to something belonging to the everyday world of his audience— of *us*. (My favorite of these crops up in a battle scene in the *Iliad*, when the poet compares a warrior who drives a spear through an enemy's head and cantilevers the poor man out of his chariot to an expert angler landing a fish.) The point of these lengthy similes is simultaneously to make the fictional action more present, more vividly knowable to the audience, and yet, by briefly returning to the familiar realities of our humdrum lives, plowing and fishing and cooking, to give the audience a respite from the world of the poem, unforgivingly violent or strange as it often is.

I talked about ring composition, that remarkable narrative technique that weaves the present and the past together, that allows the account of a specific episode in a character's life to expand to encompass his entire life.

I took a breath. Any questions?

Jack, the scruffy kid, looked sly. Uh, can you talk about the syllabus?

A bunch of the kids cracked up.

I explained how the class would work. After today's session, we'd be discussing two books of the epic per class, one before the half-time break and one after; I reminded them that next week we'd finish talking about Book 1 and go on to Book 2. I told them how to access the course website, where I'd set up a discussion board for each class session. They were required to contribute a paragraph or two about each week's reading no later than midnight on the day before class; past experience had taught me that this was a good way of priming the conversation, of getting them to articulate their thoughts about the reading before the class met. I explained my grading criteria—always a subject of tremendous concern—and answered the inevitable questions about what the midterm and final exams would cover and how much the exams, papers, and their participation in class would be weighted for the final grade.

When I'd finished with all this, it was a quarter past twelve. Fifteen minutes to go.

Anything else? I asked. Questions?

The tall boy who looked like he was outgrowing his clothes raised a long arm. Don Quixote Tom.

Um, I have a question? he said.

Are you asking me or do you have one?

This student tic always irritates me, and I was determined to quash it.

Tom laughed nervously. So, okay, you wrote us saying your dad was taking this course, but can we ask *why* he's taking this course?

All of them laughed.

I was opening my mouth to reply, to explain and dispense with what I was beginning to fear would be a serious distraction, when my father raised his hand.

Oh, Professor *Mendelsohn*, he said a little stagily, can I talk?

I winced theatrically, for the students' benefit.

Yes, Daaaad?

Some of them laughed again, but I could tell that they were curious.

As my father took a moment to look around the room, it occurred to me to wonder what he had been like as a professor. I had never understood how he spent all those days and years at Grumman, since much of what he did was classified, and none of it was comprehensible to me, who was so bad at math and science, although occasionally he'd refer to this or that project he was working on and sometimes try to explain it to us: for instance, the time in the early 1980s when he said he was working on "digital optics," which he patiently explained to me was "trying to teach computers to see" (much later I understood that this was the beginning of digital imaging, a technology that, for an aerospace corporation, meant target recognition systems); or, before that, during the 1970s, a decade during which he was away from home on business for long stretches—periods during which, we couldn't help noticing, the atmosphere in the house would ease, and Mother would regain some of her fizzy humor—when he said that Grumman was branching out from aerospace, and he was working on a project to develop an artificial heart. I was in my mid-teens; it was an awkward time between Daddy and me. *Artificial heart,* I would think bitterly, *how perfect.* And before then, in the 1960s, when we were just children, there had been the moon landing. Grumman had built the lunar module, and during the weeks of excitement leading up to the landing, all of us—not just our family but dozens of our friends and their families, since Grumman was Long Island's biggest employer—proudly felt that this was "our" achievement. We kids were all allowed to stay up late into the night to watch the landing on TV. Later, in the wet bar he'd built downstairs, my father proudly displayed the lunar module cocktail glasses that Grumman had given out, the famous vehicle outlined in blue on the crystal. We found them embarrassing, but they never budged from the shelf where he'd put them.

Given that I had ended up teaching at a college, I found it odd that my father turned out to be just as reticent about his second career, the computer science professorship, as he had been about the first; but perhaps it was because he sensed that the subject of the course was of no interest to me. After he retired from that job, when he was in his mid-seventies, I noticed during a visit home that he had taken the thick white plastic nameplate that had adorned his office door at Hofstra University and attached it to the door of his study at home, which used to be the room I shared with Andrew, with its narrow twin beds, the ones my father had built, arranged head to head. The beds had long since been replaced by a giant L-shaped desk where my father kept his papers, among which were five thick manila file folders, one for each of his children and, eventually, for our families, too, which he faithfully kept up to date with photos and clippings. On this huge desk squatted the printers and scanners and laptops, for which he had a kind of affection, as if they were pets; while underneath it the boxy computer drive hummed and bleeped, its black cables twisting thickly beneath the countertops. On the other side of the room was the only remnant of my and Andrew's days in that room: the small oak desk at which we'd done our homework. Above it he'd screwed a hanging CD cabinet crammed with jewel cases, Ella Fitzgerald and Bernstein's *Complete Mahler Symphonies* and Django Reinhardt, while on the walls, to my mother's dismay, he'd taped photographs of us and our kids and figures he admired, Billie Holiday and Einstein and Bach. So our room had become his office. PROF. JAY MENDELSOHN, read the white plastic sign on the door.

It was difficult for me to imagine what his teaching style had been like. I knew just what my mother must have been like when she was teaching kindergarten and elementary school, first in the 1950s, soon after they were married, and then again, after the two-decade interlude during which she had raised us, in the 1980s and 1990s. Mother was vivacious and outgoing and clever; she was, everyone said, a natural teacher. My brothers and sister and I benefited from this, too, although I am sure we didn't appreciate it at the time. We'd come home from school in the afternoon and on the kitchen table there'd be a single rose in a bud vase or a carefully halved orange or green pepper, and she'd gather us around and say, *Children, look how* wonderful *nature is, see how the petals, the sections, the seedpods, are perfectly geometric?*

After we grew up and she went back to teaching, she liked to call us up and tell funny stories about her colleagues and pupils, the children in the public school she'd taught in when she was just a newlywed, in Queens, who used to come to parent-teacher conferences with their "aunties" because they had no parents, or the Jewish boy she'd had in another class who, when asked to draw a picture of a fish for a class project about the fauna of lakes and rivers, had handed in a piece of construction paper on which he'd drawn a perfect oval with a single dorsal fin, and when my puzzled mother asked him to explain to the class what kind of fish it was, he'd said, *Gefilte.* It was easy to imagine her, with her brisk cheer and wild sense of humor, her talent for making striking and imaginative holiday decorations, her theatrical manner and high imagination, as a terrific teacher for very young children.

But when it came to my father, I drew a blank. I thought of how he'd look at the math quizzes and tests I brought home, the scrawled red X's like angry embroidery along the side of the paper, and I had to wonder what kind of teacher PROF. JAY MENDELSOHN had been.

Now he was sitting in my classroom on the first day of the *Odyssey* class with his hand in the air. *Yes,* he said, I'm his *father.*

Unlike my mother, my father didn't enjoy being the center of attention; whenever he found himself on the spot, whenever he was the only speaker in a room full of people, he'd stress random words as he spoke, as if these random emphases would lend his speech authority.

I'm taking Dan's *course,* he was saying now (a couple of them looked amused when they heard him call me by my first name), because I thought I'd try to read *the Classics* again, which I haven't read since high school. That was during World War *Two*, in the 1940s.

His lips tightened into a private smile.

Most of your parents probably weren't even *born* then.

My father jerked his shiny head in my direction and said, I knew all this stuff before he did.

The students were giggling.

Well, I knew a *lot* of it, he went on after a moment, vaguely tapping his iPad, onto which he'd downloaded the text of the *Odyssey*. I read Ohvid in *Latin*. I used to know the myths. I read the *Iliad* and *Odyssey*, but it was only excerpts. So I thought now I'll read the whole thing.

A couple of the students stared. They were loving this.

My father said, I figured now was my chance to read it again before I *die*.

Then he gestured toward me again and his face assumed an expression—eyes narrowed to slits, lips pinched tight, the corners of his mouth turned down, the narrow gleaming head faintly nodding as he spoke, as if reassuring himself of the truth of what he was saying or hearing—that might strike someone who didn't know him as humorous. But I knew him.

If *that* guy is a classicist, he said, jabbing a pale white finger at me, it's because he gets it from *me*.

I tried to look amused as I zipped up my book bag, which the students took as a sign that they could leave. But as they started to shuffle and stand, cramming their notebooks and texts into their backpacks, my father took another wheezing breath and cleared his throat. I turned toward him and suddenly I knew what he was going to say.

He said, I'll tell you this. You're never too old to *learn*.

He gets it from me.

Later that night, after my father had gone to sleep—climbing into the narrow bed he had built for me fifty years before and, as he settled into the sheets, fetching a great groaning sigh, something he often did when he was alone after being in company for a long time, as if the effort of being with people were a physical weight that he had at last been able to put down—later that night, as I emptied my book bag onto the desk in my study, I thought of him saying, *He gets it from me.* Maybe, I thought; but there had been others.

From the canvas book bag, I gently slid out the books I'd brought to class and had piled on the seminar table in front of me, not so much because I thought I'd be referring to them on that first day of class but because it was comforting to have them near. They were the books I had used when I myself was first reading the *Odyssey* seriously.

First, there were the two OCTs of the poem: the Oxford Classical Texts, published by Oxford University Press. The OCTs are the editions of the classical authors that English and American scholars tend to use. There are four volumes of Homer in this series, two for each epic: Volumes 1 and 2 for the *Iliad* and Volumes 3 and 4 for the *Odyssey*. The OCTs offer the Greek and Roman texts in the original languages: there is no commentary, no translation. The pale blue covers of the Greek works, the dark blue ink used for the titles—which, as always in this series, are given in Latin (*Homeri opera, Tomus III, Odysseae libros I–XII continens*, "The Works of Homer, Volume 3, Containing Odyssey Books 1–12")—the lack of any alleviating illustration, have a ferocious severity. Between the formidable covers there is an introduction, also in Latin, by the scholar who edited the volume, and then the text itself, page after page of Greek lines marching across the creamy paper, a nimbus of acute and grave and circumflex accents hovering over each word like clouds of angry gnats. And, at the bottom of every page, in tiny print, the so-called *apparatus criticus*, a list of the proposals for substitutions, alterations, and emendations to the text made by different scholars over the centuries when a word or phrase or line in the original seemed inauthentic, or where something in the original seemed to have disappeared.

That evening as I emptied my book bag, I opened the first volume of the OCT of the *Odyssey*, skimming past the Latin introduction, to the first page of Book 1, which looks like this:

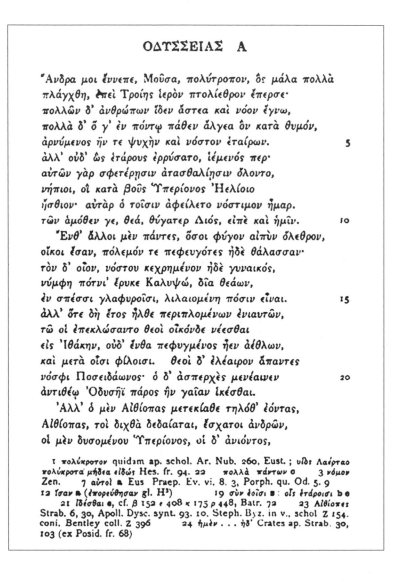

ΟΔΥΣΣΕΙΑΣ   Α

Ἄνδρα μοι ἔννεπε, Μοῦσα, πολύτροπον, ὃς μάλα πολλὰ
πλάγχθη, ἐπεὶ Τροίης ἱερὸν πτολίεθρον ἔπερσε·
πολλῶν δ' ἀνθρώπων ἴδεν ἄστεα καὶ νόον ἔγνω,
πολλὰ δ' ὅ γ' ἐν πόντῳ πάθεν ἄλγεα ὃν κατὰ θυμόν,
ἀρνύμενος ἥν τε ψυχὴν καὶ νόστον ἑταίρων.   5
ἀλλ' οὐδ' ὣς ἑτάρους ἐρρύσατο, ἱέμενός περ·
αὐτῶν γὰρ σφετέρῃσιν ἀτασθαλίῃσιν ὄλοντο,
νήπιοι, οἳ κατὰ βοῦς Ὑπερίονος Ἠελίοιο
ἤσθιον· αὐτὰρ ὁ τοῖσιν ἀφείλετο νόστιμον ἦμαρ.
τῶν ἀμόθεν γε, θεά, θύγατερ Διός, εἰπὲ καὶ ἡμῖν.   10
    Ἔνθ' ἄλλοι μὲν πάντες, ὅσοι φύγον αἰπὺν ὄλεθρον,
οἴκοι ἔσαν, πόλεμόν τε πεφευγότες ἠδὲ θάλασσαν·
τὸν δ' οἶον, νόστου κεχρημένον ἠδὲ γυναικός,
νύμφη πότνι' ἔρυκε Καλυψώ, δῖα θεάων,
ἐν σπέσσι γλαφυροῖσι, λιλαιομένη πόσιν εἶναι.   15
ἀλλ' ὅτε δὴ ἔτος ἦλθε περιπλομένων ἐνιαυτῶν,
τῷ οἱ ἐπεκλώσαντο θεοὶ οἴκόνδε νέεσθαι
εἰς Ἰθάκην, οὐδ' ἔνθα πεφυγμένος ἦεν ἀέθλων,
καὶ μετὰ οἷσι φίλοισι.   θεοὶ δ' ἐλέαιρον ἅπαντες
νόσφι Ποσειδάωνος· ὁ δ' ἀσπερχὲς μενέαινεν   20
ἀντιθέῳ Ὀδυσῆϊ πάρος ἣν γαῖαν ἱκέσθαι.
    Ἀλλ' ὁ μὲν Αἰθίοπας μετεκίαθε τηλόθ' ἐόντας,
Αἰθίοπας, τοὶ διχθὰ δεδαίαται, ἔσχατοι ἀνδρῶν,
οἱ μὲν δυσομένου Ὑπερίονος, οἱ δ' ἀνιόντος,

1 πολύκροτον quidam ap. schol. Ar. Nub. 260, Eust. ; υἱὸς Λαέρταο
πολύκροτα μήδεα εἰδώς Hes. fr. 94. 22   πολλὰ πάντων ο   3 νόμον
Zen.   7 αὐτοὶ a Eus Praep. Ev. vi. 8. 3, Porph. qu. Od. 5. 9
12 ἴσαν a (ἐπορεύθησαν gl. H³)   19 σὺν δοῖσι a : οἷς ἑτάροισι b e
   21 ἰδέσθαι e, cf. β 152 e 408 κ 175 ρ 448, Batr. 72   23 Αἰθίοπες
Strab. 6, 30, Apoll. Dysc. synt. 93. 10. Steph. Byz. in v., schol Z 154.
coni. Bentley coll. Z 396   24 ἠμὲν . . . ἠδ' Crates ap. Strab. 30,
103 (ex Posid. fr. 68)

As I scanned the page, I had a sudden vivid memory of the first day of the *Odyssey* seminar I had taken during my second year of graduate school. The professor was Froma Zeitlin, the one who later became my close friend and urged me to go on the *Odyssey* cruise. It was the early autumn of 1987, and on this first day of class Froma was standing at the head of a rectangular seminar table very similar to the one I'd stood at earlier that day. She held up *Homeri opera, Tomus III, Odysseae libros I–XII continens,* in the air with one hand as she went over some of the more important items on the bibliography she'd prepared for our use that semester. The bibliography was eight single-spaced pages long. *This* is the text we'll be using, she said, waving the OCT before our eyes, peering at us over a pair of cobalt-blue half-moon reading glasses, her huge chunky rings flashing in the air. Froma was known in those days as a pioneer in the application of feminist criticism to the Classics, and particularly to the study of Greek tragedy, which was her specialty. The first time I entered her office, which was wreathed in so much smoke from the slender brown cigarettes she preferred back then that she herself, sitting behind the immense desk from which piles of books rose like stalagmites, was, at first, difficult to make out, the soft contours of her body, the round face with its peering nut-brown eyes emerging from the shadows and smoke the way that a divinity might appear to a mortal in a myth, the artisanal jewels to which she liked to refer as her "objects" (*How do you like my new object,* she might ask as you passed her in the hallway of the Classics department as she brandished a brass breastplate or an enameled brooch in the shape of a clown or silver bangles that crawled up her arms like snakes), all of it glinting amid the tendrils of smoke like the decorations of a cult statue—the first time I entered her office I couldn't help noticing that the words "Women" and "Female" and "Feminine" gleamed on the spines of many of the hundreds of books that bowed down the metal shelves. And yet despite her focus on feminism and tragedy, Froma kept returning over the course of her long career to the *Odyssey,* as if unable to break out of its magnetic field. And indeed my most vivid memory of graduate school was that seminar on the *Odyssey,* three hours each week, once a week, over the course of a fourteen-week-long semester, from each session of which we students would emerge with dazed expressions of exhausted delight, so *scathingly brilliant,* as Froma liked to exclaim (an expression that I picked up and now use myself so often that my own students assume it is mine), so *scathingly brilliant* were the exchanges we had with her or one another, the arguments over fine points of interpretation, the insights she gave us.

Under Froma's tutelage I spent seven beguiled years, a time of pleasure and of frustration in which I both wanted to stay and wanted to leave, to move on, a span of time that bracketed the strange evolution that takes place between the moment you enter graduate school and the moment you depart as a *doctor* ("one who is licensed to teach"), as unrecognizable to yourself as the butterfly is to the caterpillar it once was.

I ran my hand over the pale blue paper and smiled as I thought of Froma that night, of *scathingly brilliant*, of so many other things I had absorbed from her over the years. Which of the young people who'd been sitting in front of me earlier that day, I wondered, would end up absorbing, digesting, teaching? Or would they be like my father and his friends in that classroom in the Bronx all those years ago, the ones who *hadn't gone the distance*? Would they, for whatever reasons, fail to pick up the thread?

Then, gently, almost gingerly, I picked two more books out of the bag. They, too, were part of a two-volume set: the "red Macmillan" edition. Distinctive for its bright red binding, this edition of the *Odyssey* is intended for the use of high school and university students: at the back of each volume, after the Greek text, there are extensive notes on the grammar and diction of nearly every line of the poem. My copies of the red Macmillan were far more worn than the blue Oxford volumes; I'd had them much longer. The deep-red buckram had long ago faded to pink, the spines were split and mended with Scotch tape that, having long ago lost its adhesive, was as brittle now as old cellophane, the covers so loose that they wobbled dangerously when I opened them. When I did, I saw my initials and a date. "D.A.M. 1979."

In the autumn of my second year of undergraduate study I read excerpts from the *Odyssey* in Greek for the first time. By this point I was a Classics major; I'd been taking Greek since the fall of my first year. A year after that first encounter with Homer, a new professor, the department's first woman, appeared, someone who, everyone was saying, was a great expert on the *Odyssey* in particular. Clay, someone said her name was, and something about the earthen monosyllable caused me to imagine a stocky woman in late middle age, with perhaps a gray bun. We immediately signed up for her course, I and the two other Classics majors: it would be devoted entirely to the *Odyssey*. And so, on a sweltering day in late August, the three of us showed up in the small classroom. There, leaning against the desk, a small smile on her feline face, a cigarette dangling from her lips, was the famous Homer scholar.

Jenny Strauss Clay. She wasn't yet out of her thirties, then. Because so many other memories have overlaid that first image of her, it's hard to summon, now, the surprise we felt on walking into the classroom. The lithe, coiled frame, a catlike calm, the Louise Brooks bob, the cigarettes. For the next year and a half Jenny taught me: Greek and Latin, of course, Homer and Herodotus, Horace and Catullus, but as we grew closer, once she started having me and a couple of other students over to dinner at her house, there were other things she introduced me to, other things she taught me. Proust, for one, the first volume of which we read aloud together during a sweltering summer when I was twenty-one, sitting on the shiny hardwood floor on opposite sides of her living room, almost too hot to speak. Modern Greek poetry, particularly a poem by George Seferis that contains the line, "The first thing that God made was love." Monteverdi's *Il ritorno d'Ulisse in patria*, which she'd often have playing as we came in the door, the odd Baroque combination of tinkling and plangency drifting into the tobaccoey air, emanating from a fancy Swedish stereo that you could hang on a wall like a painting (an object that hinted at the fantastical possibility that a Classics professor, an authority on Homer, could be cool), while she sliced limes in the kitchen. Indeed she taught me about food, too: there was the time I gawked at a tureen of linguini topped by a sauce that—miraculously to me, who had never had pasta that didn't come from a can—was not red but green, something with an Italian name that she made with leaves she had just plucked from her own garden, a small plot at the back of her house through which she would wander, snipping herbs and humming to herself like a sorceress in some old legend.

But underneath the lavishness, the generosity, the exotic sophistications acquired in a lifetime of travel—and, as I later learned, of displacement— you could feel a certain rigor, as hard-edged and unyielding as a paradigm in a grammar. It was Jenny who once said to me quite casually, when I went into her office one day toward the end of her *Odyssey* course to ask her about secondary sources for a paper I wanted to write about a certain passage in Book 4, in which a husband and a wife are bitterly arguing, *Well, you can't begin to write anything until you've read every-thing*. It was a sentence I found strangely exciting, with its promise of scholarly rigor and difficulty; I felt that if I devoted myself to a career whose training was painful, my father might approve of it. As she spoke I looked around her office: the wooden shelves neatly lined with books in Greek and Latin and French and German and Italian and English, the heavy plaster bust of an unsmiling Athena on top of one tall bookcase, a touch of humor provided by the many images and figurines of owls, Athena's bird, which Jenny loved. *You can't write anything until you've read everything.* I heard that sentence as I looked around the office, and I swallowed hard and thought, Okay.

Although I couldn't know it then, since I knew little about Jenny's family or personal history at the time, that sentence betrayed the presence of a certain intellectual inheritance as unmistakably as the curious circumflex shape of an eyebrow or the ripe Edwardian curve of a jaw can be the expressions of genes passed on from generation to generation. The intellectual DNA in this case, the penchant for rigor, was an inheritance from Jenny's father, who at one point had also been her teacher, a man called Strauss, a Classics scholar and political philosopher who had grown up in Germany and was a product of the particularly rigorous classical training for which that country was famous; and beyond that to Strauss' teacher and his teacher before him, back to Friedrich August Wolf himself, the German founder of classical philology. These chains of relationships between students and their professors—the Germans, with their combination of sentimentality and reverence for intellectual authority, rightly call such intellectual mentors *Doktorväter*, "doctor-fathers"—snake back in time as purposefully as the ever-narrowing limbs of a family tree, a lineage of study and scholarship, of intellectual tastes and idiosyncrasies, that expresses itself, just as real bloodlines do, in resemblances that persist from generation to generation.

You could, I thought as I slid the red Macmillans back into their place on my bookcase that night, trace these intellectual genealogies in a more or less unbroken line all the way back to ancient times: in my case, from Jenny to her father to his teachers and then to Wolf; and then from Wolf back to the Italian humanists of the Renaissance, who avidly collected the parchment and vellum manuscripts of the classical texts that had been copied and recopied for a thousand years and set them into type for the first time, creating the first printed versions and thereby making the Classics available to larger audiences than they had ever known; from those Renaissance humanists further back in time and space to the Greek-speaking scholars of Byzantium, who in the near millennium from the seventh to the fifteenth centuries A.D. preserved the knowledge of Greek in the eastern Mediterranean long after it had disappeared from Europe, once the Western Roman Empire collapsed, those scholars carefully copying and recopying texts such as the densely annotated copy of the *Iliad* that Villoisin had discovered in the Venetian library; past the Byzantines to the learned men of the period known as Late Antiquity, the 400s and 500s A.D., and beyond them to the enthusiasts of Greek literature who had flourished as the Roman Empire rose, a hodgepodge of highbrow critics and middle-brow popularizers (one notorious example was a scholar nicknamed Bibliolathos, "the book forgetter," because he'd written so many treatises that he couldn't keep track of them); and finally to the earliest and most authoritative scholars of Homer, the learned men who, starting in the third century B.C., served as the heads of the great Library of Alexandria, and who devoted themselves above all to the study of the texts of the *Iliad* and the *Odyssey*, the first professional scholars to address themselves to the questions that the *apparatus criticus* at the bottom of every page of the Oxford Classical Texts tries to answer: What were the words that "Homer" actually sang?

If you're a classicist, merely to open a copy of the *Iliad* or the *Odyssey* is to be reminded of this vast lineage of scholarship, of the immense hivelike labor that has slowly added drops of knowledge over the course of twenty-five centuries to our understanding of what the poems are and what they say.

All this, I understood as I turned out the light in my study after putting my books away, the pale blue, the faded red, had been in Jenny's mind that day thirty years before when she had murmured, *Well, you can't begin to write anything until you've read everything.* How lucky I had been in my teachers, who had invited me to become a link in the chain that connects the past to the present. And how much my father had missed, as I saw only now, when he turned the invitation down.

Like father, like son. Not always, I thought. Not all genealogies, I said to myself that January night after the first class session, are genetic.

With his unpredictable swings between endearing swagger and utter cluelessness, the Telemachus of the first few books of the *Odyssey* can remind you of a college freshman. In Book 1, for instance, he displays an unattractive rudeness to his mother. Stung, perhaps, by the disguised Athena's shaming words ("Any sensible man would be outraged by their behavior!" the goddess exclaims to him, looking around the hall as the Suitors gorge themselves on Odysseus' food and wine), the young prince attacks not the Suitors but his mother, Penelope, who, in her first appearance in the poem, comes down from her bedchamber in order to command the house bard, who has been singing a lay about the Greek heroes' homecomings from the Trojan War, to choose a less painful subject. (This is the moment when for the first time she takes up what will henceforth be her usual position by the doorpost, drawing the veil against her face, a maidservant standing on either side.)

Go inside and see to your own work,
the loom and distaff; and tell your maids to get
to work as well: it's up to the men—to me—
to give commands. The power in this house is mine.

Shocked, Penelope retires upstairs, where Athena drifts sleep over her weeping eyes. This is the first of many instances when the distraught queen is put to sleep by the goddess—so many, in fact, that I've had students ask me whether Penelope is supposed to be suffering from depression, a question that had never occurred to me when I was in college. It's true that this first encounter with Odysseus' queen sketches a character whose behavior seems to be at odds with her own stock epithet, "she whose thoughts are steadfast": weary and tremulous, she is first intimidated, then dissolves in tears, and is finally anesthetized with sleep. But this could well be part of a shrewd narrative strategy on Homer's part. After all, if you introduce your hero's famously strong and wise wife as a timid and helpless wreck—as a problem character—your audience can only be pleasantly surprised, as the epic moves forward, by the positive traits that gradually emerge.

Less easily cowed are the Suitors themselves. When Telemachus announces to them that he intends to call an assembly of Ithaca's citizenry the next day, they show some surprise at his newfound gutsiness even as they continue to patronize and condescend to him. "Such brave talk!" Antinoüs, the leader of the Suitors and the most hateful of them, calls out. (His name means "anti-mind": from the start, he's marked not only as the epic's archvillain but as the enemy specifically of Odysseus, who repeatedly demonstrates the power of cunning, of mind.) "Surely all this is up to the gods," purrs Eurymachus, the second most prominent of the Suitors, ostensibly less obnoxious than Antinoüs but just as hateful beneath his smooth exterior.

Telemachus' adolescent oscillation between awkwardness and braggadocio is spotlighted once again during the assembly scene in Book 2. Once the Ithacans have gathered in the assembly place, the herald who is conducting the ceremony hands the prince a scepter, thereby granting him the right to speak—which, Homer tells us, the youth "burns with eagerness" to do. He begins by replying to an elderly citizen's question about the reason for the assembly: Could it be, the old man wonders, that the Ithacans who had set out for Troy so long ago are finally coming home? Alas no, Telemachus replies: he has called the assembly not on some grand public business but on a matter of private concern. King Odysseus—who, he pointedly observes, "ruled over you all like a gentle father"—is long dead. Telemachus, to whom this vanished parent has always been little more than an abstraction, declares that he is now faced with an "even worse" problem: his household has been overrun by the Suitors, who aggressively woo his unwilling mother with no regard for the established rituals of courtship, lounging around her palace, eating her out of house and home. As Telemachus goes on, however, he begins to lose control. Unwisely, he lingers on the embarrassing fact that he isn't equal to the task of defending his home from the Suitors ("there's no man here / such as Odysseus was, to ward disaster off our house; / and we're in no position to defend ourselves"); shows his hand by openly denouncing the Suitors' outrageous behavior and the citizens' failure to react ("you ought to be ashamed of yourselves!"); veers into self-pity ("I implore you, stop! . . . Let me wallow in my baneful grief alone"); and ends by bursting into tears and hurling to the ground the scepter of state. Even after he pulls himself together later on and starts planning the voyage to Pylos and Sparta that the disguised Athena has urged him to make, he doesn't do much: it's Athena, in fact, who arranges for the ship and a reliable crew. All that's left for Telemachus is the provisioning: again at the goddess's urging, he quietly raids his father's storerooms with the help of a trusty old female servant, Eurycleia. She, as we learn, had been Odysseus' wet nurse when he was a child and will play a crucial role in the plot once the hero returns.

Perhaps because she can see how badly the assembly has gone, Athena returns toward the end of Book 2 to give the youth some encouragement. She appears this time in the guise of yet another of his father's old friends, a man called Mentor. (It is, in fact, this scene in the *Odyssey* that launched the word "mentor" on its long career as a synonym for "an experienced and trusted adviser.") Mentor asserts that the boy is likely to succeed simply because he is his father's son: "If you weren't his stock, Penelope's too, / then I'd fear your hopes might come to grief . . . But you, there's every hope that you will reach your goal."

Why does the poet devote so much space to scenes in which Telemachus fails to speak well, confuses private and public, loses control of himself and the situation? There are several possible reasons. The scene at the assembly, for instance, conveys how unstable the political situation in Ithaca is—a consideration that can be neglected by readers, overshadowed as it is by the family drama. Even more, the emphasis on Telemachus' weakness as a public speaker highlights, by contrast, the important theme of verbal cunning, one of Odysseus' greatest talents.

But there is still another reason, one that strikes me forcefully when I reread the poem now. By emphasizing the inadequacies of the son, the poet makes us, too, long for the appearance of the father, whose authority and competence are beyond dispute. In this way, the *Odyssey* enacts the truth of one of its most famous and troubling lines, which the poet puts in Athena's mouth at the end of the assembly scene: "Few sons are the equals of their fathers; most fall short, all too few surpass them."

The second meeting of the *Odyssey* seminar took place on Friday, February 4. A few days before, my father had called to say that he'd be driving up on Thursday afternoon that week rather than early Friday morning, as he'd done the week before.

That way I don't have to deal with the Friday *traffic,* he coughed into the phone. It's *awful* going toward the city in the morning! I'll get there Thursday late afternoon, and we can have dinner somewhere and then go back to your house and relax and I'll sleep over. This way I'll have more energy on Friday morning for class. Then I'll drive home after lunch.

Okay, I said, that works. Then I thought of the narrow daybed in the study, which doubled as a guest room when people came to visit. You sure you don't mind sleeping on that little bed?

Mind? he asked, drawling jauntily, as he did when he was making a joke. Through the phone I could feel his mood softening. Why would I mind? That's the bed I made!

The first time my parents visited me after I'd moved into my house on campus, my father hadn't been able to hide his pleasure on seeing that the daybed in the study was, underneath its cover and the many pillows, the bed he'd built for me when I was a child, the one he'd made out of a door. *It's still pretty sturdy!* he'd said as he leaned down and gave it a little shake. *I wasn't half bad as a carpenter.* At which my mother sighed theatrically and said, *Oh, Jay. I still have a box of things you haven't fixed from forty years ago.*

And so, for the rest of the semester, he'd come each week the evening before the seminar and sleep in the bed he'd built. Find someplace nice for us to eat, he said toward the end of the call during which he announced that he wanted to come on Thursdays instead of Fridays; which is why the evening before the second class meeting found the two of us sitting in a local steakhouse called Flatiron, arguing about Book 2—the assembly scene and Telemachus' odd behavior.

Impatiently, he dismissed any notion that Telemachus was in fact maturing, was really learning something, during the course of the first books of the *Odyssey.*

Oh, please, he said as the waitress appeared with our food. Telemachus is *always* getting help. Athena always swoops down to save him. In Book 1 she tells him to go look for his father. *She* gives him the advice. *She* tells him to call the assembly in Book 2, and then when he flounders around during the meeting she cheers him up. *She* tells him to go to Pylos and Sparta, which he does only after *she* arranges everything for him.

After a minute he added, frowning, He just has it so easy.

So? I said, even though I knew what the answer would be. What's so bad about that?

Because that's not the way life really *is*.

Although of course I'm aware that it has deep psychological sources, I think my father's reverence for struggle, for difficulty, also owes much to the circumstances in which he grew up. His earliest childhood coincided with the beginning of the Great Depression. The times were particularly hard on his own father, the union electrician. *We were always just a step ahead of the rent collector,* Daddy once said to me, half wryly and half bitterly, apropos of the many addresses his family moved among in the early 1930s. He saw the world as a rough place, hostile to the happiness of ordinary people. It wasn't easy to be *the little guy,* as he liked to say. The phrase, invariably uttered in a way that combined admiring solidarity and weary resignation, came up often when you talked to him about politics, which, with rare exceptions, he saw, as he saw most things, as a rich man's game stacked against the little guy. This habit of mind colored his pronouncements on everything from presidential elections to baseball, the sport that he loved above all others. He enjoyed its "geometries"; he relished the long reflective pauses between short bouts of action. *It's the thinking man's sport.* Because he grew up in the Bronx, people assumed he was a Yankees fan, since the Yankees are a Bronx team; but he hated the Yankees because he considered them a rich man's team. *They buy their success,* he would say dismissively. Throughout my childhood he rooted instead for the Mets, whose tendency to lose in those early years, back in the 1960s and 1970s—in stark contrast to the glittering Homeric invincibility of the Yankees—appealed to him, I now think, because however much he would shake his bald skull at a botched play or bad call, the failures of the team he had chosen as his favorite confirmed his belief that the world was somehow against him and the other little guys. (He was dismayed when my own boys turned out to be Yankees fans; once, I think only half jokingly, he offered Peter a hundred dollars to switch his allegiance. When Peter, who was then about fourteen, shook his head, grinning, and said, *I don't think so,* my father said, *What you lack in taste you make up for in character, buddy boy!* Then he turned to Lily and said, *You must have done something right.*)

Telemachus has it too easy, he was saying that night at Flatiron. All he has to do is follow Athena's orders.

I said, Well, why can't you just think of her as a teacher? She's instructing him.

My father said to me, Because a good teacher doesn't just tell you what to do, or what to think. A good teacher *shows* you how, explains things to you. A teacher doesn't just boss you around, he should help you come to your own conclusions.

I remembered myself at the age of twelve, standing in front of the wooden desk in his bedroom with a math quiz fluttering in my outstretched hand like something alive and terrified.

Now it was my turn to raise an eyebrow.

I looked at him and said, Oh?

The following Friday, February 11, we were discussing Books 3 and 4, the books in which Telemachus makes his fact-finding visits to his father's old friends. In Book 3 he visits the court of Nestor, who has long since returned from the Trojan War and resumed his rule of a seaside city at the tip of the Peloponnese called Pylos. Elderly but still in command, accompanied by his many handsome sons, he is only too happy to reminisce about the olden days, when (this is the point of many of his stories, and, it is probably fair to say, the point of many stories told by old men to their sons) men were braver and heroes were greater. Small wonder that the Greeks, hearing such tales so often, were plagued by the anxiety that few sons are the equal of their fathers.

After a warm welcome by the pious old king—when Telemachus arrives, a magnificent sacrifice is taking place on the seashore, at which thousands of citizens are present—Telemachus sits listening to the old man's war stories. Nestor starts by recalling certain events that transpired at the end of the Trojan War; then he relates what he knows about the homecomings of various Greeks who would have been familiar to Homer's audience from the *Iliad*. Not the least interesting of these home-comings is that of Agamemnon, the Greek general whose quarrel with Achilles sets the earlier epic in motion. From Nestor, Telemachus learns how Agamemnon, upon his return home, was murdered by his unfaith-ful wife, Clytemnestra, and her lover, Aegisthus, a crime that would eventually be avenged by Agamemnon's dutiful son, Orestes. Nestor's own homecoming, by contrast, was achieved with little drama: he recalls that he reached Pylos from Troy in a matter of days. As for the news that Telemachus has come to Pylos to learn, the kindly old king has, alas, no solid information.

The tales Nestor tells are examples of what are called *nostos* narra-tives. *Nostos* is the Greek word for "homecoming"; the plural form of this word, *nostoi*, was, in fact, the title of a lost epic devoted to the homecom-ings of the Greek kings and chieftains who fought in the Trojan War. The *Odyssey* itself is a *nostos* narrative, one that often digresses from its tale of Odysseus' twisty voyage back to Ithaca in order to relate, in brief, the *nostoi* of other characters, as Nestor does here—almost as if it were anxious that those other *nostoi* stories would not themselves make it safely into the future. In time, this wistful word *nostos*, rooted so deeply in the *Odyssey*'s themes, was eventually combined with another word in Greek's vast vocabulary of pain, *algos*, to give us an elegantly simple way to talk about the bittersweet feeling we sometimes have for a special kind of troubling longing. Literally this word means "the pain associated with longing for home," but as we know, "home," particularly as we get older, can be a time as well as a place. The word is "nostalgia."

In Book 4, Telemachus, accompanied by Nestor's young son Peisis-tratus, arrives at the court of Menelaus and Helen in Sparta. The good-natured king and his surpassingly beautiful wife have long since been reconciled; as if to suggest that this once-troubled household is safe for marriage again, Homer has Telemachus and Peisistratus arrive on the day a double wedding is taking place, the marriages of two of Menelaus' children. Their identities still unknown to their hosts, Telemachus and his new friend are admitted to the royal feast; when Menelaus overhears them marveling at the opulence of the palace, he leans over and explains that he amassed much of his fortune during his long and troubled trip home from Troy as he wandered from Cyprus to Phoenicia and Egypt. (Menelaus relates his *nostos* at great length, and it is almost as filled with incident as Odysseus' journey.) Yet he cannot enjoy his riches, he glumly asserts, knowing how his poor brother Agamemnon perished through the perfidy of an unfaithful wife. And then there was his most beloved companion, Odysseus! . . . As Menelaus describes his affection for his old friend, Telemachus bursts into tears, thereby revealing who he is. Menelaus and his queen then launch into a series of tales about Odysseus during the years of the Trojan War, stories that, ostensibly for Telemachus' benefit, shed light on his father's character and cleverness.

But my father didn't care about any of this. What was bothering him this week was the fact that Telemachus' voyages to Pylos and Sparta don't actually yield any useful information about Odysseus.

The weather was freakishly mild that mid-February morning; by the time we left my house for the classroom building, the thermometer read sixty degrees. Daddy was in a good mood as he drank his coffee at my apartment. The week before, he'd given my Nespresso machine, with its sleek automotive gleam, a suspicious look. You know I don't like those *little* coffees! Don't you have a normal coffee?! This week I was ready. A few days before, I'd driven across the river to the mall, where there was a Bed Bath & Beyond store, and bought a Mr. Coffee machine. At the checkout line I saw a twenty-ounce ceramic mug that said WHO'S YOUR DADDY? and I bought that, too. Then I went to the supermarket and got a giant can of Maxwell House ground coffee. Now, on the morning before the class in which we were going to discuss Telemachus' educational trips abroad, my father walked into the kitchen. I gestured like a game-show host to the Mr. Coffee machine and handed him the mug with a little bow. Steam rose off the thin brown liquid.

Awwww, *Daaaaan*! he exclaimed. There was, as often, a delicate parody in the drawled emphasis on the single syllable. What a good *boy* you are! He looked at the Mr. Coffee and said, Where did you get this?

Deathbed and Beyond, I said.

We didn't even laugh, we were so used to the joke. My mother was notorious for her malapropisms, many of which had long since passed into our family's private vocabulary. Some, I think, were authentic. I was with her the time she went to the local bakery and distractedly ordered a dozen Lafayettes, and the baker gazed at her blankly until he suddenly brightened and said, *You mean "napoleons"?!* But others, I suspect, were calculated to amuse my father, who, like her, enjoyed word games, crosswords, puns, and—the corollary—hated verbal imprecision, as if language, too, were a kind of mathematics, admitting no approximation. (*"Whooooommmm would you like to speak to?"* she would say, eavesdropping as one of us answered the phone. Not *"who."*) Every Sunday Daddy would labor over the big *Times* crossword puzzle, scowling at the clues as if he could intimidate them into yielding their secrets, and finally my mother would reach over and say, *Oh, Jay, let me have a look*, and fill in the missing word with her red Flair pen, daintily writing above the angry blue blotch that marked his failure.

My father grunted noncommittally as he swallowed some coffee and made an exaggerated *mmmmmm* sound, like an actor in a commercial. Now *that's* a cup of coffee!

We drank in companionable silence. After a minute or two he looked at his iPhone. Fifty-nine degrees! he exclaimed. He glanced out the window and shook his head wonderingly.

It can't last long, he added gloomily. God, I hate the winter. I wish your mother would let me get a condo in Florida.

He almost seemed to be talking to himself.

"Let" you?

Please. I can't go into it.

I waited a moment. How is she lately, in general?

Oh, she's fine, my father said. She sleeps *all the time*! She sleeps late in the morning, and then takes a two-hour nap in the afternoon.

He closed his eyes. After a moment, he opened them and took another appreciative sip of coffee. This is great coffee, Dan. Thanks.

But by the time we settled into our seats in the classroom, he was combative. Shaking his head, he said, I just don't see what kind of education he's supposed to be getting in these books. He doesn't find out any useful information about his father, so what does he really learn?

There were some assenting murmurs, and then a crisp-looking kid named Brendan said, Before we talk about that, I have a different problem with Telemachus, actually.

As on many small liberal arts campuses, a good number of the Bard students affect a grungy, unhygienic look. This Brendan, by contrast, was as neat as an Arrow shirt advertisement. There was something precise, almost geometric, about him: the doubled circles of his glasses, the neat verticals of the part in his thick brown hair and of the crease in his pants.

What's the problem? I asked.

Well, Brendan said smoothly, what struck me in these first few books is that Telemachus keeps wobbling in his attitude about his father. Book 1 starts with him being very sure that Odysseus is dead—he insists to Athena that his father died long ago. Then, in Book 2, at the assembly, he tells the Suitors he's going off to find information about his father to determine whether he's living or dead. *Then,* in Book 3, Athena is in disguise as Mentor and tells him that Odysseus is coming any minute, and he doesn't believe it. It's interesting because it's not a straight progression from hopelessness. Telemachus starts out hopeless, seems to get hopeful, and then goes back again to hopelessness. So why the turnaround?

Why do I have the feeling you're going to tell us?

Some of them laughed, but Brendan was serious.

I think it's psychologically true, he said. I'm starting to wonder if he actually prefers Mentes or Mentor or whoever to Odysseus. Maybe, for him, the father figure is actually preferable to the real thing.

I didn't say anything. I'd never thought of this.

What I'm thinking is this, Brendan went on. Could it be that Telemachus unconsciously *hopes* that Odysseus has died?

The other students, I noticed, had stopped doodling and were paying attention.

Go on, I said.

Well, Brendan said. For a boy who never even met his father, the question is, Which is the larger crisis: living out your life without a father, or actually meeting him for the first time twenty years later and having to get to know him?

I looked at him and said, Now *that* is scathingly brilliant.

It was at this point that my father jumped in. I just don't understand why Telemachus is supposed to be getting an "education." All he does is just follow orders. He doesn't really think for himself at all.

I looked up and down the seminar table, but no one was talking.

Well, I finally said, but there is some educational value here, isn't there? Telemachus travels and sees new cultures and meets new people, and from that he learns. And remember that *we* are learning, too—we hear stories that fill in some of the blanks about what happened at the end of the Trojan War. So what do we learn in these books?

Nina's eyes met mine. I think it's interesting that when Telemachus and Athena arrive in Pylos in Book 3, there's a big ceremony going on. Telemachus and Athena are strangers, but they're treated with the utmost respect. It's a big contrast to Ithaca, where there's a lot of feasting and drinking, but in that case, it's just freeloading. There's no mention of sacrificing to the gods on Ithaca.

Excellent, I said. Yes. In Nestor's kingdom there's proper respect for the gods, something that's sorely lacking back home.

Trisha looked up at me.

The description of the court of Menelaus and Helen also provides a compelling contrast with Odysseus', she said.

Unlike some of the students, whose comments in class were invariably interrupted by the "umms" and "likes" common in teenagers' speech and ended, more often than not, on that upward, interrogative note, Trisha's voice was invariably coolly declamatory. She spoke in complete sentences.

When Telemachus gets to Sparta, the royal family is celebrating two marriages. This feasting is part of a joyous family occasion, which is the opposite of the feasting of the Suitors in Ithaca. There, they're all feasting *against* their host's will, violating courtesy and hospitality and gorging themselves on the stores of the absent king.

Very nice, I said. The beginnings of Books 3 and 4 provide models for hospitality that are radically different from what he's known so far in his life. So yes, you could certainly say that he's getting a little education from Nestor and Menelaus.

I resisted the temptation to look around at my father. Then I said, And we learn about someone else in these books, right?

One of Trisha's hands went up, while with the other she finished writing something in her notebook.

Yes, she said. Actually, to my mind the most interesting information we get in these two books has nothing to do with either Nestor or Menelaus. It's about Agamemnon.

Good, I said. Both Nestor and Menelaus mention him as they tell the stories of their own homecomings. Why does he keep coming up?

Madeline waved her hand. Because we learn that he gets murdered at the welcome home banquet when he returns from the Trojan War?

So?

Trisha leveled her gray eyes at me and said, It's the homecoming story you *don't* want.

The story of Agamemnon's disastrous homecoming, a kind of negative *Odyssey*, weaves itself into the fabric of Odysseus' epic from start to finish: from Book 1, when Zeus, shaking his head over mortals' foolishness, ruefully mentions how stupid Clytemnestra's lover was to persist in his corrupt plan, flying in the face of the gods' wishes, to Book 24, the epic's final book, when the news of Odysseus' violent triumph over the Suitors causes the ghost of Agamemnon in the Underworld to rejoice for "happy Odysseus" and to celebrate Penelope, a "fine, faithful wife, the fair fame of whose virtue will never die." (Nothing like Clytemnestra, he viciously adds.)

Homer's skillful manipulation of the parallel homecomings reminds us of a familiar psychological truth: that a strong sense of what our own family is like, what its weaknesses and strengths are, the relative degrees of its conventionality and eccentricity, its normalcy or pathology, is often impossible to establish until we are old enough to compare it intelligently with the families of others; something we start doing only when we begin to perceive, as happens at the end of childhood, that our family is not, in fact, the entire world.

Most of the people we socialized with when I was growing up were my mother's many friends and their families. This made sense to us. My mother, after all, was the "outgoing" one—with her movie-star smile and funny stories, the uproarious phone calls as she did her nails and peroxided her hair at the kitchen table, chatting with one of the Gang of Four, as we children called the core group of friends she'd kept since college. All of these women were given the honorific of "aunt," Aunt Alice and Aunt Mimi and Aunt Marcia and Aunt Irma, and the circle expanded over the years to include certain friends of the original group, so that in time we also had Aunt Zita and Aunt Iris, too. Among their suburban houses the round of barbecues and dinners and New Year's parties cycled over the years, the old jokes and the teasing worn smooth with time, the slide shows of vacations projected onto living room walls, the men arguing about sports or politics in someone's shag-carpeted den, the women washing up in the kitchen, sharing secrets. It was to the synagogues that these women and their families belonged to, to their children's bar and bat mitzvahs throughout the 1960s and 1970s, that my father would plan to arrive as late as possible, always blaming the *traffic*.

But there were certain occasions to which he tried never to arrive late, occasions on which we were going to visit one of "his" people.

We'd arrive on time, for instance, whenever we visited his oldest brother, Howard. This wasn't much of a challenge; Uncle Howard lived in the next town over, a ten-minute drive from our house at best. I used to ride over there on my bike, pedaling up Haypath Road on a summer's day when I was fifteen or sixteen to spend a couple of hours with Howard in the living room of the split-level in which he lived with Aunt Claire and Cousin Michael and Cousin Lorri. He liked to invite me over every now and then to listen to music with him when Claire was at work and my older cousins were at their after-school jobs; in their absence, a strange, slightly melancholy hush would settle over the place. I would sit on the plush sofa in the darkened living room, staring at the large framed reproduction of Gainsborough's *Blue Boy* that hung on one wall, and we would listen to records of classical guitar music—Andrés Segovia, Julian Bream, I can still see the names on the album covers. When each of my four siblings and I reached the age of five, we had to start music lessons. These, my father declared, were part of a *real* education, and it was understood that we'd be free to stop our lessons once we were in high school (*After that, I can't tell you what to do*)—although it was also understood that to do so, to give something up, would be a terrible failure, unworthy of the principles of perseverance and dedication which my father struggled to impart to us, a dereliction particularly awful since my father himself had never given up on anything. The one major exception to this, as far as we all knew—his abandonment of high school Latin didn't quite count—was the dissertation he had never managed to finish, which is why he had a Master's degree but not a Ph.D. in mathematics. But that solitary failure didn't seem to bother him very much, since what had prevented him from finishing it was, in a sense, us. Occasionally, when I was growing up, he'd mention that he had finished his course work for the doctoral degree but wasn't able to write the thesis because Mother had gotten pregnant with Andrew just as Daddy was getting ready to start work on the dissertation, and because he had to make a living, to provide for a family, he'd had to leave graduate school and go back to work, which is why the unfinished dissertation was the only thing, as far as I ever knew, that my diligent father had never completed.

So we stuck with our music lessons, with the instruments he assigned to us.

The instrument that my father decided was right for me, when I was five years old, was the classical guitar. Perhaps he already thought of me as a loner, someone who wouldn't fit easily into an ensemble. Anyway, although I was never more than mediocre, had never really loved the weekly lessons to which my father drove me all through the 1970s, often in silence, him listening to the grim news of the Vietnam War on the radio, the endless broadcasts from the "Paris peace talks," and me miserably looking out the window to my right, wishing I were going anywhere else, I did enjoy those quiet sessions with my father's brother on the velvet sofa across from *The Blue Boy*, not least because I found myself enjoying the idea, which was novel to me then, that I could have a relationship with a relative that was based on something other than a sense of obligation.

Uncle Howard was nearly a decade older than my father. A bit stooped, as tall people can be who aren't terribly outgoing, he would make his way around his own home tentatively, as if it were a house he was only visiting and the host had gone upstairs to take a nap. As with my father, there was something slightly rueful about his face, as though he were privy to some irony about life that only he could appreciate. His close-set eyes were brown, like my father's, and below the prominent, curved nose, which he had inherited from his father, quiet Poppy Al, was a dapper mustache that always gave this modest man an improbable dash. There was, come to think of it, something about him of an RAF pilot in a war movie. And why not? We knew that he had joined the air force at eighteen, in 1938, and flown missions all throughout "the war," so perhaps that was it— perhaps he had seen and done things that had earned him the slightly rakish quality I would notice every now and then. This face, which I'd sometimes peer at surreptitiously as we sat listening to Segovia under the wet girlish gaze of *The Blue Boy*, bore faint worn scars that were the traces of the acne that had ravaged it when he was a teenager.

So Howard was quiet and seemed to enjoy quiet times. How different he was from raucous Aunt Claire! As different as my father was from my mother.

Claire. *Clairesie!* as she sometimes called herself with a guffaw, throwing her head back and laughing the throaty, racy laugh that may have been natural but may, then again, have been the product of the packs of cigarettes she smoked each day, the improbably long "women's" filtered cigarettes of the 1960s and 1970s. Claire wasn't one of those women who closed her eyes when she took her first drag; more likely she'd be looking right at you, jabbing the cigarette in your direction as she recounted the dispute she'd had with someone at the beauty parlor (which, inevitably, she had won) or outlining one of her schemes, an investment opportunity someone at work had told her about, the free toaster ovens and blenders you could get if you moved some money from one bank to another, a surefire way to win LOTTO. My father, who in general disliked flamboyance of any kind, seemed nonetheless to enjoy Claire, to have granted her, of all the women he knew, some special grudging indulgence. I sometimes wondered whether they shared some secret that had bonded them long ago.

The house I grew up in was crisply well organized, the contents of every closet, bookcase, refrigerator, and freezer hung or shelved or stacked with rigid rationality. Claire's house was as exciting and unpredictable as her schemes and plots. Her basement, crammed with the refuse of many long-dead relatives, was a paradise for me, the bony lampstands and old brass candelabra and chunky Lionel trains winking and gleaming in the dark with as much promise as the contents of King Tut's tomb. There were many noisy pets, including three excitable dogs, one of which was a hyperactive Chihuahua named Benny B. Boychikl. This dog tormented my poor father, who, we all knew, had been bitten by a rabid dog when he was a small boy and had had to have those horrible shots in the stomach for two weeks afterward. Because of that childhood trauma he was never comfortable around even the friendliest canine; he'd cross the street to avoid our next-door neighbor's toy poodle. So it was torture for him to go to Aunt Claire and Uncle Howard's house. He'd sit miserably on the sofa beneath *The Blue Boy* while the dogs jumped and snapped and snarled somewhere down around his legs, his head arced up and back above the yapping like that of a drowning man above the waterline, his mouth set into a tight horizontal, the eyes narrowed, the hollow cheeks sunken beneath the staring cheekbones. Then Claire would walk into the room holding a mug of coffee, a long white cigarette dangling from a pink-glossed lip, and the dogs would suddenly grow quiet and, after an inquisitive moment in which they looked from my father to her, would trot over as quietly as if she'd put a spell on them, dainty as ballerinas, and lick her outstretched hand. None was daintier than Benny B. Boychikl . . . *Boychikl,* which is Yiddish for "little boy," was what Claire called me, too. *Boychikl!* she'd cry as I entered a room, chuckling throatily as she started brewing another pot of coffee, using the special "Spanish" (as we called it) grind she liked—a coffee so inky and strong that it was like a drug. Both hands held high, like a cartoon illustration of *amazement,* the bright mascaraed eyes opened wide, and the flawlessly arced brows comically raised, she'd shout *Boychik!* and throw back her small head with its reddish mane and guffaw with rasping delight. On a whim, I recently searched the Internet for the word *boychik.* When you do so, a wiki appears offering a definition ("a term of endearment for a young boy, or a young man"), followed by this sample sentence: "Boychik, your daddy would be proud of you if he were alive."

Besides Howard, the person whose house my father was eager to get to on time was Uncle Nino. Nino, who lived farther east on Long Island (only about an hour away—well, if the traffic was good), wasn't a "real" uncle. He was Italian, and Catholic, but such a close friend to my father that he became one of our many honorary uncles and aunts, a phenomenon much commoner in the case of my mother's friends. But then, my mother, we knew, was an only child, and we understood that unlike my father she "needed" these pretend siblings. Like my father, Nino was a mathematician, and my brothers and sister and I had always silently assumed that math was what bound them together, because any superficial resemblance, any hint of common tastes or interests, seemed to stop there. Because we grew up knowing that my father was a mathematician, we had, inevitably, thought that he must be the model for all mathematicians: the gray hooded sweatshirts, the polyester short-sleeved shirts, the too-wide or too-narrow or simply wrong ties, the embarrassing "comfortable" dress shoes with rubber soles, the hopeless cars, pieces of which would start falling off soon after he bought them, something that never seemed to happen to the cars belonging to our friends' fathers. And then there was Nino, with his tiny feline convertibles and suave Italian slacks and sports coats, the beautiful soft loafers, his enormous wine cellar and his knowing way with food, and Aunt Irene, his glamorous long-haired Greek wife, who would have platters of strange appetizers waiting when we finally got there, the grape leaves and "fresh" anchovies—an unimaginable concept to us, for whom the natural habitat of most fish seemed to be tin cans. Nino, my father's good friend, a man who we knew was, more than anything else, a great traveler, who went to Europe as casually as we went to bar mitzvahs in New Jersey, who had lived abroad, had taken the long-haired wife and the dark-eyed children to Italy, where he taught at some university for a year, and who came back from this sojourn with gifts and food and stories, tales of cathedrals and vineyards and daylong meals, anecdotes he'd tell with a gleam in his blue eyes, his sly, pink-cheeked, humorous face creased in laughter, the mobile mouth opening to let escape his staccato *Ah!*, a sound inevitably accompanied by a downward shake of the head and a small gesture, both hands spreading out before him, then dropping into his lap, as if in futility: his characteristic expression of delight at some remembered pleasure too large and complicated to describe. *But, Jay, Jay! You should go sometime!* Nino would say after returning from one of his trips, and my father would look down at the floor, shaking his head, and say, *You don't understand.* And we knew that what Nino didn't understand was that Mother didn't want to travel—didn't like to leave the neighborhood, really, unless Daddy was driving. And so my father didn't go anywhere, either.

And yet, as different as the two men were, my father loved Nino. *Your father adores your uncle Nino!* my mother liked to say each year as we prepared for our visit, uttering the words to no one in particular as she carefully wrapped the gifts for him that she'd so exactingly chosen: special, rarefied things we wouldn't dream of giving to other friends, gold-flecked Italian glass decanters with improbable swanlike necks and Orrefors crystal cordial glasses in unemotional colors, smoky gray, cobalt blue; *Your father adores Nino,* my mother would say aloud as we were getting ready to leave, as if the trip we were about to embark on were so exotic, so arduous, that it needed a justification this dramatic, this grandiose, although what struck our ears as strange wasn't so much the announcement itself as the collocation of the words "your father" and "adores." We were unaccustomed to thinking of my father as a person of great passions, even as someone of strong affections. He had, at best, a handful of close friends, the relatively small number of which stood in reproachful contrast to the vastness of my mother's circle, which may or may not have been the result of her emotional extravagances, she who was so entertaining and funny, who brought flowers from the gardens to checkout girls at the supermarket and to the receptionists at the doctor's and dentist's offices, who had so many friends. When I was young this contrast seemed a confirmation of my sense that my father was somehow the inverse of my mother . . . Some of my father's few close friends, it was true, were men he'd known much longer than he knew Nino. There was Eugene Miller, for instance: a gangly, soft-spoken, beak-nosed accountant who could be seen at the big family functions, the bar mitzvahs and weddings at which the "Bronx crowd" would gather, stalking around the room like a long-legged bird, someone who didn't quite fit in with my father's scientist friends from work and yet with whom my father was, uncharacteristically, physically affectionate. Every now and then my father would, without saying a word, throw an arm around Eugene's high stooped shoulders or give him a little sideways hug, and we imagined that this unusual physicality reflected Eugene's special place in the small constellation of Daddy's friends, since, as people would say in approving whispers, *Daddy has known Eugene since he was five years old!*

So yes: my father had some people to whom he obviously felt close. But "adore"? Certainly he himself had never said aloud the words *I adore*; or, to my knowledge, *I love.*

———

Book 4 is the longest book in the *Odyssey*—twice as long as most of the other books. This is, in part, because it contains some lengthy tales by means of which Homer ingeniously teaches its young hero a certain important lesson.

At the beginning of the book, not long after Menelaus' reference to his great love for his old comrade Odysseus reduces Telemachus to reve-latory tears, Helen of Troy enters to take her place at the wedding feast. Unlike her husband, she instantly recognizes the youthful visitor:

> *I declare, I've never seen a likeness quite as close*
> *in either man or woman—astonishing!—*
> *as the one that this man bears to Odysseus' son,*
> *Telemachus, whom that man left—a newborn babe—*
> *when you came to Troy, you Greeks, to launch your war—*
> *all for my sake, shameless bitch that I am!*

In lingering on the physical resemblance between the youth, who is a stranger to her, and the man she once knew, a likeness that she alone has been able to perceive, Helen gives Telemachus the confirmation of his identity for which he has been yearning since he first appears in Book 1. It would seem that she is still a woman who knows how to give men what they want.

A great deal of weeping ensues as Menelaus, Helen, and Telemachus recall the absent Odysseus. Even young Peisistratus, Nestor's son, works up a few tears—not about Odysseus, of course, since he never knew him, but about a brother of his who died at Troy; weeping, the Greeks knew, can be a kind of pleasure. Ostensibly because all these tears are getting to be overwhelming, Helen decides, before launching into her remi-niscence about Odysseus, to lace the wine with a powerful drug. This potion—which, we are told, the Spartan queen obtained in Egypt, home to the greatest sages and healers in the world—has the effect of severing the cord between inner emotion and outward expression: to drink it is to lose the ability to weep, to shed a tear, even if one's mother and father were to die, even if one's brother or darling son should be killed before one's eyes. The drug is called *nepenthê*, which means "no grief," the *penthê* in *nepenthê* deriving from the noun *penthos*, "grief." It is, indeed, a word formed much the same way that *anodyne*, "without pain," the word that points to the origins of Odysseus' name, is formed.

Helen's remarkable ability to recognize people is, in fact, the subject of the story she now proceeds to tell, apparently to satisfy Telemachus' desire to learn more about the father he has never known. She recalls how, toward the end of the war, Odysseus infiltrated Troy disguised as a beggar, wearing filthy rags and, more extraordinarily, having whipped himself with a lash first, for the sake of verisimilitude. She alone, she now declares to her drugged husband and her drugged guests, was able to recognize him, and after doing so she bathed and dressed him, questioning him all the time about the Greeks' plans. She finishes her tale by further recalling how, toward the end of her odd encounter with Odysseus, he had made her swear not to give his identity away until he had slipped out of Troy and returned safely to the Greek camp. It would seem from this that he didn't quite trust her; but now, to her husband and her guests, she hints that the oath was unnecessary. For by this point in the war, she assures her narcotized listeners, her "heart had changed": she regretted having run away to Troy with Paris and wished only to sail back home with the victorious Greek army. She ends her narrative with a graceful reference to her husband Menelaus' brains and good looks and laments the "madness" that distracted her from them in the first place.

Menelaus seems to applaud his wife's long story—"Well done, my dear, a very becoming tale!"—and then launches into a war story of his own. On the night when he and the other Greek soldiers were concealed within the Trojan Horse, he begins, waiting to spring their ambush on the Trojans, Helen emerged from the royal palace and went down into the center of the city where the Horse had been dragged. Three times, Menelaus recalls, she walked around the giant wooden construction, and as she did so she cried out the names of the Greek warriors hiding inside, as if testing to see whether anyone was there; as she did so she disguised her own voice, mimicking those of the warriors' long-lost wives. Meanwhile, inside the horse (Menelaus recalls) a number of the Greeks were on the verge of crying out in response to what they thought were their wives' voices; they had, after all, been at war for ten years by this point, sick with longing for their homes. But the canny Odysseus wasn't fooled: he clapped his hand over the mouths of these weaker men whom Helen's ruse had duped. And so, Menelaus concludes, Odysseus "saved us all"—with a little help from Athena, who finally lured Helen back to the palace.

During the second half of our session on Books 3 and 4, as noon approached and the bizarrely mild day grew even warmer, I briefly summarized these two stories and then said, So what's going on here?

There was a Belgian boy in the class whom I'd called Damien Half-Beard the previous year, when he was a freshman in the Great Books course I had taught. As if out of some perverse desire to mask himself—he had the marmoreal oval face and solemn expression of a nineteenth-century diplomat in a portrait—he liked to play tricks on his face. Occasionally he'd grow opulent Victorian whiskers on one side only, the left or the right, the effect of which was that he sometimes looked like both halves of a before-and-after illustration: *The Boy; the Man.*

Now, as we discussed Book 4, Damien raised his hand.

For me the funny part is how Helen was putting drugs into their wines.

Why is it funny? I said.

Jack cried out gleefully, The Greeks did drugs!

Because they're telling sad stories about the Trojan War? Madeline said.

Over in his corner my father muttered, *All* war stories are sad.

Damien said, It's funny! Menelaus is being sarcastic to Helen when he says "Well done, my dear, a very becoming tale!"

Yes, I said, you're right. But what's he being sarcastic *about*?

It's just . . . funny, Damien said. Like he doesn't really believe her.

But why doesn't he believe her?

Nobody said anything.

I said, You're not reading closely enough if you're missing what's actually at issue between Menelaus and Helen in this scene. Don't just accept what the characters are saying; read between the lines. You have to tease the meaning out of the text. What's really going on here—the drug, the stories, the sarcasm?

But the fact is that my incredulity was disingenuous. I hadn't seen it right away, either.

The first time I read this passage from Book 4 of the *Odyssey* in Greek was in the Homer seminar that Jenny taught when I was in my third year at Virginia. One day, when we had finished struggling through the speeches of Helen and Menelaus, Jenny, taking a drag on her cigarette, asked us the same thing: What does Telemachus actually learn from this passage?

There were only two other students in that class: David, a graduate student who was going to be writing a thesis on Roman poetry but had to improve his Greek in order to get his degree, and a terrified boy who simply disappeared one day from the class and, for all I know, from the university. For whatever reason, they both spoke before I did that day. David, who had grown up near Boston and rather endearingly affected a tough-guy Humphrey Bogart air, said, He learns that his father was clever at disguises and was willing to hurt himself if it meant success.

The terrified kid said, He learns that his father saved all the Greeks on the night of the wooden horse, that he was a hero.

Jenny looked at each of us in turn, as she would sometimes do when waiting for a translation or a comment, and then, using the nickname that, until then, had only been used by my father, said, *Dan?*

I don't know what kind of houses the two other students had grown up in, but I suspect, now, that I was able to answer Jenny's question correctly that day because I had grown up in the house of my mother and my father, listening to their terse back-and-forthing every night during dinner and afterward, the clipped allusions to certain events and people (*Oh your father, your father, he wasn't such a hero, believe me*); and, during one particular period when I was in my teens, had learned how to read the fraught silences, too, as my father stalked off after dinner to sit at the tiny desk in his room with his head in his hands and my mother cleaned up the floor on her hands and knees, muttering to herself, and we all slunk off to our rooms to do our homework. During that period, it was as if you could smell ozone in the atmosphere of the house, as if some terrible storm were always threatening to break. It made you want to walk on tiptoe.

So I answered, It looks like they're sharing these happy memories of Odysseus, but actually it's pretty tense.

Jenny smiled, then, and made a tiny motion with her sleek brown head. She wore a silver ring on her forefinger, made from an ancient Athenian coin and designed so that you could swivel the coin around to display either the obverse or the reverse, Athena's profile or the owl, the goddess's special animal.

Go on, Dan, she said.

Well, I said, the point of Helen's story is that she's sorry for having run away with Paris by now. She wants everyone to believe that she's come around to the Greek cause, that now she's helping Odysseus on his spying mission.

Jenny nodded.

But the whole point of Menelaus' story is that it shows she's lying.

How?

Because she was trying to get the Greeks who were hiding inside the horse to betray themselves. Which means she was still actually on the Trojans' side.

She looked pleased. *Now* tell me why she drugs the wine.

I suddenly sat up straight in my seat. It's as if she and Menelaus have told these stories before and she knows that his story exposes her as a traitor, and so she drugs the wine because after taking *nepenthê* no one can react to anything, no one can become outraged, no one can do anything about what the stories reveal . . . they're eating and drinking and it looks like a nice feast, but underneath it all they're actually fighting.

Cocking her head again, Jenny exhaled. Then she looked us over. I'll repeat my original question, then. What does Telemachus learn in Book 4?

Into the silence she finally said, Remember, this is the first adult couple he's ever encountered.

Then it came to me. He's learning about *marriage*, I said.

My father wasn't the only one who questioned the educational value of Telemachus' trips to Pylos and Sparta. Some ancient commentators weren't persuaded, either. "Preposterous," one sage harrumphed in his marginal note to Book 1, line 284—the line in which Athena urges the prince to "Go first to Pylos and question godlike Nestor." Among other things, the sage noted, by going abroad Telemachus leaves his home unprotected and his mother more vulnerable than ever to danger. That scholar further complained that the fact-finding trips anyway turned out to be fruitless, since Telemachus returns home from his journeys without any hard information about his father's whereabouts. It was in response to these doubts that still other ancient savants proposed that the purpose of the Telemachy and certain other ostensible digressions was to add "variety" to the plot of the *Odyssey*, to help prevent it from becoming too uniform—too (to use the word of one of these commentators) *monotropos:* that is, the opposite of *polytropos*.

Such complaints are likely to strike us as odd, accustomed as we are to the commonplace that travel can be a "learning experience" for young people; and so we moderns tend not to question the wisdom of Athena's instructions to Telemachus in Book 1 of the *Odyssey*. Most readers have taken it for granted that his voyages to Pylos and Sparta will somehow be, in and of themselves, educational—that (like going away to college, say, or taking a junior year abroad) the mere fact of leaving home and being on his own will play a crucial part in Telemachus' maturation. And indeed, since ancient times many scholars and ordinary readers have seen the first four books of the *Odyssey* as an early if not indeed pioneering instance of the genre the Germans would later call the *Bildungsroman*, "formation novel": that is, a tale that charts the ethical and moral growth of a young person. The term was coined by a nineteenth-century German literary scholar called Johann Karl Simon Morgenstern, who happened to be the star student of Friedrich August Wolf, the founder of philology, until the two fell out bitterly: Wolf thought that Morgenstern, with his growing emphasis on the practical uses of literary texts as ethical models, had become a vulgar popularizer, while Morgenstern thought his *Doktorvater*'s emphasis on scientific method was in danger of obscuring the broad humanistic implication of literature, whose aim should be the "harmonious molding" of a young person's soul.

Those who see the Telemachy as a proto-bildungsroman approvingly cite another ancient commentator on line 284 of Book 1, who remarks that Athena sends Telemachus to Pylos

in order to be educated (for [Nestor] had the experience that comes with age), then to Sparta, to Menelaus (for he has recently returned from eight years of roaming); more generally, in order to gain glory on account of his search for his father.

Yet another of the ancients who saw the Telemachy as a tale of a young man's growth was a pagan Greek philosopher called Porphyry, who wrote a number of treatises on Homer. In one of them he remarks that the first four books of the *Odyssey* constitute the story of a young man's *paideusis*, "education." Embedded in *paideusis* is the word *pais*, "child," which is indeed the root of the Greek verb *paideuô*, "to educate." Education, in other words, is what you do for children.

As it happens, this word *paideuô*—no doubt because it is extremely regular in all its forms—is used as the "sample verb" throughout a slender volume called *A New Introduction to Greek*, which was the textbook used to teach Greek 101–102, the introductory language sequence offered by the Department of Classics at the University of Virginia during the 1978–79 academic year, my first year at college. I had come to this university unwillingly, at first. I had wanted to go to another Virginia school, the College of William and Mary, which I thought was prettier, and whose early associations with British royalty I found obscurely exciting. *But Daaan!* my father cried as we made the long trip down South in the spring of 1978 to see the campuses of the two colleges. Come *on!* U. Va. was founded by an American *president!* Look at the architecture, it's everything you love—classical, Tuscan, Doric, that's what he wanted it to be about! The Age of *Reason!*

But the truth was that the brick-and-stucco neoclassical pavilions, grouped around a central building inspired by the Pantheon in Rome, left me cold. I declared myself an admirer of Christopher Wren, and ostentatiously played a cassette tape of Purcell's *Funeral Music for Queen Mary* as we drove along the Virginia interstate. There were other things, things I didn't mention to my father. The preppy boys, lounging proprietarily around the stucco porticos in their button-downs and khakis and rep ties, ambling along the herringbone brick walkways, exuded a confidence I was certain I would never feel. I was determined not to go.

But my father was adamant.

You want to go to the other place because it's <u>pretty</u>, he said while we were driving home, his left shoulder hunching spasmodically as we raced up I-95. As he spoke I was surprised to see that he was working hard not to lace his words with too much acid. But *pretty* isn't everything, he went on. U. Va. is a *great* school, it has a *big* Classics department, there's everything you wanted. And Charlottesville is a real college town, you know.

(He had looked grim when we took the tour of Colonial Williamsburg, with its reconstructions of eighteenth-century life, the chipper girls in hoopskirts churning butter. *Phony,* he'd muttered as a college kid in a white powdered wig showed us around a low-ceilinged room and talked about beeswax candles.)

You'll find things you . . . you won't find in a small place like *Williamsburg*. He paused. This time, his tone put sarcastic little quotation marks around the name of the city.

Look, he said a few hours later, in the awful restaurant at the WELCOME TO MARYLAND rest stop where we wolfed down crab-cake sandwiches. Look, go to U. Va. for a year, and if you hate it, you can transfer to William and Mary. And if you love it, you can just thank me. How's that?

I was surprised to see how deeply he felt about the whole thing. The force of his conviction pushed hard against the resistances I'd built up over all those years. A few days later, after we'd returned home, I walked into his bedroom and said, Okay.

He looked up warily from the teak desk.

Okay, I repeated. I'll do it your way. I'll try it for a year.

And he was right: I found what I wanted at Virginia, which was, as he had intuited, big enough, diverse enough, to satisfy all my interests, intellectual and otherwise; the place where I found Jenny, and others. I stayed.

I eagerly signed up for Greek 101–102 during my first year at Virginia, after years of excited anticipation. Neither my junior high nor high school had offered anything but Spanish and French, and although I was already avidly reading books about Greek mythology and archaeology and history, I could do nothing but take French and wait until I went to college. This is why, when I finally returned to my dorm room from the university bookstore one afternoon late in August of 1978 and opened *A New Introduction to Greek*, the dark buckram boards slightly scratchy in my hands, the pages as cool to the touch as sliced apples, it was with the special joy it's possible to feel only when you are a student about to embark on a course of study that you have long anticipated, an excitement in which satisfaction and yearning, plenitude and lack, are curiously mixed. As I flipped through the chapters, my uncomprehending eyes hungrily roved over the stacked paradigms and conjugations, the black Greek characters marching across the page like insects. But because the class moved swiftly—we covered one chapter per class session, each chapter covering an entire grammatical principle; the class met five times a week from 9:00 to 9:50 each morning—what had at first appeared to be random markings soon coalesced into words, nouns, adjectives, adverbs, verbs, in all their possible forms.

More than anything I loved the elaborate richness of the verbal system. Partly this was because of the additional features that bespoke an alluring obsession with precision. For instance, the Greeks have a form, neither singular nor plural, called the "dual," which is used only for things that typically come in pairs—oxen, eyes, hands—and made the paradigms familiar from high-school French (I, you, he/she/it, we, you plural, they) seem inexact, deficient. And partly it was the fascination exercised by that strange "middle" voice, neither the active nor the passive that I knew about from English class in school but something that is both at once, a verbal mode in which the subject is also the object, a folding over that Greek elegantly achieves in the space of a single word but which English can only accomplish by means of the awkward addition of the reflexive pronoun ("I x'd myself," "they y themselves").

What thrilled me above all were the fantastically metastasizing verb tenses, the shifts in time signaled by prefixes that agglomerated like crystals, by endings that pooled at the ends of the words like honey that has dripped off a spoon onto a saucer:

paideu-ô I educate
e-paideu-on I was educating
paideu-sô I shall educate
e-paideu-sa I educated
pe-paideu-ka I have educated
e-pe-paideu-ka I had educated

It seemed wonderful to me that by means of such tiny additions at either or both ends of the stem, *-paideu-*, such remarkable leaps in time could be achieved: the present morphing, by the mere addition of an *e* to the beginning of the word, into the hazy past of the imperfect, or, just as easily, slithering its way into the future by the insertion of a sigma, *s*, between the stem and the personal ending; or, rather comically, entering the hall of mirrors that is the "perfect" past by means of a double augmentation, first the stuttering reduplication of the initial consonant, *p-p*, and then the annexation of the cruel *k* sound at the end: *pepaideuka*, "I have educated." And, indeed, you might say that the progress from the hesitant prefix to that authoritative suffix mimics the trajectory that education itself is meant to set in motion.

So the first paradigm of *paideuô* that I encountered was exciting for me. It was not so for everyone. When the Greek 101 class began, in the last days of August of 1978, a boy with solemn features and bright red hair—clearly a prep-school kid, I thought enviously, with his blue blazer, his rumpled pale blue oxford button-down shirt and blue-and-orange rep tie, a uniform worn with a confidence so blandly unself-conscious that it didn't even seem like confidence—took a seat on the other side of the classroom. After the first few class sessions I'd find a way to stop him and chat for a few moments. *I took Greek at my school so I thought I'd give it a try again*, this boy, each of whose pale cheeks had a ruddy patch so highly colored and distinct that it looked painted on, like the red circles on the cheeks of a doll, said to me vaguely one humid afternoon, *but I'm not so sure . . .* His voice trailed off as I stared at him with dismay. His high school had offered Greek! As I stood there, amazed, his eyes slid away to the far end of the hallway, where some other kids wearing blue blazers and ties and button-down shirts were lounging. They waved at him. *Oh, there are my friends*, he drawled, and he walked toward them, loose-hipped, and a few days later he stopped coming to class . . . The first paradigm of *paideuô*, as I was saying, was exciting to me.

And that was only the active voice in the indicative mood! But there were also the subjunctive and optative moods, the former indicating, as my dictionary puts it, "a state of contingency or unreality," the latter "a wish or prayer," verbal modes of which only the barest traces survive in

English, for instance when you say "Be that as it may" or "God help us," but which in Classical Greek are ubiquitous and indispensable.

And so on. During the first year of my university education in Greek I learned that, like *paideuô*, every other Greek verb exists in each of these moods and tenses and forms and voices, which means that every verb has literally hundreds of forms, each beautifully tailored to describe with fanatical precision the action to which the verb refers: who is doing it, how it is being done, in what circumstances, with what aims. Because I grew up in a house organized in accordance with my mother's insistence on neatness and order, all this seemed natural to me, and I absorbed it hungrily; all this precision was comforting. It was as if the implacable rigor of grammar, with its implication that there was a place and a function for everything if only one could master the system, was a kind of armor that could protect me from things that were less easily classified and ordered.

At the root both of *paideuô*, "to educate," and of the corresponding noun *paideusis*, "education," the word that Porphyry, the third-century A.D. philosopher, chose to describe the theme of the first four books of the *Odyssey*, is the Greek word *pais*. When compounded with other words, *pais*, which means "child" or sometimes just "boy," becomes *paed-* (or *ped-*), as for instance in such English words as "pedagogy," "the leading of children into knowledge," and "pederasty," "the erotic desire for *paides*, 'young boys'" (boyhood, for the Greeks, being a state that ended when the first traces of the beard appeared)—the latter being the kind of yearning that, as Plato expounded in one of his dialogues, represented the lowest rung of a ladder which with any luck might lead to a love for higher concepts.

A millennium and a half after Porphyry, in the nineteenth century— when, as I'd explained to the kids in my introductory lecture, there was suddenly a great fashion for dividing the *Iliad* and the *Odyssey* into discrete episodes—some classicists held that the first four books of the *Odyssey* had once formed an independent mini-epic that had only later been grafted onto the *Odyssey*. So strong, they argued, was the narrative arc of its young protagonist's development from passivity to activity, from mere observer to energetic seeker; so forceful was the novelistic trajectory of the Telemachy, that mini-bildungsroman in which the character of Odysseus' young son comes to be molded, *educated*, in the course of his search for his father.

2. HOMOPHROSYNÊ

(Husbands and Wives)

A nother thing that my father didn't like about Odysseus was the fact that the hero weeps.

He's always crying! he exclaimed as we drove to campus on the third Friday in February. We were going to be discussing Books 5 and 6 that day. *Crying!* He shook his head in bemusement. What's so heroic about that?

It was bitterly cold that morning; the thermometer outside the back door had read nineteen degrees when we left my house. My father muttered and cursed as he fumbled with the buttons of his bulky coat.

Dad, I said, maybe you should try doing that *before* you put your gloves on?

Don't tell *me* what to do, he said; another familiar refrain from our childhood. I know what I'm doing. Without looking up from the buttons he added, Sometimes you sound just like your *mother.*

It is in Book 5 that the poet at last turns his attention fully to his main character, abandoning Telemachus (who will not reappear until Book 15) and his search for his father and zeroing in on the lost hero himself. Odysseus, as we know from Book 1, is stranded on Calypso's island. Now, as the epic zooms in on him, the hero is described as "wailing" with grief every day while he sits contemplating the seemingly infinite sea that separates him from home, "groaning" because he cannot see the home fires of his native Ithaca. The culmination of this portrait of despair is the information that Odysseus has lost the will to live: he "longs to die."

As we started our discussion of Book 5, I asked the students what they thought of this long-delayed fuller glimpse of the epic's main character.

Nina lifted her hand.

It's even more surprising than in Book 1, she said. He's totally passive and depressed. He's suicidal!

Jack guffawed. Not very heroic!

This was when my father jumped in.

I agree with her, he said, motioning to Nina. (Did he even know their names? I wondered. Would he ever make even some small effort to get to know them?) He's a complainer, he says he wants to die. I just don't understand why he's supposed to be such a great hero.

He pronounced the word "hero" with slight distaste, turning the long *e* in the first syllable into an extended *aih* sound: *haihhro*. He did this with other words: "beer," for instance. I remember how, not long after his father died, after they had flown the body back down to Miami to be buried with my grandmother and her sisters and their husbands, after the pathetic funeral at which, my father told us, he couldn't bear to look into the open casket because they had rouged his father's cheeks, and as he spoke I could hear how shocked and disgusted he was from the way he said the word "rouged"—I remember how, after all that, my father turned one day to me and my brothers and said, *When I die, I want you to burn me up and then I want you boys to go to a bar and have a round of beers and make a toast to me, and that's it.*

A round of *baihhrs*.

I don't know why he's supposed to be such a haihhro, he was now saying. He cheats on his wife, he sleeps with Calypso. He loses all of his men, so he's a lousy general. He's depressed, he whines. He sits there and wants to die.

He shook his head. So why does everyone keep saying "the hero" this and "the hero" that? He's supposed to be a soldier. A father! A leader! A king!

Well, I said after a moment, he is. The *Iliad* has lots of scenes that show Odysseus as both an effective military leader and an honorable fighter.

Well, I was in the army, and I knew some guys who were real heroes. And I can tell you, *nobody* cried.

There were some amused looks.

I coughed. I'm actually glad that my father is bringing this point up, because one of the *Odyssey*'s agendas, as we'll be seeing during the course of this semester, is to redefine what a hero is. In the *Iliad*, which is a poem about war, heroes die all the time, but they're willing to die if their heroism on the battlefield brings them glorious renown, which the Greeks called *kleos*. The most famous instance of this is the choice of Achilles, the greatest of all the heroes, who chooses a short, glorious life over a long, undistinguished life.

Some of them were nodding.

But the *Odyssey*, I went on, is a poem about a postwar world. It's set in the aftermath of war, and one of the things it explores is what a hero might look like once there are no more wars to fight. Achilles is renowned for his physical prowess, his speed and strength. Odysseus, although he's a distinguished warrior, is renowned above all for his stratagems, his intellectual brilliance. Achilles dies, but Odysseus survives. One question posed by the *Odyssey* is, What might a heroism of *survival* look like?

The students, who'd reacted with amusement when my father said *I was in the army, and nobody cried*, had quieted down. I took advantage of the subdued mood to make a point. So yes, I said, Odysseus cries. But crying wasn't an embarrassment for Homer's Bronze Age characters. Tears flow freely in both the *Iliad* and the *Odyssey*.

I paused and said, And *no one* thinks the characters any less manly for crying.

I turned and gave him a look.

I never saw my father cry. Certainly throughout my youth I went to great extremes to avoid outward displays of emotion. My father hated signs of weakness—even of illness, for which he displayed a kind of contempt, as if being sick were an ethical rather than a physical failing. If we had to stay home sick from school, he'd poke his head into our room before he went off to work and make a disgruntled face, sighing wearily, as if this case of flu or chicken pox were the beginning of some irreversible moral decline. We sensed obscurely that this attitude had something to do with his childhood and Uncle Bobby's polio. In our childish minds, Daddy's quarrel with Bobby, whatever terrible thing that had caused him to stop speaking to his older brother, had become conflated with the illness that had crippled him. To be ill was to be like Bobby. Only much later did I learn the whole story: how close they had been as children, how my father, when still a small child, had accompanied Bobby to all the doctors, taken the buses and subways with him to the consulting rooms and hospitals; all that, the drudgery and the doctors and the disappointment when it became clear that Bobby was never going to get better, was surely the source of his horror of illness . . . So you weren't allowed to be sick. To show any kind of vulnerability in his presence seemed somehow dangerous, an invitation to reproach. Once, on a blazing summer afternoon when I was about thirteen, I was sent outside to cut the hedges with the electric hedge clipper, but when my father came out to check on my progress I was taking a break, sitting in the shade. *It's too hot to do anything now,* I said, a little challengingly, and my father said, *Don't be such a* <u>*sissy*</u>. After that I took off my shirt and hacked away with the electric clippers at the boxwood until I fainted. I was lying on the lawn with the clippers still buzzing when my mother found me. For some perverse reason, this made me want his approval all the more. Once, when I was around fifteen and had begun secretly writing anguished short stories about doomed and passionate friendships between teenage boys, one of whom would invariably die by the end of the tale, I took advantage of some sense of a thaw in my father's attitude toward me, some gentling, to shyly show him my latest work of fiction, sliding it onto the teak desk so he'd find it when he came home from work. Later that evening, after dinner was over and my father had retreated to his desk, he called me into their bedroom and said, *It's beautiful, Dan.*

I was so surprised that I couldn't think of anything to say in reply.

Then he suddenly made one of his faces and said, almost to himself, *But this idea about perfect love is <u>shit</u>,* and thrust the sheaf of papers back to me.

So I never let my father see me cry.

Even on the day his work friend Bob McGill had died, my father hadn't cried. Bob and Daddy would play tennis every Tuesday night after they left the office; apart from those weekly matches, as far as I knew, my father didn't see Bob much outside of the office. The odd blank pall that seemed to obscure the substance of his working life hung as well over the men he worked with, which is why I knew so little of what his friendship with Bob McGill might have been like.

There was, we knew, terrible pain in Bob's life, and this dark sorrow somehow fenced him off from the rest of us even farther, making him both special and frightening to think about. Bob was married to a tiny woman called Anne, who had rheumatoid arthritis. At her terrifying hands, their fingers as twisted as roots, I would sneak hot shamed glances at the rare parties my parents gave, back when I was a teenager. Her feet, of course, were covered, but it was easy enough to infer how horribly they, too, had been contorted, from the agonizingly slow and lumpy way she walked. It was of this stunted gait that we all immediately thought on the morning in 1975 when Bob suddenly died just after he'd returned home following an impromptu morning tennis match with my father. Bob had walked into the house, Anne later told my parents, and then he just fell down to the ground. A *massive coronary,* everyone later whispered. But it took her too many minutes to hobble to the phone, and then she was so frantic that she couldn't manage the special dialing mechanism that Bob had attached to it, and then it was more minutes before she could get outside to call for help, and so he died.

This happened one morning when I was in the tenth grade. That evening I was supposed to be inducted into the National Honor Society. The ceremony had been scheduled weeks in advance, and afterward everyone was going to go, as usual, to Friendly's for ice cream. But that day, after I got home from school, I'd nervously gone into my parents' room, where my father, who'd come home from work early, was sitting at his desk, his head bowed, both hands gripping his cranium, staring unseeingly at a pile of bills and papers, and I shyly told him that it was okay if we didn't go to the ceremony or the after-party. But he just shook his head grimly and said, not looking at me, *You got in, and we're going. An honor is an honor.* He wasn't crying then, and he didn't cry later on, either during the ceremony in the school auditorium or at Friendly's, where my school friends and I sat around the Formica tables, guzzling milk shakes and root-beer floats. From time to time, during the hour or so that we sat there, a group of tenth graders gossiping and guffawing, I would furtively glance across the room at my father and mother, who were standing against a wall not saying anything, and would notice that there seemed to be no emotion at all on his face, let alone tears.

This was the moment that sprang to my mind that frigid February morning a few years ago when we were discussing Book 5 of the *Odyssey* and my father said that he didn't understand why Odysseus was supposed to be such a great hero because he cried all the time.

I turned to the class. In Greek epic heroes do cry. You just have to accept it. Remember, this book represents the product of a different culture.

My father's mouth was a horizontal line. Well, in *my* book, he finally said, he's no hero. When I was in the army, I knew some pretty heroic guys, and they never cried.

That night, as I typed up the notes I'd taken in class, I asked myself whether my father had been showing off to the students that morning. Heroes he'd known in the army? On the rare occasions when my father had talked about his military service to us, it was in the way of a joke. *I peeled potatoes in Petersburg, Virginia,* I remember him telling me once, *that was my time in the army.* When my father did talk about the military, it was usually either about Uncle Howard's long service or the fact that Bobby, because of the polio, hadn't been able to join up in World War II. *It killed your uncle Bobby not to be able to fight,* he said once in the 1990s, after he and Bobby had reconciled . . . and he and Howard had stopped speaking. Given the tragedy of the one and the heroism of the other, his own boring time in the army must have been embarrassing. But then, we knew that the only reason he'd joined was the GI Bill: in exchange for his potato peeling he'd get a college education.

Recently, when I was asking my siblings what they remembered Daddy saying about his military service, it turned out each one of them had heard something different. "I thought he was at Fort Hamilton, at the base of the Verrazano Bridge," Jennifer wrote me, adding, in a second e-mail, "Oh, and he told me he was a clerk of some kind. That the smart people were separated out or something and he got picked." Matt wrote that he was pretty sure that Daddy had been stationed at the Aberdeen Proving Ground in Maryland. Andrew, always the closest to Daddy when we were children (which is why, I'd always secretly thought, Daddy was able to forgive him for being the reason he couldn't finish his dissertation), wrote the longest e-mail:

> I once asked him what he learned in the army and he answered that what he learned was that he "was the smartest person in the army."
>
> There was some story about how he had to flush deer out of the woods so that the officers could shoot them for dinner but I'm fuzzy on the details.

When I read this, I couldn't help enjoying the idea of my father involved in what is, in fact, a very Homeric scene. Often in the *Odyssey*, when Odysseus and his men land on some unknown island, the first thing they do is to go hunting or foraging for food. In Book 10, for instance, when they land on Aiaia, the eerie island where the nymph Circe lives, Odysseus—who is momentarily torn between satisfying his irrepressible curiosity and investigating the terrain, on the one hand, and

seeking out food for himself and his crew, on the other—spots a huge
stag. He takes down the animal with one cast of his spear and brings it
back to camp to his men. This long and strangely detailed preliminary
to the encounter with Circe herself is, perhaps, justified by the fact that
it shows the hero deciding to provide for his men's needs before satisfying himself, a priority that, as my father was always quick to point out,
doesn't always influence his decisions.

This is why the reference to my father's having had to "flush deer" put
a smile on my face as I read Andrew's e-mail. I also grinned when I read
the other thing Andrew had written: "what he learned was that he 'was
the smartest person in the army.'" Leave it to Daddy, I thought, to make
his service in the army a story about *intellect*.

If Book 4 and the visit to Helen and Menelaus provides a discomfiting
glimpse of one of the most notoriously troubled marriages in Western
literature, Books 5 and 6 seem designed to provoke questions about marriage more generally—about why some couples are better suited to each
other than others, and about what special qualities distinguish a successful match.

Book 5 begins with part two of the gods' plan to bring Odysseus home:
rescuing him from Calypso. They send the messenger god, Hermes,
down to her island, and there he finds the nymph in her dark cave, which
is perfumed with burning herbs and surrounded by dense growth. After
he conveys to Calypso the gods' order, she explodes in a rage, denouncing their infamous sexual double standard: the male gods, she declares,
often take mortal women as their lovers, but never allow female deities to
remain with *their* mortal lovers—and indeed often kill these unfortunate
young men. Yielding to Zeus' will, however, Calypso promises Hermes
that she will set Odysseus free. When she goes to bring her lover the
news, she finds him on the beach, weeping—weeping because he has
tired of sleeping with her. (Students invariably find this line amusing; but
Homer goes out of his way to mention that the goddess has "compelled"

the mortal man to make love to her each night, a detail intended, perhaps, to let Odysseus off the moral hook that my father was so eager to
hang him on. *He cheats on his wife, he sleeps with Calypso!*) It is in this
scene that we learn a crucial fact: Calypso had once offered Odysseus
immortality and eternal youth on the condition that he stay with her, but
he had refused—because he wants to return to the mortal Penelope and
"see the smoke of his own chimneys" again.

The great question here, I said to the kids as we began class that
morning toward the end of February, is, Why doesn't Odysseus stay with
Calypso? She's a goddess, she is more beautiful than Penelope can ever
be, she offers him divinity. So we have to wonder why he says no.

Jack called out, It's crazy! The sex had to be *great!*

They laughed. But he was right: Even on the night before the hero
finally sets sail for home and Penelope, he and his immortal lover "revel
and rest softly, side by side"—not, this time, by compulsion.

This seemed to irritate my father.

The whole poem, *obviously*, he began, is going to lead up to his
reunion with his wife. Fine, we all know that. But he keeps cheating on
her! How's that supposed to be heroic?

When I was a teenager, he'd once taken me aside to tell me that my
mother's father had had a mistress at some point in the 1940s. *Oh, your
grandfather, your grandfather,* he said dismissively one Sunday afternoon
after he'd been arguing with my mother, who in those days liked to cite
her father as a paragon of those qualities of urbanity and uxoriousness
that, she thought, my father lacked. *Your grandfather isn't such a haihhro,
believe me.* And then, making the same face he would make forty years
later as we discussed Odysseus' adulteries in my *Odyssey* seminar, he
said, with vicious quiet, *When I was your age my mother told me she'd
heard that your mother's father had a "lady friend."*

I was bewildered. Really? But how do you know it was true?

He looked at me. *Because I knew your grandfather.*

And you? I thought. I knew my father, and was certain that he had
never strayed, never sought out another woman to (I am sure this was the

reason for Grandpa's affair) feed his vanity—in part because he had so little vanity, but mostly, I thought, because to have betrayed my mother would have been to have betrayed something even larger, for him: that rigorous code which allowed for no gray areas, in which *x* was always and only *x*, marriage was marriage, your wife was your wife, no matter how strained things could be, no matter how many times you stalked off after dinner to seek refuge in your little bedroom while she cleaned up the kitchen, weeping. Men often tried to pick up Mother, we knew— although we were fairly certain that she didn't even notice, the pickup lines and the meaningful looks that they'd give her in supermarkets and dentists' offices and (once) at the end of Yom Kippur services evaporating within the high theatrical haze of her laughter and her stories. Imagine, she'd say a bit breathlessly on coming home from the supermarket, the *nicest* man helped me with my grocery bags and, oh, he was so nice, he wanted me to come over to his house for coffee, but I told him of course I couldn't, I have to get home and make more flyers—(this was when she was leading a grassroots movement to shut down a nearby toxic-waste dump) and take Matthew to that new barber, well, it's not a barber, it's a *salon* . . . She would tell these stories and we'd all sit there grinning, even my father, in whose dark eye the smallest spark of some primitive emotion—pride? possessiveness?—gleamed.

Odysseus' relationship with Calypso bothered some of the students as well. Jack said he didn't like "the casual manner," as he put it, in which Odysseus refers to Penelope during a delicate exchange he has with Calypso, once she has informed him that the gods have decided at last to send him home. Trying to soothe the nymph's offended vanity even as he makes it clear that he'd rather be with a mortal woman, Odysseus acknowledges to Calypso that Penelope "is far less impressive to behold in her size and appearance."

It's kind of weird that Odysseus admits that Penelope can't compare to Calypso, Jack said. It doesn't seem very loyal.

Well, I said, but is it necessarily disloyal to tell the truth—to acknowledge that your spouse is no longer the beautiful girl you'd married twenty years before? The point is—and this is a *big* point—that his preference for Penelope, who could never be as beautiful as a goddess and who anyway is now aging, maybe approaching middle age, means something. What?

Madeline waved a hand at me; the red hair shimmered. That physical beauty and good sex aren't the basis for a marriage?

Right, I said. Remember last week? Remember Menelaus and Helen, how we said that Telemachus gets to see what a difficult marriage is like, it's part of his education? Now, in the next book, we see Odysseus himself trapped in a bad, one-sided relationship, too. The question is, What does a good marriage look like, according to whoever composed the *Odyssey*?

The answer to that question is given in Book 6. After Odysseus finally leaves Calypso's island, he sets sail on the open sea and eventually washes up on the shores of a fabulously lush island called Scheria, inhabited by people called Phaeacians—a race of expert seafarers who will, eventually, bring Odysseus back to Ithaca at last. In order to facilitate this outcome, Athena engineers an elaborate scheme to maneuver Odysseus into the good graces of the Phaeacian royal family. The goddess appears in a dream to the daughter of the house, a charming young princess called Nausicaa, and suggests that she go down to the seaside that morning to wash the family's clothing—the kind of chore, she chides, that a marriageable young woman ought to be doing. Nausicaa obeys. Accompanied by a flock of her friends, she goes down to the water's edge and there stumbles upon Odysseus, fresh from his latest shipwreck, with nothing but an olive bough to cover his salt-grimed, naked body. He then proceeds, cannily, to simultaneously calm and charm her. He starts by declaring that he can't tell if she's a mortal or Artemis herself, a compliment few girls could resist, and then proceeds to drop hints that he's not, in fact, a penniless nobody but a man of some importance, a soldier with a glorious past—the kind of man, perhaps, that she might think of marrying . . . Naturally Nausicaa melts, promising to convey him to the town and introduce him to her parents.

It's at the end of Odysseus' shrewd appeal to the princess that Homer reveals what constitutes a good marriage: the kind of match, in other

words, that is the opposite of those we've encountered thus far in the
Odyssey. "Mistress," Odysseus implores Nausicaa,

> *"Pity me: for you are the first to whom I come*
> *after suffering many woes: I know no one else*
> *of those who hold this land and dwell in it.*
> *Point me toward the town, give me some rag*
> *to wrap around myself, from the clothes you brought.*
> *And then may the gods fulfill whatsoever you desire:*
> *a husband and a home; may they grant you, too, like-mindedness,*
> *that noble thing. Nothing stronger or better than that—*
> *when a man and wife hold their home together*
> *alike in mind: great trouble to their foes,*
> *a joy to all their friends, the source of their renown."*

The Greek word that I've translated as "like-mindedness" is *homophrosynê.* The *homo-* root comes from the adjective *homoios,* which means "the
same" and which makes itself felt in such English words as "homeopathy"—
to treat a disease, *pathos,* with the same, *homoios,* thing that causes it—
and "homosexual." The *phron-* root has to do with the intellect, the mind;
our word "phrenology" derives from it. (The word I've translated as "alike
in mind" a few lines later is, in the original, a form of the verb that's connected to *homophrosynê: homophronein,* "to think in the same way.") Not
least because of the central place of the *Odyssey* in the Greek tradition,
homophrosynê has become the canonical word in the study of Greek literature for the quality that is the sine qua non for a successful relationship
between two people.

As we discussed Books 5 and 6 and pondered the *Odyssey's* troubled
pairings, we talked about *homophrosynê.* I pronounced it aloud for them:
ho-mo-fro-soo-nay.

Think, I said to them. Why do you think a perfect like-mindedness is
the most important thing a couple can have between them, according to
Odysseus in Book 6?

My father broke in and exclaimed, It's like that line in "That Old Black Magic"! Suddenly, to everyone's astonishment, he started singing, his gravelly high baritone floating into the dull morning air. *For you're the lover I have waited for / You're the mate that fate had me created for . . .*

His voice trailed off and he nodded to himself in private satisfaction. It's like Johnny Mercer knew his Homer. There's that one person made just for you by fate, and nobody else will do.

The kids were looking at him blankly.

"That Old Black Magic"! he cried. Music by Harold Arlen, lyrics by Johnny Mercer?! Flapping a dismissive hand in their direction, he said, You kids don't know *anything* about your own culture.

In a cooing radio announcer's voice, I said, Thank you for the musical interlude, Jay Mendelsohn. And now, back to our regularly scheduled programming.

I turned back to the students. Now let me ask again: Why do you think *like-mindedness* is the most important thing according to Odysseus in Book 6? Especially in light of what we know about the relationship between Calypso and Odysseus, about how after a while she had to compel him to sleep with her, how sexual desire, even with the most beautiful of females, can fade after time?

Madeline wiggled her hand. Because the physical isn't enough? Odysseus and Penelope will both be so much older when they reunite than they were when he left. I guess the question is, How will they be able to recognize each other, physically, when he comes home?

Yes, I said, and how *will* they be able to recognize each other, do you think?

Jack said, Spoiler alert!

They cracked up. I said, I doubt there's anyone here who doesn't know the ending . . .

Trisha was serious. She stopped writing in her notebook and said, It will be something in their minds, not their bodies?

Jack said, *Homo . . . ?*

Homophrosynê, I said. Do you see how it's being set up? Do you see what's coming? Your physical appearance can change with time, but nobody can take away *what*?

Brendan's hand shot into the air. What you know, he said.

Over in his corner on the left, my father had grown serious. Your *memories*, he said.

The students bent over their books and started writing furiously.

There was something else my father enjoyed complaining about in class, something he liked to describe as a "real weakness" in the epic. I knew as soon as he said those words what this gripe would be and wasn't surprised when he suddenly raised his hand and started talking on the last Friday of February, when we were discussing Books 7 and 8. These books give an extraordinarily detailed picture of Scheria and the Phaeacians, the last of the places and peoples that Odysseus encounters before he finally reaches home. It's the most extended account of any place mentioned in the poem, apart from Ithaca itself, and the poet takes his time with it, letting the details and oddities sink in.

Book 7 describes the curious circumstances of Odysseus' arrival at the Phaeacian court. After charming Nausicaa, he bathes in a river by the seashore in order to "wash off the brine" and make himself present-able; the princess then lends him some clothes belonging to one of her brothers. Then—not for the last time in the epic—Athena steps in to help her protégé, giving him a divine beauty treatment:

> *Athena, daughter sprung of Zeus, made him*
> *taller to look upon, more massive, too;*
> *hair curled down his head, like the blossom*
> *of a hyacinth. Just as when an artisan*
> *lays a golden rim around a silver vase—*
> *a man to whom Hephaestus and Pallas Athena have taught*
> *every skill—putting the finishing touches on his lovely work,*
> *so did she pour loveliness around his head and neck.*

Immediately afterward, Nausicaa returns to the city with her ladies-in-waiting. Only much later does Odysseus himself set out, made invisible by a mist that Athena helpfully pours around him; the Phaeacians, the princess advises him, don't like strangers. As the hero approaches the outskirts of the town, Athena steps in once again: disguised this time as a little girl with pigtails—an incongruous disguise for the warrior goddess, to say the least, but then, the *Odyssey* is not without a sense of humor—she materializes and offers directions to the royal palace, which is set among uncannily lush gardens and orchards whose flowers are always in bloom and whose trees are always fruiting. The detail is significant: there are no seasons here. It is as if Time itself had relaxed in order to provide ceaseless abundance to this languid and playful people.

In this paradisiacal setting Odysseus is courteously received by the royal family: the king, Alcinoös, and his queen, Aretê—her name resembles the Greek word for "virtue"—whose good favor Nausicaa has particularly advised him to seek. (The queen is indeed no fool: she can't help noticing that the foreigner who flings himself as a suppliant at her knees is wearing freshly washed clothing that belongs to one of her sons.) At the palace Odysseus is lavishly entertained at a feast that features, among other things, not one but three performances by the court bard, a blind man named Demodocus. Two of these, as it happens, are about the Trojan War, and as the hero listens to these artful re-creations of his own history, he is reduced to tears—much as Telemachus had been reduced to tears by Menelaus' reference to his absent father at the Spartan court in Book 4.

Like father, like son.

There were important points about Books 7 and 8 that I wanted to make that day. Not least, I wanted to draw the students' attention to the second song that the bard Demodocus sings. This song, known as the lay of Ares and Aphrodite, is a charming mini-epic that takes up fully one hundred lines of Book 8. On the face of it, Demodocus' song is an amusing trifle: it tells the story of how Hephaestus, the blacksmith god—the lame and cuckolded husband of Aphrodite, goddess of love—once entrapped his wife and her lover, the war god Ares, *in flagrante delicto* by means of a golden net of cunning design that he had fashioned: invisible to the naked eye but unbreakable even by a god. After trapping the two adulterous lovers, who writhed miserably in the fine but indestructible mesh, Hephaestus called all the other gods to witness their adultery, shaming them publicly. However much casual delight this risqué story brings to the Phaeacians (and to us), this poem-within-a-poem parallels crucial elements of *Odyssey* itself: abuses of hospitality, anxiety about adultery, the superiority of cunning to brute strength, the satisfactions to be had from vengeance. The lay of Ares and Aphrodite is, therefore, an excellent example of how the *Odyssey* uses what may at first appear to be digressions, material that is extraneous to the "plot," to underscore its most important themes.

But I didn't get to talk about Odysseus' incognito arrival at the palace, or the suggestive opulence of Scheria's landscape—another alluring distraction for the homeward-bound hero, another enticing alternative to Ithaca; didn't get to talk about Demodocus' choice of song that rainy last Friday in February, because as soon as the students had settled into the wooden chairs and I opened my text to Book 7, my father's hand went up.

Another reason I can't call Odysseus a *hero*, he said, as Blond Tom looked across the table at him, nodding, is that he keeps getting help from the gods! Everything he does, every bit of success he has, is really because the *gods* help him.

I'm not so sure, I said. The poem also makes clear that even without the help of the gods he's very clever—

No, my father said, with a vehemence that made some of the students look up from their note-taking, *No*. The whole *poem* happens because the gods are always helping him. It starts because Athena decides it's time to get him home, right? And then the reason he's able to get away from Calypso is because Zeus sends Hermes to tell her to let him go . . .

Well, yes, I said, but—

Let me finish, he said, in a tone I recognized from many years earlier, although the students merely thought it was funny. He took a breath, and I noticed that Trisha was now nodding, too, along with Blond Tom and Jack.

So it's really just the gods, my father pushed on, the dismissive rhythm of his argument, the jackhammer emphasis on certain words, familiar from other, much-older arguments, arguments whose climactic, clinching phrases I could remember years later, *Oh, what do you know, that's just a college-boy argument* or *Trust me, I know what I'm talking about, numbers aren't your strong point.* And now· *It's really just the gods.*

And it's Athena, my father went on, who dolls him up for his visit to the palace.

He made a little face when he said "dolls him up." The students chuckled.

It is funny, Damien declared. Now he is having curls like a flower petal?

I looked at him; he was clean-shaven today. I resisted the temptation to point out that his own appearance changed on a weekly basis.

Hyacinths! Jack snorted. Not very manly!

It does seem a bit artificial for him to get this total makeover, Trisha said levelly, looking up at me. Why isn't it good enough for him just to wash off and put on some nice clean clothes?

It was hard to answer. I myself have never been totally comfortable with these physical transformations of the hero. Several times in the poem, Athena dramatically enhances Odysseus' looks—before his reunions with his son and wife, for instance—or makes him unrecognizably ugly and wizened, as she does when Odysseus, finally back on Ithaca, needs to infiltrate his own palace incognito. In the story about Odysseus that Helen shares with her drugged guests in Book 4, she recalls how he had sneaked into Troy during the war by making himself look like a beggar, which he'd achieved by whipping himself. But that was different: an example of his cunning ability to disguise himself and of his willingness to suffer in order to make his stratagems work. But to be magically transformed by a god did seem a little too easy.

My father wasn't finished with his damning list of instances in which Odysseus had gotten help from the gods.

Athena dolls him up, he pressed on, and then wraps him in a magic cloud so he can sneak into the city and then gives him directions to the royal palace, right? So it's pretty obvious that he gets a lot of help directly from the *gods*.

His vehemence took some of the students aback. But it didn't surprise me. *The religion thing*, I thought to myself. *Here we go.*

He abhorred religion—the real cause of his loathing for rituals and protocols. Having to attend ceremonies of any kind would reduce him to adolescent sulking. He would slouch down in the pews at the weddings or bar mitzvahs or confirmations he worked so hard to arrive late at, covering his eyes with the slender fingers of his left hand, the way you might cover your face during a slasher movie, wincing like someone with a headache, the horizontal furrows across his sunburned forehead rippling; and all the while he'd be muttering his atheistic invectives to me or my siblings or, sometimes, to no one in particular as the rabbi or priest or cantor droned on. *They can't prove any of this crap! It's like voodoo! These guys are no better than witch doctors!* Sputtering and grimacing, he would leaf through the prayer books as if their pages were evidence of a crime, stabbing a finger at this or that passage of the scripture or a hymn with an incredulous shake of his head, and my mother would try to shush him. *Jayyy!!* she would hiss—a bit halfheartedly, it must be said, because after all wasn't this part of the secret reason she had married him: to get away from her overbearing, emotionally extravagant Orthodox family? *Jayy! Be quiet!*

After repeating *He gets a lot of help from the gods,* my father sat back in his chair and frowned triumphantly.

Blond Tom said, Well, yeah, I have to agree with what, uh, Mr. Mendelsohn said.

As had happened before when explicit reference had to be made to my father's presence in the classroom, a current of amusement rippled through the room.

Tom looked across the room at my father, as if for support, and went on, My question is, Is all the hype about Odysseus validated? Has he really done that much so he should be considered a hero? I mean, your father is actually right, I think. The thing that stuck out to me the most this week was how much Athena intervenes in the story, it's like she's holding Odysseus' hand even when it seems unnecessary. After all, if Odysseus can trick his way into Troy, like the story Helen tells about him, why can't he trick his way back home on his *own*? If everything is predetermined to go his way, then why should I be impressed by his masterful cunning or physical abilities?

Again, he was looking over at my father.

Tom went on, It's just that when *I* read about the deeds of great men, I want to read about them overcoming the gods—not the gods making everything easy for them. So I think it's questionable at this point whether it's through his own merit that Odysseus has survived so far, or whether it was all because of the gods and Odysseus is just as helpless as the rest of us

My father was beaming. Exactly! Without the gods, he's *helpless*.

It was when he said the word "helpless" that I suddenly understood. Since the semester began, I had been thinking that his resistance to the role of the gods in the *Odyssey* was connected to his loathing for religion in general—which, I had come to see over the weeks of the seminar, extended even to extinct religions. But when he said the word "helpless" that morning on the last Friday of February during the spring semester of 2011, as we talked about Books 7 and 8, I saw that the problem, for my father, was that Odysseus' willingness to receive help from the gods marked him as weak, as inadequate. I stood there in front of the open text and thought of all the times he had growled, *There's nothing you can't learn to do yourself, if you have a book!* I thought of the Colonial armchairs he had painstakingly assembled from kits in the garage, having laid down several layers of newspaper so that the Colonial Pine and Salem Maple wood stains wouldn't spill onto the concrete floor (*What does it matter if it gets dirty, it's a fucking garage*), of how he had huffed into his white plastic recorder while scowling at the sheets of music that lay open on the wobbly stainless-steel stand. And of those many afternoons I'd returned home during fall or spring break to find him frowning at *Latina pro populo,* the teach-yourself-Latin book he had bought himself after I decided to major in Classics, silently mouthing the paradigms of noun and adjective forms, the tables of verbs, that he'd once known so well. And I recalled, too, the people who, he obviously thought, were incapable of doing things without *help,* most of whom, I had come to understand over the years, were on my mother's side of the family, not least my mother's father, him with his hypochondria, his doctors and pills and regimens, his fears and anxieties and breakdowns, the three wives he had taken in rapid succession after my grandmother died, because *he just wasn't someone who could be alone,* as my mother once put it.

I thought of all this, of all the things he'd done *with no help from anyone,* all except the dissertation, the one thing he'd never managed to complete on his own but which, after all, wasn't his fault, *by that time your mother was pregnant and I had to work;* I thought of all this and said to myself, No wonder he can't bear the fact that the gods intervene on Odysseus' behalf. If you need gods, you can't say that you did it yourself. If you need gods, you're cheating.

And the one thing we knew about my father, the thing that more than any other defined him, was that he never cheated and never lied.

APOLOGOI

(Adventures)

———⊰●⊱———

MARCH / JUNE

Clearly if one wished to examine the wanderings of Odysseus closely, he would find that they are allegorical.

—PSEUDO-HERACLITUS, *Homeric Problems* (first century A.D.)

A few months later, we were aboard a ship in the middle of the Aegean, telling stories and singing songs. We were on the "Retracing the *Odyssey*" cruise.

Sometimes, it was as if my father had become a different person on the ship. As we moved farther and farther from home—first the long flight from New York to Athens, then the rattling bus ride to the port, then the smooth journeys out to sea, the Aegean and then the Dardanelles and Asia Minor, then the Aegean again and around to the Tyrrhenian Sea and then back to the Adriatic, tracing the undulating shorelines of five countries, zigzagging among the small islands, most memorably tiny Malta, seemingly lost in the middle of the sea, like something out of a dream, with its hulking medieval fortresses and its strange language bristling with X's—as we moved farther away from home, my father seemed to shed some hard outer surface and soften.

At the start of the trip, he'd been tense. He was prickly when he picked me up in front of my apartment building in New York for the trip to JFK and our flight to Athens. It was mid-June—five weeks after the end of the *Odyssey* class—and the day was miserably hot and humid. I had offered to arrange for a car to pick him up on Long Island and drive him into Manhattan to meet me, so he wouldn't have to take the commuter train in. *Nah*, it's fine, he said, I know a guy here with a taxi service, I'll get him to do it. When the battered old cab pulled up, the windows were wide open. He doesn't have *air-conditioning*? I moaned as I sat down next to him. He glanced sidewise at me and said, You're just like your *mother*, and looked away.

We landed in Athens late the next morning. As we stretched and yawned and started to gather our carry-on bags, I looked at my iPhone. Sunday, June 19. It's Father's Day, I exclaimed, and he said, No kidding! and smiled. But after we collected our luggage and boarded the air-conditioned coach that would take us to Piraeus, the port, he seemed as coiled as a spring. The bus lurched and twisted its way through the traffic, which had been snarled by demonstrations protesting the country's desperate economic crisis. A representative from the cruise line took advantage of the bus's leisurely pace to give a brief orientation. We'd board the ship around midafternoon; at cocktail time there'd be a welcome reception, followed by a short introductory lecture about Homer's epics given by one of the professors who'd be our guides throughout the cruise. After dinner we'd start our twelve-hour voyage across the Aegean toward Turkey, where lay Çanakkale, the site of Troy's ruins. We'd spend all the next day visiting the site.

When the coach halted on the quay, my father looked out the window at the ship. CORINTHIAN II, read the white letters on the navy hull, which sat very low in the water, almost invisible beneath the teetering white superstructure, the three decks bristling with radar stanchions and antennas and orange-shrouded lifeboats. It's smaller than I thought it would be, my father said.

When we'd booked our tickets a few weeks earlier, he had insisted, to my surprise, on paying for one of the more expensive cabins. It had a private balcony. When we entered the cabin for the first time he looked around, surveying the sleek furnishings, and then walked out past the beds and the little living area onto the balcony. As he stood on the balcony he sniffed loudly at the Mediterranean air. But even though he seemed to approve of the little luxurious touches, the orchids and cocktails waiting on a gleaming wooden side table, I could feel in him a kind of resistance, as if he were going to prove to me by the end of our ten days at sea that the *Odyssey* wasn't worth all this effort, all this luxury.

That edge of combativeness, which I recognized from certain kinds of comments he'd made in the seminar, made itself felt through the first days of the cruise. As the *Corinthian II* glided into the pier at Çanakkale the next morning, he and I were standing in the breakfast buffet line on the open aft deck. Curious, I surveyed the crowd. Who exactly goes on an *Odyssey* cruise? In addition to a sizable contingent of well-heeled retired couples—the cruise was the kind of thing you see advertised in the backs of alumni magazines—there were, to my surprise, a large number of passengers like me and my father: pairs of parents and children, women and men in their forties and fifties accompanying what could only be their fathers or mothers. I pointed out one such couple to Daddy: a handsome blond woman speaking in some guttural northern European language to her dapper, white-haired father. Do you think this is a "thing"? I joked. My father humphed and said, What thing? I said, Adult children taking their parents on the *Odyssey* cruise. He made a musing face and said, tonelessly, Maybe.

Bright blue awnings snapped and fluttered in the stiff morning breeze. As we shuffled along the buffet, I noticed a boy of about nine or so, his fair hair crisply parted, his white polo shirt neatly ironed, standing next to my father and moving along in sync with us. Teetering at the corner of the boy's breakfast tray was a fat paperback translation of the *Odyssey*, one of the long list of titles, both translations and secondary reading, that had been suggested by the organizers of the cruise. A few weeks earlier, when my father received the orientation packet in the mail, he called me, approval in his voice. This is a *serious* cruise, he said.

The *Odyssey* on the boy's tray was impressively dog-eared.

I smiled and said, Oh, so you've read the *Odyssey* already?

The boy leveled his clear blue eyes at me. I'm here with my family, we're from New Orleans. We travel to different destinations every summer. Of course, we all read the *Odyssey* before this trip. I liked a lot of it, but it was pretty clear that Homer needed an editor. There are a lot of repetitions.

My father was impressed. Good for you! he said.

I assumed he was applauding the fact that this child had already read Homer, but then he turned to me.

He's only a kid, but he's not intimidated by Homer! He thinks for *himself.*

Then, almost imperceptibly, Daddy started to ease into the rhythm of the cruise. Mornings were for trips ashore to visit the sites associated with the epic. Many of these were not easy to get to: it seemed that we were always scrambling up a donkey path or skidding down a rocky embankment or trudging across a dirt access road, baked by the sun to the hardness of concrete. We'd return from these trips exhausted and dusty, grateful for the tall glasses of lemonade or iced tea that were always waiting for us in the ship's reception area after we'd climbed back up the gangplank. Early evenings were for bathing and changing; then there was dinner. After a couple of days at sea, a small group started to gather after dinner, at around nine o'clock, in the ship's bar, where we'd pull up some armchairs in a semicircle near the piano and order cocktails.

These sessions were presided over by two members of the ship's team, whom by the end of the voyage we'd affectionately dubbed the "King and Queen of the Cruise": Brendan, a Classics professor who was the cruise's resident archaeologist, and Ksenia, the cruise director, a lithe blond Ukrainian who liked to laugh. Although he must have been in his forties, Brendan was strikingly boyish; with his easy confidence and neatly parted hair and preppy clothes, he could have been the older brother of Brendan, my student. Sometimes he would play the guitar and Ksenia would sing folk songs and everyone would join in. But most nights we listened as the ship's pianist, who had a glass eye, played. This pianist took requests, and my father would invariably ask for one of the classics of the Great American Songbook that he liked so much. It was this more than anything, I think, that started to mellow him as the days and nights passed. As far as we were from home, as strange as some of the places were and as incomprehensible as the languages we were hearing (*I never saw so many x's outside of a quadratic equation*, he exclaimed as we scrutinized a poster at a bus stop on Malta), these reminders of home, the words he knew so well, the echoes of the culture of his past, reassured him. He seemed almost visibly to unclench once he was settled into a chair with a martini, singing along in a raspy Sprechstimme as the one-eyed pianist played.

On the first night that we found ourselves in the lounge, he was half singing along to "My Funny Valentine"

> *Is your figure less than Greek?*
> *Is your mouth a little weak?*
> *When you open it to speak, are you smaaaart?*

Ah, what a great song! He took a sip of his drink and smacked his lips.

Brendan smiled. Why is it great?

The *lyrics*, my father cried. They have just what we like in mathematics: simplicity and elegance. It says the maximum with the minimum amount of resources.

Brendan said, The maximum about what?

My father shook his head. The . . . strangeness of love, he finally said, looking down into his glass. A person can be flawed, you know everything about them that's wrong, but you love them. *Your looks are laughable / Unphotographable / Yet you're my favorite work of aaart . . .*

So great, he said after a moment. It tells you everything about real love, real relationships. Not what you see in the *movies*.

To my surprise, it soon became clear that he was enjoying the cruise itself—the dressy ritual of dinnertime, the late-night cocktails and the piano playing, the desultory conversations with strangers over drinks or breakfast—far more than he did the sites. I had worried, at the start, that the physical demands would be too much for him; he was three months shy of eighty-two, after all, and there was a great deal of walking—which, in Greece, usually means walking uphill. But this didn't bother him. I'm fine! he would say when I offered a steadying hand as we struggled up a steep hill. But a number of sites, beginning with Troy itself, left him cold. *It doesn't really look that impressive!* he'd muttered on the morning we walked around Çanakkale, listening to Brendan lecture about the history of the site. As the lenses of Brendan's round, steel-rimmed spectacles flashed in the sun, he explained that there had been a number of successive Troys over the millennia, each rising and falling in turn. Among the ruins of these, he went on, there was evidence of a "major catastrophe" that had occurred around 1180 B.C.—the traditional date of the Fall of Troy. As he said this, people murmured knowingly and wrote in their notebooks.

My father listened attentively but looked skeptical as we scrambled among the dusty paths and walkways, the giant inward-sloping walls, the heaps of gray stones rising out of patches of parched, yellow grass. In the obliterating sunlight the stones looked weary and porous, as insubstantial as sugar cubes.

My father looked around. Obviously it's *interesting,* he said. But . . .

His voice trailed off and he shook his head.

But what? I was curious.

He looked at me and then, to my surprise, threw an arm around my shoulders and patted me, smiling crookedly. But the poem feels more real than the ruins, Dan!

Over the next week this became a refrain of his. *The poem feels more real!* he'd say each evening as people discussed the day's activities. When he did so, he'd cast a quick sidelong glance at me, knowing how much the thought pleased me. He said it after we sailed from Turkey to the southern tip of the Peloponnese, where we traipsed around the ruins of the palace that tour guides have dubbed "Nestor's Palace." (But the Nestor episode comes in Book 3, Robert, the boy we'd met on the first morning, piped up as we disembarked at Pílos. And we hear about Odysseus at Troy in Book 4. We're not going in the order of the poem! Brendan laughed. If we went to these sites in the order they occur in the poem, he said, we'd run out of gas!) It was nearly one hundred degrees outside; the air was so hot it felt like fabric. Somebody made a joke about wanting to get into the deep stone tub that Brendan was pointing out to us. Some guides, he said, will tell you that this tub is the very one that Telemachus bathed in while he was a guest in Nestor's palace, in Book 3. My father peered into the tub and said into the darkness, I doubt it. Standing up straight again, he turned to me. I don't necessarily think much of Telemachus, he said, but I doubt he was so small.

That night, as our little group settled into the lounge, the pianist started playing "Where or When." Daddy raised his martini glass and crooned along raggedly. *It seems we stood and talked like this before . . . But I can't remember where or when . . . Some things that happen for the first time seem to be happening again . . .*

Obviously, he said to the group after a moment, obviously I'm glad I got to see the places and be able to make a connection between the real places and what's in Homer.

People nodded.

If I would have read Book 3 now, for instance, he went on, I would know exactly what the seashore of "sandy Pylos" looks like—he wiggled his fingers to indicate that he was quoting verbatim—where Telemachus landed. And now we all have a sense of the landscape of Troy, the way it's sited, how it looks out with the water in the distance. That's great. But for me it's a little bit empty compared to the story. Or maybe half empty. It's like these places we're seeing are a stage set, but the poem is the *drama*. I feel that that is what's real.

I beamed and said, Don't tell me we've come all this way to retrace the *Odyssey* and now you're telling me that we could have stayed home!

Ksenia laughed loudly. Don't tell *me* that, she said. I'm supposed to be keeping you all happy!

Maybe it's like *The Wizard of Oz*, my father said jauntily. "There's no place like home . . ."

There was a small silence, and then Brendan turned to me. Would you say that that movie is actually an *Odyssey*-based story?

It was a book first, my father interrupted. L. Frank Baum!

I thought for a moment. Sure, I said. Totally. The protagonist is torn from home and family and experiences fabulous adventures in exotic locales where she meets all kinds of monstrous and fantastical beings. But all the time she's yearning to go home. It's amazing, actually, how similar the structure is.

The fortyish blond woman whom I'd seen several times in the company of the dapper gentleman who must be her father said, Yes, but in the movie it turns out to be all a dream, no? It's all in her mind. All of the people she meets there are just fantasies based on the people from her drab life on the farm, no? But the adventures of Odysseus are all *true*. So it's a bit different, don't you think? He really has trouble coming home, but for her it was just a dream.

I shot my father an amused look, but he was staring down into his martini. That movie came out just before the war started, he said wistfully. Weeks before, as I recall. My dad was working away from home that summer on a big project, but he was home just then, and he took me and Uncle Bobby to the Loew's Theater to see it. Man, in those days when you saw a movie, it was really an experience. There was a floor show with Judy Garland and Mickey Rooney! An organ came out of the floor! And then the movie—well, no one had ever seen anything like that before.

The small group huddled around the bar had grown quiet as he reminisced. Every now and then he'd share with my siblings and me some story like this, some anecdote about his childhood that wasn't about struggle, wasn't pointedly contrasting the hardship of the Depression with how easy we kids had it—something about his mother's circle of clever, card-playing friends, or how his father liked to sit in a chair by the radio and listen to Jack Benny, or Thanksgivings in the countryside at an aunt's house. To me such stories were the more precious because they were rare; but as far as the people in the ship's lounge knew, they were the only stories he had to tell.

To them, I suddenly realized, this was who he was: a lovely old man filled with charming tales about the thirties and forties, the era to which the music tinkling out of the piano belonged, an era of cleverness and confidence and sass. It was as if he *were* the Great American Songbook. A spasm of dark emotion coursed through me, something primitive, childish. If only they knew the real him, I thought. Glancing around at the others as they listened to Daddy, at the charmed smiles on Brendan's and Ksenia's faces, and then back at his face, relaxed and open, mellow with reminiscence, a face so different from the one he so often presented, at least to his family, I wondered suddenly whether there might be people, strangers he had met on business trips, say, bellhops or stewardesses or conference attendees, to whom he showed only this kindly face, and who, therefore, would be as astonished by the expression of contempt that we knew so well as we were by the rare glimpses of the other, softer side. How many sides did my father actually have, I asked myself, and which was the "real" one? Perhaps this expansive and charming person, so different from the crabbed and coiled man whom only a month or two earlier, I ruefully thought, my *Odyssey* students had come to know, this song-singing old gentleman who could be so affable and entertaining with total strangers on a ship in the middle of the sea, was the person my father had always been meant to be. Or, perhaps, had always been, although only with those others, the bellhops and stewardesses. Children always imagine that their parents' truest selves are as parents; but why? "Who really knows his own begetting?" Telemachus bitterly asks early in the *Odyssey*. Who indeed. Our parents are mysterious to us in ways that we can never quite be mysteries to them.

Or, I thought a moment later, maybe both were his true selves. Maybe Daddy, too, was *polytropos*; maybe, as that adjective suggests so powerfully in the *Odyssey*, identity is less a matter of binary oppositions, the contemptuous or the kindly, the father or the husband, the father or the son, than it is of kaleidoscopic perspective. Maybe it's a question of which section of the circle, the loop, you happen to be in a position to see.

My father twisted around in his seat and motioned to the pianist.

How about "Over the Rainbow"? he said. The one-eyed man grinned and nodded and smoothly segued from whatever he'd been playing into the first few bars of the famous song. My father swiveled back toward us.

Harold Arlen! And Yip Harburg! What a great American songwriter. He closed his eyes and half hummed, half sang along. *There's a land that I heard of once in a lullaby* . . .

Then he looked at me. Dan and I know all the old songs, don't we? All my kids do, we used to sing them around the piano while my son Andrew played. Rodgers and Hart, Harold Arlen, George and Ira—all the greats! That was when a song was a *song.*

He took another sip of his martini and made a little sound of satisfaction. *Ahhhh.*

He's happy, I thought.

Behind him, huge plate-glass windows looked onto the sea. The sky was violet; the water was black.

The blond woman gestured to the view and said, The days slip by just like the sea is sliding by us. What are we seeing tomorrow? I barely know what day is it!

I knew what was coming next. My father started to sing the Rodgers and Hart song "I Didn't Know What Time It Was." *I didn't know what day it was*, he rasped, *youuuu held my haaaaaand* . . . A few of the passengers clapped delightedly.

Someone said, We're in the middle of the ocean drinking wine and listening to music. Who cares what day it is?

Daddy said, Yeah! *We're* not desperate to get home.

It is during the course of a great feast held at the court of the Phaeacian king that Odysseus finally gets to relate to his spellbound hosts the tale of all the trials he has undergone, starting from the day he and his men left behind the ruins of Troy and ending on the morning he was discovered, naked and alone, by the princess Nausicaa on the beach at Scheria. The telling of these tales takes up nearly four books of the *Odyssey,* from Book 9 to Book 12.

The Greek name that tradition has assigned to this part of the poem—the long-awaited narration of Odysseus' adventures, which, for many readers, are the most memorable part of the *Odyssey*—is the Apologoi, the "Narratives." This title reflects a crucial fact: the narrator of these tales is none other than Odysseus himself. Thus far, everything we know about Odysseus, his imprisonment by Calypso, the shipwreck after his departure from her island, his discovery by Nausicaa, his arrival at the palace of the Phaeacian king and queen, is narrated by the poet of the *Odyssey*. But the adventures that have become so famous that even people who haven't read the *Odyssey* know about them—his encounters with the Lotos-Eaters, addicted to a drug that can make men forget their homelands; the fearsome monsters Scylla and Charybdis, who inhabit opposite sides of a narrow strait, preying on the sailors who pass through; his encounter with Circe, who turns his men into pigs; the one-eyed monster Cyclops— are related by him. Hence "Narratives": a title that underscores Odysseus' wondrous way with words, his sly expertise as a raconteur and fabulist.

As if to emphasize that role, the revelation of his identity to the Phaeacians occurs at the moment he starts telling his stories. Throughout his stay on Scheria, Odysseus has been anonymous, an honored guest of the royal household, none of whom, as per the convention of this society, has dreamed of asking his name. Then, toward the end of Book 8, when he is a guest at the banquet during which Demodocus has performed the Lay of Ares and Aphrodite, the hero asks the bard to sing about the end of the Trojan War—specifically, about the Trojan Horse. As Demodocus sings his song, Odysseus is overcome by memories of the real-life event and bursts into furious tears, which Homer describes in striking terms: they are, he says, like the tears of a woman who flings herself on the body of her husband, a warrior fallen in battle defending his city. (When you read the *Iliad*, you encounter women who do just this: but they are Trojan women, mourning husbands who died fighting Greeks—Greeks like Odysseus.) Alarmed by his guest's distress, the Phaeacian king gently asks the stranger to reveal why this particular story has affected him so strongly; perhaps, he wonders, he had a kinsman who fell at Troy?

It is in response to the king's kindness that Odysseus at last reveals his identity:

But first I'll tell you my name, now, so that you too
will know it; and if I escape the fatal day we'll be
bound in friendship, though my home lies far away.
Odysseus I am, Laertes' son: known to all mankind
for my way with tricks, my renown reaches even to heaven.

At the beginning of class on the first Friday in March, when we began to discuss the Apologoi, I emphasized that the famous adventures of Odysseus are, in fact, narrated by their own hero. Why, I asked as the students settled down around the table, weren't these episodes related by the narrator of the poem? What is the poet accomplishing by having the protagonist of the tales narrate them?

My father raised his hand.

Am I the only one who thinks that his bragging here is strange?

I'd noticed, as the weeks passed, that my father had begun to preface his comments in class this way: *Am I the only one who thinks . . . ?* At first I'd thought it was a sign of insecurity; but then I'd started noticing how, when he said that, a couple of students would nod, as if emboldened by the phrase. Blond Tom, for instance; Jack, quite often.

Tom nodded just then, in fact, and said, Yeah, it's weird that he kind of goes from zero to sixty here—ten minutes ago he was nobody, he hadn't told them who he was the whole time he was there, and suddenly he's, like, "This is my name, oh and by the way, I'm so incredibly famous that even the gods know who I am."

A few of the kids laughed.

Agreed, I said. It's weird. What do you think that's about?

My father said, I don't like it. Why does he have to brag about how tricky he is? If the stories show that he's so brilliant and clever, then he should just tell them and let the stories prove it.

As he spoke, a very clear mental picture of him in the mid-1960s sprang to my mind. I would have been six or seven or eight years old at the time, back when some of my maternal grandfather's siblings were still alive and would descend on my parents' house when Grandpa came to visit us. Invariably the climax of these gatherings would find us all crammed around my mother's dining room table as my grandfather told one of his stories, the common theme of which was his ability to bend the rules, to cheat a little here and there, in order to succeed or, occasionally, to survive: the one about how, when he was eighteen, he'd sneaked onto the boat that took him to America by crying *Fire, fire* and rushing up the gangplank in the resulting confusion; about how, when he was a teenager, during World War I, he and his family had had to hide for a week in the forest outside their town because the town center was being shelled, and while they were camping in the woods he'd shot and killed a deer, which they had then eaten, although they all knew that the meat of an animal killed in this way was not kosher. *But then,* as he would say as he reached the climax of this story, *you bend the rules and God forgives.* We assumed, naturally, that there was a strong element of embellishment in these tales, that my grandfather had taken something that had really happened, a clerical error on the part of some immigration officer, some sporadic shelling and, perhaps, a few hours in the dense woods outside of his little town, which his active imagination had populated with all manner of wildlife, and had given those simple and banal events an iridescent sheen of drama and excitement. But the stories were so good that nobody wanted to question them, nobody wanted to dig too deep to find out just how much invention there was . . . Nobody except my father. I remember the expression of skeptical impatience he wore as he sat way off on the side somewhere, his chair pulled away from the table, his face shut like a door, stony and impassive, as if to react in any way to my grandfather's stories, to show pleasure or delight, would be a defeat, a failure.

Now, as we talked about how Odysseus begins the story of his amazing adventures, my father was saying, *Why does he have to brag about how clever he was?*

But it is, in fact, Odysseus' bragging about his talents that causes his homecoming to take so long, as we learn during the greatest of the adventures he relates in the Apologoi: his encounter with the Cyclops.

There are, to be sure, other significant adventures in Books 9 and 10, the books we talked about that day. When Odysseus and his men leave Troy, they arrive in the land of a people called the Cicones. What follows will be familiar to anyone who's read the *Iliad:* the Greeks storm the town, kill the men, enslave the women and children, and take plunder back to their ships. The surviving Cicones run inland for reinforcements, who arrive while Odysseus' men, heedless of his warnings, are feasting and drinking on the beach after their victory. ("Fools!" Odysseus exclaims as he relates this incident to his Phaeacian audience: it's the same word the poet uses to describe Odysseus' comrades in the proem, when the narrator mentions their blasphemous eating of the Cattle of the Sun.) The unsuspecting Greeks are overwhelmed and sustain many casualties; the survivors eventually retreat in their ships.

The resemblance between this first adventure and the kind of fighting that the Greeks did at Troy is not accidental: it is as if, at the beginning of his journey, Odysseus were still subject to the gravitational pull of Troy and the *Iliad*. But as time passes and his adventures accumulate, they become more fantastical, supernatural, otherworldly. The next adventure, for instance, is an encounter with the Lotos-Eaters, a peaceable people who live off plants that are harmless to the locals but pose a mortal danger to Odysseus and his men; for the flower of the lotos makes anyone who eats it "forgetful of his homecoming." Not all the threats that Odysseus and his men fend off during their years of struggling to get home are violent in nature.

In the next book, Book 10, the supernatural element predominates. First Odysseus sails to the floating island of Aeolus, the ruler of the winds, who gives the hero a bag of winds intended to bring him home; but as they voyage toward Ithaca, his suspicious men, convinced that the bag contains treasures that their leader is concealing from them, open it while Odysseus is asleep, and the winds escape. This is one of a number of incidents, culminating in the men's eating of the forbidden Cattle of the Sun, that suggest considerable tension between Odysseus and his men. When we discussed this episode in class, my father said, Am I the only one who's noticed that he's got problems with his troops?!

Afterward, Odysseus and his men land on another strange shore, this one belonging to a race of giants called the Laestrygonians. Like the curiously lush land of the Phaeacians, where trees and flowers are always in bloom, the territory of the Laestrygonians is distinguished by an anomalous temporal foreshortening: there is no night here, the dusk leading seamlessly each day into dawn. Other, more sinister resemblances to the Phaeacians mark this episode. After mooring his ship, Odysseus sends ahead three scouts whose reception by the royal family grotesquely echoes Odysseus' happy reception by Nausicaa and her parents: they meet a princess on their way to the city, and then meet the king and his queen, but this queen is monstrous, "towering like a crag," and the king is eager to eat the flesh of the Greek men. In the ensuing battle the Laestrygonians destroy all the Greek ships save one, and kill most of Odysseus' men.

In the one remaining ship, Odysseus, accompanied by whatever men are left, makes his way to Aiaia, the tree-shadowed island inhabited by Circe. The story of Circe is populated by uncanny animals: lions and wolves pad around her palace, beasts that she has tamed with her potions. And in the sties outside rut swine who once were men—Odysseus' men, on whom she has worked her awful magic. Eventually Odysseus rescues them, armed with an antidote that Hermes has given him, a magic herb called *moly*. Knowing, at that point, that Odysseus enjoys the favor of the gods, Circe yields her palace and her bed to him. He and his men remain with her for a year.

And so the first few adventures that Odysseus narrates in the Apologoi trace a progression from straightforward violence to enchantment, from the natural to the supernatural. They have in common, too, a disorienting blurring of the boundaries between animal and human, between human and divine; abuses of hospitality; and the persistent motif of the self-destructive foolishness displayed by his gluttonous crew, chronically

unable to suppress their impulses, their greedy craving for food and drink
and treasure, in the service of their own survival.

But the Cyclops episode may be the most significant of Odysseus' adventures because it sheds the greatest light on the hero's personality, its
strengths and weaknesses.

It also turned out to be the episode that my father liked best.

After escaping the Lotos-Eaters, Odysseus and his men come to the
land of a race known as the Cyclopes, who are described as being

> *arrogant and lawless*
> *who place such great trust in the immortal gods*
> *that they neither plant their crops nor plow;*
> *but everything grows unsown and unplowed,*
> *wheat and barley too, and vines that bear*
> *a rarefied wine, which Zeus' rainstorms water.*
> *They hold neither assemblies for council nor have laws*
> *but live in the peaks of lofty hills*
> *in hollow caves, each a law unto himself*
> *ruling children and wives, and care not a whit for their neighbors.*

These brutes represent the low end of a spectrum of civilized behavior whose upper end is occupied by the Phaeacians themselves—who, we
must remember, are the audience for this tale—with their languid poli-
tesse, their love of dancing and games and poetry and feasting. Violent,
lawless, ignorant of agriculture, strangers to the preeminent institution of
Greek political life, the civic assembly (such as the one that Telemachus
calls in Book 2), the Cyclopes are, literally, cavemen.

What saves Odysseus' life in his encounter with one of these brutes, a
cyclops called Polyphemus, is his mind; what gets him in trouble, at the
conclusion of this episode, is his mouth.

After the Greeks arrive in the land of the Cyclopes, the hero and a small detail of his men go to investigate a great cave that, they immediately see, is the solitary home of a "huge man." Some "foreboding," as he later describes it to the Phaeacians, inspires him to take along a skin of very powerful liquor he'd received as a gift once, a grateful tribute from the family of a priest whose life he had saved. (The hospitality theme again.) Soon enough they enter Polyphemus' cave, which happens to be deserted at the moment. The men urge Odysseus to make off with the sheep they find there and return to their ships, but this time it's Odysseus whose greed turns out to be fatal: he wants to wait for the Cyclops to return home, he tells them, in order to see what guest-gift he might get from the inhabitant of the cave. But whatever hopes he may have that the Cyclops adheres to normal standards of hospitality are immediately, horribly dashed. When Polyphemus returns, he seals the opening of the cave with a huge slab of stone ("which twenty-two wagons couldn't budge") and proceeds to eat two of Odysseus' men. Here, then, is a grotesque inverse of proper hospitality: the host eating, rather than feeding, his guests.

There is a passage in the *Iliad* in which an elderly man who was once tutor to the hero Achilles declares that his educational mission had been to turn the boy into a "speaker of words and a doer of deeds": in the Cyclops episode of the *Odyssey*, Homer portrays Odysseus as both. Realizing that he can't indulge his fury and kill the monster in revenge for eating his comrades—because only the Cyclops is strong enough to lift the slab of stone that seals the entrance of the cave—he bests his enemy with both words and actions. When Polyphemus leaves the cave to tend to his flocks, Odysseus and his men cut a length from a giant club that's lying in the cave—the trunk of an olive tree, which the giant uses as a staff—and sharpen it into a stake. After the monster returns, Odysseus plies him with the liquor that he's brought along. There follows some clumsy banter that proves to be crucial. When the drunken Polyphemus tries to wheedle information about the identity of the humans in his cave and the whereabouts of their ship, Odysseus replies that they've been ship-wrecked, and that his name is "Nobody." Unused to wine—he belongs, after all, to a race that knows neither agriculture nor viniculture—the huge creature passes out, vomiting up bits of human flesh.

This is where the trap, with its entwined elements of violent deeds and clever words, springs shut. Taking up the stake they have prepared, Odysseus and his men plunge it into the Cyclops' one eye. When, in response to his cries of agony, the wounded monster's neighbors gather outside the cave to ask what's going on—"Is anyone rustling your sheep?" they cry out, "is anyone trying to kill you, either by guile or violence?"—all he can reply is "*Nobody* is killing me," at which point his would-be rescuers return to their homes, advising him to say a prayer to his father, Poseidon, if he needs help. The next day, Odysseus and his men escape by clinging to the woolly underbellies of Polyphemus' sheep as they file out of the cave, leaving the wounded and humiliated monster to wonder how a puny human, a "tiny, no-account weakling," could have bested him.

It's just after this triumph that Odysseus makes his deadly mistake. The Greeks begin to sail away from the Cyclops' island, but while they're still within shouting distance of land, Odysseus turns back to taunt the creature whom his cunning intelligence had trounced:

> *Cyclops, so he wasn't a weakling after all, the man*
> *whose mates you devoured so brutally in your hollow cave,*
> *but your foul deeds came down on your own head,*
> *fiend, since you failed to honor the guests within your house*
> *but ate them: a crime avenged by Zeus and the immortals!*

At this, the monster erupts in rage. Tearing the peak off of a mountain crag, he hurls the huge boulder at the escaping ship; the backwash threatens to drive the ship back toward land. But despite the entreaties of his terrified crew, Odysseus continues to taunt the Cyclops:

Cyclops, if any mortal man should ask you how
your eye became so hideously blind,
tell him Odysseus, sacker of cities, blinded you—
Laertes' son, who dwells in Ithaca.

This is the only time during his adventures that Odysseus impetuously gives away his full name and identifying details, and it has disastrous consequences. For once he has this information about his enemy—a "nobody" no longer—the Cyclops is able to call down a terrible curse on him. Raising his huge hands heavenward, he invokes his father, Poseidon:

Hear me, Poseidon, black-maned shaker of the earth,
if indeed I am your son and you my father, as you claim,
then grant that Odysseus, sacker of cities, not come home—
Laertes' son, who dwells in Ithaca.
But if he's fated to see his own again, to return
to his well-built house and to his fatherland,
then may he be much-delayed, may he lose all of his men,
sailing on some stranger's ship to a house that's filled with woe.

This, in fact, is why it takes Odysseus ten years to come home.

The combination of canniness, dashing improvisation, and outrageous daring that Odysseus shows in the Cyclops' cave always provokes a deep satisfaction in audiences.

Jack said, This is so cool! It's like he's Hercule Poirot and James Bond all in one!

Even my father had something good to say about Odysseus. He beats him with a *pun!* he cried out happily.

But the wordplay in this remarkable passage is more intricate than any translation can convey, as I went on to explain. Odysseus tells the Cyclops that his name is "Nobody." Now, the Greek word for "nobody" or "no one" is *outis: ou* means "not," and *tis* is the indefinite pronoun "one." *Ou-tis*, "no-one." *Odysseus, outis.* The name Odysseus gives to the Cyclops is actually a kind of slurred version of his actual name.

Nina said, It's an alias, but it's also sort of his real name. He's both lying and telling the truth at the same time.

Yes, I said. That's a great point. But it's even better than that. Think about the word "nobody." In English, when you ask a question to which the answer will be "nobody," you have to use the pronoun "anybody"—as in "Is *anybody* home?" "No, *nobody's* home." Greek has more or less the same syntactical feature. In Greek, one way to convey "is anybody" is actually a two-word phrase, *mê tis*, pronounced *may tiss.* That, in fact, is the phrase the Cyclops' neighbors use when they rush up and ask him if anybody is stealing his sheep or trying to murder him: "Is anybody [*mê tis*] killing you?" To which he replies, "No, nobody [*outis*] is killing me."

I paused for breath and was pleased to see that they were a bit breathless themselves, waiting for whatever the payoff was going to be.

I asked them to think about what Nina said, about how by calling himself Outis, "Nobody," he's both telling the truth and lying at the same time. This was not only because *outis* and *Odysseus* sound a little alike but because at this point in the epic he actually is both "somebody" and "nobody": he's Odysseus, himself, but also a nobody, a man who has to reclaim his identity.

They were nodding. Good, I thought, they're getting it.

In fact, I now told them, the same doubling of meaning goes for *mê tis*, the words that the Cyclops' neighbors use when they ask if anyone is hurting him. For in Greek, *mê tis*, "any body," is pronounced identically to a certain noun, *mêtis*, which means "tricky intelligence." Hence there is a double layer of double entendre in this scene. On the one hand, Polyphemus has been undone by *outis*, nobody/Odysseus; but he's also being undone by *mêtis*, anybody/trickery. And as we know, the single trait that distinguishes Odysseus is *trickery.* So here again, he is both nobody, anonymous, and also his truest self, the man famous for his trickery.

When I got to the end of my explanation, Brendan whistled and said, Whoa. That is *totally* cool.

I turned to the students. *Now* do you want to say anything about why he starts the recitation of his adventures by boasting about his reputation for trickery?

Madeline hesitated, but only for a moment. Because the adventure itself is about trickery? And it's a trick that's wrapped in language. So it's all about tricks and words.

Yes! I said. Words! In the end, what dooms the Cyclops is his inability to distinguish between two homophones. It's funny, and it's also kind of brilliant.

Brendan's hand went up. I wonder if you think we could say it's a story about listening? About how your own perspective affects how you hear things? I mean, the real problem in this story is that from the very start Polyphemus hears what he wants to hear. If someone came up to you and said "My name is Nobody," you'd do a double take, right? It's so obviously weird. But he doesn't take the Greeks seriously, because he's bigger and stronger than they are, and so he doesn't actually hear what Odysseus is saying.

I'd never thought of this before. I was opening my mouth to take up his point when my father cut in.

I have to say this part is just *great*. Intellect beats the bullies! The little guy beats the big guy with his brains.

It was nearly twelve-thirty, but we still hadn't talked about the end of the episode—Odysseus' foolish outburst.

This adventure, I said, shows Odysseus at his best. But before we go, does anyone want to say something about how it ends?

Jack said, He totally fucks it up!

Excuse me?

Sorry! . . . But he does screw up, he added.

Yes, you're right. What screws it up for him?

Before any of the students had a chance to speak, my father raised his hand.

He said, His cunning and his trickery save him, but in the end, his bragging about how smart he is gets him into the worst trouble he's ever known. Before he starts telling all his stories, he boasts about how clever he is, and that's what dooms him. He's a braggart. No matter how ingenious he is and how entertaining his stories are, his *personality* is a real problem.

He was nodding to himself as he said this, as if in some private satisfaction, and I knew that he wasn't thinking about Odysseus.

The only time my father didn't cap off an evening aboard the cruise ship by saying *The poem feels more real* was after we'd gone to Gozo, off Malta, to see Calypso's cave. This, in fact, was where we were heading on the night my father hummed along and sang "Over the Rainbow."

We'd been warned the day before that the descent into the cave was rocky and difficult, and that only a few people at a time could go inside, given how cramped it was. Elderly people and people who had "mobility issues" were advised not to visit the site.

When I heard all this, I was determined not to go. I suffer badly from claustrophobia: simply being in an elevator sets my teeth on edge. When the boys were little, Lily and I took them to Disneyland, where they insisted on going on a complicated space-simulation ride; only too late did I realize that it involved being sealed into a chamber that was spun around in a centrifuge to create the feeling of zero gravity. When the ride finally ended and we scrambled out of the tiny cabin, between the terror of being in the thing and the effort of having to pretend I was enjoying it, I burst into tears. Thomas, who was six and already fearless, put his arm around me and actually said, *There, there.*

So there was no way I was going to go into Calypso's cave.

What are you talking about? my father exclaimed when I told him. You have to go! Seven-tenths of the *Odyssey* takes place there!

Seven-tenths? I had no idea what he was talking about. It's twenty-four books long, I began—

Math, Dan! *Math.* Odysseus spends ten years getting home, right?

I nodded.

And he spends seven years with Calypso, right?

I nodded again.

So in theory, seven-tenths of the *Odyssey* actually takes place there! You can't miss it!

Well, I protested weakly, actually no. The poem isn't actually equal to his life. They're two different things.

But he wasn't convinced. You can't argue with *numbers*, he said.

We got on the bus and went. As the big coach rattled and bumped along the rocky roads, it was touchingly clear that my father was trying to distract me. Look at those beautiful blue flowers! he would say, pointing. The windows were so coated with road dust that it was hard to see. Wow! Look at those purple bushes, what do you call those? Look at the sea, it's like a piece of glass! But I looked without seeing; I was thinking about the cave. Already, flickering at the edges of my consciousness, there was the familiar prickle of panic. As I do when waiting for elevator doors to open or after fastening my seat belt on a small plane, I was focusing on pushing back against the prickly feeling. This required an almost physical effort. I was sweating.

We pulled up at the site and everyone got out of the bus. We were standing on the brow of a brown, lifeless hill; scrub clung to the dun-colored dirt like scabs to diseased skin. A narrow stair descended steeply from where we were standing to an uneven rocky surface fifteen feet below. Below, the face of the cave looked like a sheer wall of stone with a low, dark cleft in the middle; it was clear you'd have to stoop to get in. A few passengers had already made the descent and were disappearing into the cleft. The boy I'd seen on the first day, the one who declared that Homer needed an editor, had just entered, along with a taller kid who must have been his brother.

A clammy terror seized me. I shook my head. No, I said to my father. Nope, sorry. I'm not going. You go, you'll tell me what it's like.

Oh, come *on*, Dan, my father said. I'll be with you, it'll be fine.

I felt like I was five years old. I said again, No. You go. I'll stay up here.

Then my father did something that astonished me. He reached over and took my hand. I looked at him and burst out laughing. *Daddy!*

You'll be *fine*, he said, holding my hand lightly, a thing I couldn't remember him having done since I was a small boy. His own was light and dry and slender. I looked at it awkwardly.

I will *be* there with you every step of the way, my father was saying. And if you hate it, we'll leave.

I looked down at our clasped hands and to my surprise found that it made me feel better. As I looked around to see if anyone was watching, I realized, with a complicated feeling of relief, that whoever did see us would assume that I was leading my father by the hand. He, after all, was the one at real risk; he was the one who was terrified of falling.

And so it was that I visited Calypso's cave with my father holding my hand. He held it as we made our way gingerly down the stairs. He held my hand as we crouched down low to squeeze through the opening; he held my hand as we shuffled around inside, my heart thumping so hard that I was surprised the others didn't seem to hear it; held my hand as I said firmly that, no, I didn't want to go through a passageway in the center of the rock to see the spectacular views of the bay below, visible from the other side of the cavern; held my hand as I shuffled at last out into the dry hot air, not even bothering to conceal my panicked haste. Only after we reached the top of the stairs again and started walking toward the waiting bus did he let go of my hand.

You okay, Dan?

I grinned shakily. I think this is one time when we can say that the poem does *not* feel more real, I said.

Ha! my father said. Then he looked at me and said, You did good, Dan.

That night, in the lounge, people were talking about Calypso's cave.

So? Ksenia asked, turning to me. That morning, as people were gathering in the reception area for the excursion, I'd told her about my claustrophobia. You know, she had said, you really don't have to go! A lot of people are staying aboard because for them it's too difficult.

The flood of relief I'd felt when she said "A lot of people are staying aboard" had been so intense that it was vaguely shaming; a pale memory of a gym teacher in elementary school, saying, *You don't have to climb the rope all the way to the top if you don't want to,* rose up from some long-buried place. But something had stopped me from accepting the excuse she had been offering, and after a moment I realized what it was: I didn't want my father to see me afraid. Later, after we'd returned from the excursion, I bumped into Ksenia on deck and told her what had happened: my panic attack, Daddy holding my hand.

Wonderful! she had cried.

Now, as people sat sipping their cocktails in the lounge, she was looking at the two of us warmly. See? You survived!

Some of the others glanced at her quizzically. "Survived"? someone asked.

I was trying to think of something funny to say when my father cut in.

We had a *great* time, he said loudly.

I looked over at him, but he was leaning forward, facing into the ragged semicircle of armchairs like a teacher addressing a study group.

I didn't want to go, my father said to them. The stairs are hard for me. I thought it would be too much for me physically. But Dan helped me, and I'm glad I went. After all, Odysseus spends seven-tenths of his adventures there!

He paused and said, not looking at me, It was one of the more impressive things I've seen, actually.

The pianist was playing the song he'd sung the night before: "I Didn't Know What Time It Was." Daddy closed his eyes and started humming along. *I didn't know what year it was / Life was no prize . . .*

Ksenia smiled. Your father is a very charming man, she murmured.

———

The last class before what would be a two-week hiatus fell on March 11. The following week the students would be taking the midterm examination, and the week after that was spring break. We wouldn't be convening again until April 1, when we'd start on Book 13 and the second half of the *Odyssey*—Odysseus' return, at last, to Ithaca, his stealthy plotting against the Suitors, the violent revenge, and the climactic reunions with his son, wife, and father. All this we would cover in six sessions, from the first Friday in April to the first Friday in May—a period that, I knew from past experience, would feel much shorter than the first six weeks of the semester had felt.

The students noticed this, too. Toward the end of the semester, I recall, one of them—I think it was tall Tom, Don Quixote Tom—remarked that the first half of the *Odyssey* felt twice as long as the second half. I understood what he meant. The revenge plot gives to the last twelve books of the epic a propulsive forward momentum, whereas the convoluted narrative of Books 1 through 12, heavy with reminiscences and flashbacks, storytelling and digressions, digressions *within* digressions, makes it move more slowly, feel more dense. But then, none of the climaxes of the second half, nor the long-delayed outburst of violence, nor the emotionality of the reunions and recognitions, would be satisfying had they not been so carefully, laboriously prepared for in the first.

On the second Friday of March, then, we would finish the first half of the epic, which concludes with a twin climax. In Book 11, Odysseus describes to the enthralled Phaeacians the most harrowing of his adventures—his visit to the Underworld, the land where the souls of the dead reside and where, Circe has instructed him, he must speak with the ghost of a famous seer, Teiresias, who will provide crucial information about his voyage home. In Book 12, after bringing the Apologoi to an end, he embarks on the Phaeacian ship that will bring him home at last to Ithaca. This double climax, in other words, gestures dramatically to the past even as it nods to the future.

The second week of March was mild, and my father was in a good mood when I picked him up at the station.

By now he was coming by train. I was a little surprised by this, given his secret love for the aggravations of traffic; but by early March he'd given up driving altogether. I suspected that he didn't like to admit he'd been bested by the weather.

This way I can relax and do some rereading on my iPad, was all that he'd said when he called to tell me he was coming by train. He always made a point of mentioning that he was reading the *Odyssey* on his iPad. Books are an obsolete technology! he'd say. Get with the times. Homer on an iPad, now *that's* an adventure.

And so instead of listening for the sound of his tires crunching on the gravel outside my house late every Thursday afternoon, I'd pick him up at the station in the early evenings and we'd go have dinner at Flatiron. I would pull up in the tiny parking lot at the entrance of the old-fashioned country station, careful to keep the engine running so that the car would be warm for him, since my father, as he aged, was constantly cold, always complaining about the cold in coffee shops and the local library and trains and, most of all, at home, in the house he shared with my mother, who, in a perfect, disastrous symmetry, always complained of feeling hot, of feeling a little *flushed*, was always wanting to open a window, *to get some fresh air* even in the winter months, the months when my father would sit downstairs watching the Giants games, cocooned in his hooded sweatshirts, a woolen cap with a comical little peak teetering on his naked head. He'd emerge from within the brick station into the cold that he hated so much, looking incongruously small in the big padded coats my mother bought for him, like a child in a snowsuit, and we'd drive straight to Flatiron, where he'd order his filet and his glass of red wine.

On the evening before the class in which we'd be discussing Books 11 and 12, my father was clearly feeling expansive.

I love the Underworld! he exclaimed.

I laughed. What do you love so much about it?

I like that it isn't *under*! I always thought it was like hell—you know, below the surface of the earth. But these guys just sail there, like it was

just an ordinary place on the map. You don't need the gods to get there—
it's a normal trip that anyone can make. That's really neat, Dan.

Well, I said, by now "Underworld" is just a conventional way of referring to his destination in Book 11. You're right, it's not actually "under."
After all, they can't make it too hard to go there. Getting to the Land of
the Dead is a trip that everybody makes, eventually.

My father looked at me for a moment and then stared down. Ha, he
said tonelessly. You got *that* right.

Odysseus' journey to Hades, the Land of the Dead, in Book 11 is
traditionally known as the Nekyia. Strictly speaking, this Greek term,
derived from the word *nekys*, "corpse" (the English "*nec*ropolis" is related
to it) refers to the dread rites by which the living summon the ghosts of
the dead in order to speak to them; Homer's description of these rituals, which involve some shivery, unexplained arcana, has the unsettling
power you associate with the best horror movies. After arriving at the spot
designated by Circe—a level shore marked by a rock at the meeting place
of two rivers—the hero first digs a pit, each side the length of the distance
from the tip of the third finger to the elbow; around this pit he then pours
a libation of milk, honey, wine, and water; afterward he sprinkles barley
around the perimeter; and finally he cuts the throats of a ram and a black
ewe, turning their heads in one direction as he turns his own head in the
opposite direction, and then letting their blood fill the pit. Only after the
ghosts drink this blood is the power of speech granted to them.

Over time, *nekyia*, the word for the rites that summon these inarticu-
late zombies, has come to stand for the entire episode, which occurs just
before the halfway point of Odysseus' long journey home. The strategic
positioning of this episode suggests an important moral: In order to move
into the future, we must first reconcile ourselves with our pasts.

It is in the "House of Hades and of Persephone," as Homer refers to
this gloomy place, that the hero, expecting to see Teiresias, encounters a
surprise: the ghost of one of his sailors, Elpenor, who, unbeknownst to his
comrades, had fallen drunk from a roof and broken his neck while still
on Circe's island. The ghost of this young man now approaches Odysseus

and begs his erstwhile captain to return to Circe's island, once he has finished his errand in Hades, and recover his body:

> *Don't go off and leave me behind, abandoned and*
> *unburied and unmourned, lest I become a reason*
> *for the gods to visit their awful wroth on you;*
> *no, but burn me up, together with such armor as was mine,*
> *heap up a grave for me on the gray sea's strand,*
> *so even men to come will know of me, unlucky man.*
> *Do all of this, then plant upon my grave the oar*
> *that I plied while still I lived, rowing with my mates.*

Moved by his crewman's entreaties, Odysseus eventually does what Elpenor asks.

Many ingenious interpretations of Elpenor's role in the *Odyssey* have been advanced over the centuries. He is, after all, only introduced in Book 10, at the end of the Circe episode, and his fatal accident, which we hear about immediately afterward, is quite patently engineered so that we can meet his ghost in Book 11. The most persuasive explanation for this plot twist is that Elpenor functions as a kind of emotional and narrative human sacrifice: he is a figure whose death, which can mean nothing to the audience since we never really got to know him, nonetheless serves as a bridge between the worlds of the living and the dead, easing Odysseus' (and the poem's) passage from the familiar world of the present narrative into the history- and tragedy-haunted world of the dead whom Odysseus encounters in Hades: not only the thronging spirits about whom we hear right away but, a bit later on, his own mother, dead comrades from the Trojan War, a gallery of famous heroines, and mythic wrongdoers serving out their eternal punishments. Homely Elpenor's presence among these figures somehow makes this unsettling book easier to bear. Somehow, too, the death of a minor character makes bearable the thought of the death of the main character, which is, in fact, foretold in this episode.

Book 11 contains a wonderfully poignant scene. Circe has warned

Odysseus that he must speak to Teiresias first; and yet as our hero waits for the old man's spirit to appear, he notices with shock the shade of his own mother, Anticleia: shock, because she had been alive when her son left for Troy. It is here, in this awkwardly public way—Odysseus is, after all, standing in front of his companions, surrounded by the rustling, flitting spirits of the dead—that he learns his mother has died. The ache of an unfulfillable yearning pulses through the encounter that ensues between the living child and the dead parent. When Odysseus catches sight of Anticleia, he rises and attempts to embrace her, only to find that she sifts through his grasp like a shadow. Three times he tries to hold her; three times the embrace comes up empty.

Madeline's hand went up when I asked what aspects of Book 11 they wanted to discuss.

The pain Odysseus feels in the Underworld is incredibly palpable, she said. The passage about him trying to hug his mother who can't be held was just heart-wrenching.

I wondered how many of them could know grief well enough, so early in their lives, to appreciate the devastating aptness of the symbol Homer contrived for the gulf between the living and the dead: the armful of air, the impossible embrace.

Why is it three times? Don Quixote Tom suddenly asked.

I thought for a moment. Well, three is a kind of magic narrative number, right? Think of how jokes are organized around triplets—a rabbi, a minister, a priest—and the structure is tripartite, too: *x*, *x*, then *y*; and *y* is always the punch line. There's something structurally satisfying about the number three, I suppose. Imagine if he'd tried to embrace her just once, the scene would have no impact.

From off in his corner my father quietly said, Yeah. That scene is just great.

I wondered if he was thinking of his mother, my clever card-playing grandmother Kay, who'd died in the 1970s of Alzheimer's, her mind vacant, her body wasted. *She's already like a ghost,* my father said wearily to my mother at the top of the stairs one night after he returned from another weekend in Miami watching her die. She weighs seventy-eight pounds, it's like she's made of paper. There's nothing to hold on to. It was, in fact, my grandmother's awful death that had first inspired one of those sayings we would tease him about. *Don't ever let me get like that! Just pull the plug and then go out and have a round of baihhrrs!*

I looked around. Anyone else? What other encounters are noteworthy?

Nina said, I thought it was interesting that he meets the ghost of Agamemnon. There's been so much about Agamemnon's story, but finally we hear from him what happened when he got home, so it's like proof of that. His story shows Odysseus what to avoid.

She was right: it is in Hades that we get the fullest narration thus far of Agamemnon's homecoming—this time, from Agamemnon himself. We must remember that at the time the two heroes of the Trojan War meet, Odysseus has no knowledge of Agamemnon's fate: we, the audience, have heard about it, and Telemachus hears about it in Books 3 and 4, but Odysseus knows nothing. This encounter in Hades represents the first time that the hero of the *Odyssey* hears the tale that we have been getting from the start: the story of Agamemnon's return home from Troy, that inverse *Odyssey* in which the wife has yielded to her suitor and betrays her returning husband. Agamemnon's bitter description in Book 11 of the ambush at the welcome-home feast—the dead bodies bleeding among the plates and goblets, he himself cut down "as if (he tells Odysseus) I were a fat beast in a slaughterhouse"—gives the most detailed account thus far of that awful narrative, one that is sure to be at least as instructive for Odysseus as are the warnings that he gets from Teiresias. And indeed, Agamemnon concludes his account with a double admonition to Odysseus to avoid the mistakes that he made: He must not trust his wife, and should return home in secret, rather than publicly. It is advice that Odysseus takes.

I asked, Who *else* does he meet in the Underworld?

Jack said, The drunk guy who fell off the roof!

Yes, I said, good. The drunk guy has a name, for which you will be responsible on the midterm. Elpenor.

We talked about the significance of Elpenor for a few minutes. Then I said, But who *else?*

The night before class, as I read through their postings on the discussion board, I'd been perplexed that no one had mentioned the most remarkable encounter that Odysseus has in the Land of the Dead: the one with the ghost of Achilles, hero of the *Iliad*. It is the last conversation Odysseus has with someone he knew personally.

The climactic quality of this meeting is heightened by an astonishing admission on the part of Achilles. In the *Iliad*, Achilles recalls how he had willingly exchanged the possibility of a long life in return for a short life with undying glory, *kleos*, that paramount motivation for heroic action. In the *Odyssey*, Odysseus meets his former comrade in Hades and is eager to assure the dead hero that his choice was the right one:

> *But never before has a man been more blessed by fortune*
> *than you, Achilles, nor will there ever be again.*
> *While you lived we Argives honored you as if*
> *you were a god; and now you wield great power here*
> *among the dead. So do not let death grieve you, Achilles.*

And yet Achilles disagrees:

> *Don't sweet-talk me about death, brilliant Odysseus.*
> *I'd rather serve another as a land-bound serf,*
> *some man without a portion, no livelihood,*
> *than be the lord of all the withered dead.*

The exchange represents a shocking rejection of the values embraced by Achilles and endorsed throughout the *Iliad*. For the hero of the *Iliad*, a poem that celebrates the dark glamour of early death, to announce to the hero of the *Odyssey*, a poem that celebrates the overriding drive to survive at all costs, that life at any price, life even as the servant of an indigent farmer, is preferable to glory among the dead, is both devastating and something of a dark joke. It's as if the *Iliad* were saying to the *Odyssey, You win.*

But not a single one of the students had posted about the Achilles-Odysseus exchange on the online discussion board the night before class. This was why I was pressing them to think about it as the seminar got under way the next morning.

Who else does Odysseus meet in the Underworld? I repeated.

Jack said, Lots of people. It's practically a party!

Come *on,* you guys, I said. There's a *major* encounter in the Underworld. Major! You can't not have noticed it.

They looked up at me blankly, and I made a frustrated noise.

You're not trying hard enough, I finally said. Who *else* does Odysseus meet in the Land of the Dead, and why is this meeting important?

Finally, my father grunted off in his corner and waved his hand. He meets Achilles, he mumbled.

The students' eyes swiveled over to the place under the window where he sat.

Okay, I said, and so?

It had occurred to me that my father would appreciate this important scene. Last night, at Flatiron, he had talked about how much he wanted to read the *Iliad* after the seminar was over—to reread it, rather, for the first time since high school. I'm a war kid, I grew *up* during the war. War is something I *get.* Your uncle Howie was in the war. I grew up with soldiers on the streets. You knew who the good guys were; you knew who the bad guys were. So I think maybe the *Iliad* is a better fit for me.

Now my father was raising his hand and saying, He meets Achilles.

Trying to lead him to make the point I had in mind, I said, So what's the meeting about? What gets revealed here?

It's an impressive moment, my father said. It certainly tells you a lot about Achilles, he said.

Good. I nodded. Tells you what?

It turned out that my father wasn't interested in what I was interested in. He didn't want to pursue the literary implications of Odysseus' meeting with Achilles, of the strange symbolic encounter between the *Odyssey* and the *Iliad.*

Glumly he said, It reveals that you can spend your whole life believing in something, and then you get to a point when you realize you were wrong about the whole thing.

Three months after this exchange my father and I were standing at the entrance to the Underworld—Hades, the Land of the Dead.

I love that you don't actually go *under,* he said again as he slowly made his way down the steps of a bus in Italy. It was the fifth day of the cruise, and he was still leery of falling.

We were at the Campi Flegrei, the Phlegraean Fields: the site that the ancients identified as the portal to Hades. The ship had docked that morning in Naples; after breakfast, we'd all clambered onto the big air-conditioned coach. Although it was early, the group was unusually animated. Despite our joking, we were unsettled by the uncanny nature of our destination, and a reactive hilarity had set in. At the front of the bus, Brendan was sharing a joke in Italian with the dark-haired young Italian archaeologist who would be taking us around the *campi.* Just behind us, the blond woman who was traveling with her elegant old father was having a *fou rire* in response to something he'd said; as she nodded and wiped the tears from her eyes, she said something in what I thought might be Dutch or Flemish. On the other side of the aisle the brothers from New Orleans were giggling conspiratorially while their parents and aunt talked above their heads, shushing them. I leaned over and smiled at their mother. Everyone's so punchy this morning! I said.

She grinned back at me a little wearily. I don't know what's got *into* everyone, it's like they put something in the coffee this morning!

Half an hour later the bus stopped, and we all got out.

For a few moments, everyone stared in silence, clearly thinking the same thing: No wonder the Greeks and Romans thought that this must be the portal to the abode of the dead. We were standing at the rim of a huge shallow crater; stretching away from us in every direction was a landscape that could have been the moon. Beneath our feet the ground was flinty, scattered with rocks and pebbles. Farther away, as the ground sloped up into some low hills, giant boulders lay scattered, powdered with saffron-colored dust. It was hard to imagine that anything had ever grown here. From fissures in the ground, spumes of white smoke rose into the air. It was overcast that morning, and it seemed as though the plumes were feeding the clouds from below. A rotten smell filled the air.

Sulfur, one of the young brothers announced.

My father looked over, nodding appreciatively. Smart boy, he said to me.

Sì, the young archaeologist said, looking over at the boy, smiling. Yes, it's sulfur pits. Is why this place is called Solfarata. The place of sulfur.

Everyone wrinkled their noses.

The archaeologist smiled and said, Is the smell like death.

The woman with the elegant Dutch father said, Ugh!

I looked around for her father. Where's your dad? I said.

Oh, he stayed on the bus, she replied. He has a bad leg and didn't want to walk around too much.

I'd never have guessed about the leg, I said. He's been so intrepid!

She smiled. But so has yours, no?

I turned and saw my father crouching down to the ground, sniffing at a handful of dirt.

Yes, I said finally, I guess you're right.

Then the woman looked at me. You know, I think you need to talk to my father. He has a very interesting story about his life and the *Odyssey.* I heard that you're a Classics professor, I think you will be interested. It's why we're here on this cruise!

Before I had a chance to ask her about her father and his story, Brendan and the Italian archaeologist called out for us to follow. We trudged along behind them, inhaling the aroma of death, and saw the sights in the Underworld.

Later that day, after we'd returned to the ship, I sought out her father.

He's up on the sundeck, the woman had told me as we milled around the reception area after the tour of Solfarata, gulping our cold tea and lemonade. You can't miss him. He has a big scar on his leg.

I burst out laughing and said, You're joking. I was thinking of the passage in Book 19 about the telltale scar on Odysseus' leg and how he got it—the passage that exemplifies the uses of ring composition.

She laughed and shook her head. No, I'm not, really! It's just like in the book!

I went upstairs and found her father, and he told me his story.

On our first evening at sea, Daddy and I had sat on our little balcony, nursing our cocktails and wondering what kind of person takes an *Odyssey* cruise. Over the next few nights, the answers had trickled in: the New Orleans family traveled together every year, as the precocious boy who thought Homer needed an editor had announced at breakfast that day, although this year had a special poignancy for them, as his mother later told me, since this was the first summer after her sister, the boy's aunt, had died. We wanted to do something really *meaningful,* she said to me one evening, and what could be more meaningful than Homer? Some people had read the Classics in high school or college and wanted to visit the sites. But the blond woman's father had the best story of all.

You probably want to know how I got this scar? he said to me, smiling, after I found him on the sundeck. I nodded. He was lying on a deck chair, wearing only some bathing trunks. The scar had long ago faded to a pale brown but was deep enough to be clearly visible: a furrow that traveled from the top of the shin down to the ankle.

I got this scar during the war, he began.

I made a quizzical face: he didn't look any older than my father.

Oh, I wasn't a soldier! He laughed. I was a teenager. But I was in Europe.

I nodded.

I am Belgian, he said. He looked at me. Have you been there?

I nodded. To Antwerp once, I said. And Brussels.

Ah, so you've been to my hometown! We lived in Brussels, not far from the museum. You know it?

I said, Yes, I knew it well. I told him that one of my favorite paintings, Brueghel's *Landscape with the Fall of Icarus*, was in that museum.

Ah, yes. A very famous work, which you, as a Classics scholar, must enjoy.

Yes, I said, smiling. It's about hubris, about the foolishness of challenging the gods.

He gave me an amused look. I think it is about the foolishness of challenging your father!

We chatted about Brussels. Then he said, My story about this scar is in fact about studying Classics.

I looked at him.

Now, the last winter of the war was very hard, terribly hard, the old man said, very cold. Nobody by that point had any food. My cousin in Amsterdam told me that there they called it the Winter of the Tulips, because people were digging up tulip bulbs and eating them, they were so hungry.

I nodded again.

My parents were fairly well-to-do before the war, and we had a big house. And in that house several people were living with us by this point, people who had lost their homes, people who were afraid.

He looked at me. Yes, I said. I know what you mean. Go on.

Now, I was a teenage boy, and I and all my brothers had taken Latin in school from a very brilliant teacher. Eccentric, he was. A bit of a maverick. To my knowledge he never married, but he was wonderful with students, even with his odd habits. He was a bit unkempt, not so clean. One of my brothers used to say that when he went to his house to be tutored before the war he would only eat the foil-wrapped chocolates that he offered because he wouldn't eat anything our teacher had actually touched.

He laughed softly to himself.

He knew *everything* about the Classics, he went on. If all of the classical literature we have today were destroyed tomorrow, I think he could have reconstituted eighty percent of it from memory. Anyway, at some point during the Occupation he came to live with us. He lived in a small attic. My parents fed him breakfast and lunch and dinner and kept him clothed and warm. In return for this he would continue to tutor us. I recall that he kept his mind active by making up Latin words for modern things—"butterfly bomb," "air raid," things like that. Quite amusing.

He paused.

The last year of the war, as I have said, was a winter of terrible hunger. And cold! Unless you found something to burn, you froze. So we all learned to wield an ax and chop wood. Now, one day I went to cut some wood. Although I was only fourteen, I thought I could do it. But in fact, I was very slender and also weak from hunger. So I lifted the ax to chop the wood, but I was overcome by weakness, and instead of chopping the log I hit my leg! It was a very deep cut, not to the bone, but very deep. As you can see.

I looked again and nodded.

He beamed. What has this to do with this cruise? you must be wondering!

I smiled but said nothing.

I will tell you what happened. Because of the wound to my leg, I fell very ill. Remember, we were malnourished; I had not the strength to fight off an infection. It was quite serious, and for days I lay in bed, delirious. And my tutor, he sat by me every day and every night. He never left my side. And what do you think he did while I lay there?

I shook my head. I can't imagine, I said.

He read to me the *Odyssey* in Greek! He spoke to me in Latin! He was reciting the Classics all the time, just to have the sound in my head. I should say that I understood a good bit, since I had been studying classical languages with him already for two years. And I think that hearing that sound, the sound of a human voice reciting poetry, helped me to heal. Yes, I do think that is true. So I feel in some way the *Odyssey* saved my life.

He paused for a moment and suddenly looked straight at me. And I can tell you that it sank in!

Then he opened his mouth and, in flawless, rhythmical Homeric Greek, began reciting Athena's speech to Zeus from Book 1:

> *But my heart is torn in half for brilliant Odysseus,*
> *The wretched man who far from all his friends endures such woes . . .*

He stopped.

I said, So that's why you're on the cruise—because you love the *Odyssey*?

The man with the wound on his leg said, I am here because I loved my *teacher*. I always thought that someday I should find a way to honor him, and to me this seemed the best way: to experience the journey of Odysseus.

He paused and then said, He is long dead, but I hope he would approve.

When I got back to our cabin, my father was stretched out on the bed, reading the *Iliad* on his iPad. You have got to hear this, I said. He put down his device, and I told him the Belgian's story.

In a million years you could not make this stuff up, I finished.

Daddy was quiet.

Oh, c'mon, Dad, you have to admit it's uncanny—the leg wound? The *Odyssey*?

Yeah, he finally said, it's amazing. No one will believe you.

There was a little silence.

The Winter of the Tulips, he said presently, in the appreciative tone he always used when speaking of the Second World War, that time when things were really tough, when the good guys were good and the bad guys were bad and you knew what was what.

He said, I knew a Dutch kid when I was in high school.

He wasn't looking at me. He was staring at his darkened screen.

Joop, he said. It's spelled *J-o-o-p*, but you pronounce it like *Yupe*. To tease him I used to call him Joopy. He came with his family just before the war started.

He was a friend of yours? I said. I couldn't understand what this was about. I'd never heard about a Dutch friend.

Nah, my father said, exhaling loudly. Nah, he wasn't part of our gang, Walter, Eugene Miller, those people. But we had refugee kids in the neighborhood, sure. As you know. Wolfgang Grajonca was a buddy of mine—you know, the rock promoter, Bill Graham. He changed his name. But he was a refugee, he lived in our building.

I nodded. He loved telling that story.

We hung out, but not Joop. He wasn't—wasn't really one of us.

Something prickled at the back of my neck.

You mean—

But he *liked* me, my father said.

What do you mean, "he liked" you?

He liked me in . . . in, you know, that way.

I stared at him.

You mean he was gay?

Yeah. I guess he was. Yeah.

And you were the object of his affections? I tried to lighten the tone, but he stayed somber.

He liked me. He would hang around me, but he didn't really join in our stuff, stickball, ball games, stuff like that. But he liked to hang around, and he was smart, so I liked him. He read a lot of books and we would talk about that.

He looked thoughtfully at the iPad. I called him Joopy, and he called me Loopy. But it was only him, nobody else ever did. Of course.

Of course, I repeated. I thought, Daddy Loopy!

That's where it came from?

Anyway, he said, ignoring my question, finally I figured out what—*how* he liked me.

I couldn't believe he'd never told me this. So what happened?

My father looked at me. What do you mean, "What happened?" It was the Bronx! Nothing "happened" in those days.

I burst out laughing. Uh-huh, I said. Sure.

Well, nothing happened with anybody I knew. Anyway, I wasn't that way, as you know.

He shook his head.

But how did you respond? I asked.

Oh, I was nice to him. What else could I do? It didn't bother me. You heard about guys like that, people would make fun, I guess, but what the hell. I guess at first I pulled back a little, when I realized what was going on, but it didn't really bother me that much, and I got used to it. Anyway, I think he found a friend of his own after a while.

A friend. I remember him and Mother talking about my high-school teachers. *He has a "friend," doesn't he?*

A minute passed. Daddy, I said. Was this what you were thinking about when I came out to you and Mom, and you said, "Let me talk to him, I know something about this"?

He nodded. I remembered how horrified I'd been when he'd said it, too. It would have been easier for me to think he had no experience at all of what I was going through, of what I was; the idea that my coming-out would be the basis for some kind of intimacy with him had bewildered and frightened me at the time. I'd walked hurriedly out of the room that day and somehow the moment had passed. I'm *fine*, I told my parents later. We don't need to talk about it.

Daddy, I said again. Let me get this straight. You had some gay Dutch boy in love with you in the Bronx who I'm pretty sure gave you the name "Loopy" and it never crossed your mind to tell me about this before?

My father looked down. Ah, Dan. I just didn't know how to talk about it.

I couldn't think of anything to say. In the end, I did what my father had done: I was nice to him.

Okay, I said. Well, now you do. Jesus, Dad.

He pushed a button on his iPad and the *Iliad* glowed bluish in the darkened room. Yeah, I guess so. Then he looked up and said, It's an *Odyssey* cruise. Everyone has a story to tell. And everyone has . . . has a *flaw*.

Yes, I said. I guess everyone does.

Then he added, lightly, Some stories just take longer to tell.

Despite its aura of finality, Odysseus' sojourn among the dead isn't the last adventure that he narrates to the spellbound Phaeacians in the Apologoi. The last adventure he has is, in fact, the first one we hear about in the *Odyssey*: the episode of the Cattle of the Sun, the climax of Book 12 and the only one of his remarkable exploits mentioned in the proem.

I was eager to devote as much class time as possible to this crucial episode. As we wrapped up our discussion of Book 11 and the Land of the Dead, I told them to take a short break so that we'd have lots of time for the Cattle of the Sun.

By the time Odysseus and his men land on the coast of a place called Thrinakia, his crew has been warned by both Teiresias and by Circe—warnings repeated, now, by Odysseus—to avoid touching the beautiful cattle that roam there, enormous herds of cows and sheep that belong to the sun god Hyperion. Each herd, the poet goes out of his way to point out, numbers precisely three hundred and fifty head. At first the men take pains to obey the orders they've had, but after they're stranded for some time on Thrinakia because of bad weather, they succumb to their hunger. Taking advantage of a moment when Odysseus has gone off to pray to the gods for help, they slaughter some of the animals, roast the meat on spits, and eat it. But the all-seeing Hyperion takes offense and cries to the other gods that the Greeks must be punished; if not, he threatens, he will go to Hades and shine among the dead—a grotesque, a horrible, inversion of the natural order of things. The gods oblige him, sending a terrible storm at sea as the Greeks set sail from Thrinakia. Odysseus is the sole survivor of this final calamity; which is why, in the end, he gets to make his *nostos* alone, gets to be the hero of his epic.

I wanted to discuss the Cattle of the Sun, which shares with the trip to the Underworld some of the poem's spookiest moments. (For instance, after the cattle have been slaughtered, the dead animals' skins continue to move, and the flesh that is roasting on the spits baas and moos.) Above all, I wanted them to grasp how the episode fits into the overall structure of the epic. For the story of the Cattle of the Sun, which comes in Book 12 and explains how Odysseus came to land alone on Calypso's island, in fact loops us back to the opening of the poem: to Book 1, which finds Odysseus, wailing and yearning to go home, at the end of his seven-year sojourn with the nymph, ready to move on at last.

Which is to say that by the time the *Odyssey* reaches its exact mid-point, it's made a gigantic three-hundred-sixty-degree turn: after all that travel, you end up right where you started from. *How can you travel great distances without getting anywhere? By going in circles.*

But try as I might that morning, I couldn't get the students interested in the Cattle of the Sun—or, at least, couldn't get them interested in what had interested me, in what I had once learned. (*Think,* Jenny had said thirty years earlier. *They belong to the sun, they cannot die. There are three hundred and fifty of them, which is very nearly the number of—what?* And then I said, *Days of the year?* I was confused, and she smiled. *It's about _time_.*)

As it turned out, the students' ideas were more interesting than mine.

Brendan said, Before we get to the cattle I actually want to go back to Circe in Book 11. It's interesting how many similarities she has to Calypso.

Jack said, Yeah, I keep getting them mixed up. They're both so into Odysseus.

A few of the others made rueful assenting noises. As if taking courage from this, Brendan pressed on.

I actually compiled a list of the ways in which the two characters are

both similar and different, he declared, picking up his yellow pad. He
began to read aloud. *Similarities*, he said:

> Both on isolated islands with animals and lush flora.
> Both are lovers of Odysseus.
> Both offer Odysseus assistance upon departure.
> Both are nymphs, a specific kind of Greek demigod.
> Both possess supernatural capabilities.
> Both are daughters of Titans (Circe of Helios and Calypso of Atlas).
> Both of their names begin with K in Greek.
> When translated from Greek, Calypso means "conceal," while
>   Circe means "encircle." So both names relate to captivity.
> Hermes plays a role in both encounters. He appears in Book 5 to
>   demand that Calypso release Odysseus. He appears during
>   Book 10 when Odysseus arrives on Circe's island to protect
>   Odysseus from her power to change men into animals.

Brendan took a breath.

I said, All right. So what are you getting at?

Well, we *know* he was with Calypso on her island because Homer
tells us. It's the part of the poem that he gets from the Muse, right? But
he tells us about Circe as part of the story he's telling the Phaeacians
about his adventures, and she's an awful lot like Calypso. And there are
other weird parallels. I know this may seem contrived, but I was going
to say that what I noticed in Book 10 was how much the Laestrygonians
were like the Phaeacians. Odysseus lands on their island and then right
away meets the royal princess, then the queen, then the king, but with
the Laestrygonians it's like a nightmare version of the Phaeacians.

Yes, that's right, I said. We talked about that last week.

Blond Tom was nodding. It's true. So many stories that Odysseus tells
to the Phaeacians are like dark parallels to something we know for a fact
that Odysseus experienced in the earlier part of the book.

Nina looked over from her seat next to Jack. Pretty much everything he tells in the adventures stories comes off as a kind of lurid dream. It's familiar and bizarre at the same time.

I dunno, Brendan interrupted. I guess it feels like—okay, so I'm just going to say it. Do you think it's possible that the stuff he's telling the Phaeacians is totally made up? To me it feels like he's just making it up as he goes along, basing the Apologoi on what actually happened to him.

I pondered this. I see where you're going, I said, and I will say that it's really interesting, very intriguing. You've come up with some interesting points, some notions. But for it to be a real interpretation you have to have a theory that explains the notions. Let's say that Homer wants us to think—or maybe just suspect—that the stories in the Apologoi are totally invented, that they're tall tales based on actual things he's experienced but wildly exaggerated and dramatized—that, like Homer himself, Odysseus is composing on his feet, improvising his story to suit his audience. The question then is why. What would be the point of hinting that the Apologoi are fictional?

They'd grown a little subdued.

Then Jack blurted, I'm sorry, Professor, I don't mean to offend you. I don't. But sometimes—right now I have the impression that you have some interpretation in your head that you think is the right one, and you want to lead us to see things your way, and you just sort of squash anything that doesn't fit that interpretation. I think this idea is pretty cool actually. So can't it just be cool that he's maybe making a lot of stuff up? Why does everything have to "mean" something?

The room became still.

Of course my first instinct was to be defensive. Of course I was surprised that Jack, the blithe jokester, had erupted in this way.

My father, I knew, was looking at me.

I said, carefully, First of all, don't be sorry. This is a seminar, you're allowed to express yourself. Yourselves. I'm sorry you think I'm imposing my interpretations on you—it's not what I *think* I'm doing.

Even as I said this, I wondered whether that was perfectly honest.

Jack started to make an apologetic noise, but I held up my hand. It's fine, really—if that's what you think, we should address it. Now, I do think that there are certain elements in the poem that should be illuminated, certain ways of seeing the poem that people have come up with and passed on for centuries, millennia even, and I think it's important for you to come away from this class having been exposed to those, if possible. Like the meaning of the Cattle of the Sun, which we *still* haven't gotten to.

There were a few nervous giggles.

And I do think that although it's great to notice interesting features in a text, your job as readers is to make sense of them, to figure out how they contribute to a larger meaning. That's how I was trained, and that's how the people who trained me were trained. If the work has real coherence, all these details will add up, even if they're not noticeable at first and even if the big picture isn't clear. Only by means of close reading can we understand what that big picture is and how the pieces, the small things, fit into it. That's what interpretation is about, and this is what philology is for. Interpretation isn't some mushy subjective enterprise, it has to arise from meticulous examination of the data, and that data is what's in the text.

I looked over at my father, then. He was nodding and frowning at the same time.

Then I glanced around the seminar table. It felt as if they were all holding their breath. I raised my eyebrows at Jack as if to say, *Okay?* He nodded.

That said, I went on, I *am* intrigued by this idea, as I said. So I'll try to keep an open mind. Just as I hope you'll try to listen to what I'm saying. Are we good?

They nodded. Suddenly Jack looked mischievous and said, Are we having a "moment"?

Everyone laughed.

It's fine, I said, although I realized then that my knee was jerking uncontrollably under the table. I'd had contentious encounters in classes before; why had this one gotten me so riled? And then I realized: my father was sitting there, watching.

I'm glad we aired that, I said finally. Now, does anyone want to take this idea and run with it? Believe me, I'm all ears.

They looked around at one another.

Blond Tom said, I actually think there is a point. I think it's really philosophical. We're always talking about storytelling and how important it is in the *Odyssey*, how you have to read between the lines of people's stories, like with Helen and Menelaus in Book 4. So maybe by presenting the Apologoi as based on truth but not representing the *whole* truth, Homer is making you wonder what "truth" is to begin with.

Madeline said, slowly, It's funny that we're even having this conversation about what adventures are "real" as opposed to the adventures that may be "fiction," since the whole poem is a fiction.

Tom nodded and then looked up at me again. So I think, he said, I think this is the climax of the whole storytelling theme that we have talked about so much. If you read the whole thing this way, by the end of Book 12 you're, like, how do you know what's *true*?

It was half past twelve, and I had no answer. As the students started collecting their books, I made a mental note to call Jenny that evening and see what she thought of their idea.

I went on thinking about it after I drove my father to the station. As a writer, certainly, I could see the attractiveness of this interpretation of the Apologoi—could appreciate the advantages of the narrative games the kids wanted to attribute to Homer. As a writer, I could see the appeal of a Homer who was interested in raising profound questions about the uneasy border between fact and fiction; of a poet who wanted Odysseus' tales to serve as a meditation on storytelling, on how a good storyteller need not be bound by the facts of what happened, which after all have a bony authenticity that often resists the meanings we would like to impose on them, but instead simply takes things that have really happened and then—because the storyteller wants his audience to think about this or that theme, travel or teaching or education, say, or marriage, or fathers and sons—elaborates and embroiders the actual events with touches that would better highlight those notions.

But when I finally got around to calling Jenny late that night, she was skeptical.

So basically, I summed up after retailing the points the students had made that day, they're saying that the Apologoi are inventions fabricated by Odysseus but based on things we know happened to him because they're things the poet narrates. The assumption is that the best storytellers are like the best liars: there's always a grain of truth in the tale.

Jenny exhaled slowly into the receiver.

Yeeeah, she said. It's a fun idea. But in the end, how could you *prove* it?

It had been thirty years since I'd been her student, but I was still accustomed to deferring to her, especially when it came to the *Odyssey*. I was about to let the matter go when something occurred to me.

Well, I said, that cuts both ways, doesn't it?

She made a little interrogative noise.

I said, How could you prove that he *didn't* make it all up?

For a few days after this exchange I felt very pleased with myself. Then, about a week later, Jenny called.

You know, she began, I forgot to make the obvious objection.

To what? I said.

The thing about the Apologoi being made up, about Circe being a fabrication based on Calypso and so forth.

Yeah, the kids have been excited about their little theory since then, I said.

(I'd been excited, too.)

Mmmm. But if that's true, what do you do with 8.447?

8.447? I repeated, uncomprehendingly.

Yeeah, Jenny said. Book 8, line 447. Before the Phaeacians take Odysseus home, they give him farewell gifts, and the poet says that he puts them in a chest that he seals "with an intricate knot that he learned from the lady Circe."

She paused. And that's *Homer* talking, not Odysseus.

Oh, I said. Well, so much for that bright idea.

Jenny made a soft noise on the other end of the line. The text is the text, it says what it says. The answers are there. You just have to read more closely.

Of course, I replied.

But I waited awhile before I told the students. They'd been so happy with their discovery.

On a blistering Mediterranean afternoon in June, the *Corinthian II* was sailing south from Naples toward the Strait of Messina, the narrow strip of water that separates southern Italy from Sicily. Here, according to legend, is the site of Odysseus' dreadful encounter in Book 12 with Scylla and Charybdis, the most abominable and terrifying creatures he and his men will meet during their journeys—the end point, so to speak, of the spectrum that began with the raid on the Cicones in Book 9. The two monsters are said to have occupied opposing headlands across the Strait. Scylla is, at first sight, the more grotesque, with her dog's body, serpent necks, twelve legs, and six heads, their mouths filled with triple rows of razor-sharp teeth; but Charybdis, a vast whirlpool that thrice daily swallows and then vomits back the waters of the Strait, is ultimately deadlier. In Book 10, when Circe warns Odysseus about this perilous part of his route, she advises him to steer closer to Scylla, since she can take six men at most, while Charybdis can sink the entire ship; and "it is better by far / to mourn six companions than the whole company." Odysseus ends up taking her advice but withholds from his men any information about what is in store for them.

On the second-to-last full day of the cruise—the next day we'd see Ithaca, and the morning after that we'd be back in Athens for our flights home—the waters of the Strait were as glassy and smooth as the ice in a rink. My father, who had found in Book 12 an occasion to object to Odysseus' captainship (*Am I the only one here who thinks that that's a crappy way to treat your men—to keep secrets from them, to fail to warn them about imminent danger?!*), looked around skeptically.

Hard to believe anything could sink in these waters, he announced with an air of satisfaction. I said nothing. Atop one jutting headland were the squat ruins of what looked like an old fort. He looked at the ruins and said, Everything's always about *war*.

As we shuffled back on board after our excursion and stood around sipping our iced tea, the loudspeaker squawked. It was the captain.

The economic crisis in Greece, he began, had led to nationwide strikes this week, and I have just learned that the Corinth Canal is going to be closed.

The voice on the loudspeaker paused, and a ripple of consternation ran through the small crowd. Corinth? We weren't going to Corinth anyway. What . . . ?

The loudspeaker twanged again. The Corinth Canal, the captain's voice explained, allows swift passage between the western and eastern sides of the Greek mainland. The island of Ithaca lies off the west side, which is not far from where we are now, sailing as we are from Italy. But Athens is on the east side of the country. Going from west to east is a straightforward affair if you use the canal. But as the canal is now closed, we must now make a rather big detour—we must sail all the way down the west coast of Greece, and then around the tip of the Peloponnese, and then back up again along the east coast. Imagine if the Panama Canal were shut: the only way to get to the Pacific from the Atlantic would be to sail around all of South America. It's quite a long detour, he said.

Oh my *God*, someone said.

My father looked at me. Whaaa—?

I suddenly understood. We're not going to have time to go to Ithaca, I said. We're going to have to spend all day tomorrow sailing back the long way to Athens.

I'm afraid, the captain's voice was saying, that this means that we must begin sailing back to Athens this evening. Tomorrow will be a day at sea. We will not, I am sorry to say, have time to stop at Ithaca.

The drawn-out vowels of disappointment began to fill the air. *Oh no . . . No Ithaca? Not going to Ithaca? But it's the grand finale of the whole trip! Oh my . . . !*

At the other end of the room, the Belgian gentleman with the scar on his leg stood murmuring with his daughter. As if in telepathic response to my catching sight of them, at that moment they both looked up and saw me. I tugged at my father's arm, and we strolled across the deck. My latter-day Odysseus, his scar hidden beneath a pair of white trousers, made an amused face.

So? he said, stroking his polka-dot ascot. It must be a big disappointment to you—you, a Classics scholar! Not to get to Ithaca!

I found myself genuinely happy to be talking to him right now. The memory of our recent conversation, the recollection of the drama of his own past sufferings, were helping to put today's news into perspective. It was for his sake, I realized, that I wanted to seem philosophical.

Disappointing, yes. Although I have to say there's something kind of great about *not* getting there, too. You know—the idea of an infinitely receding horizon.

My father sounded grumpy. But in the poem it doesn't recede infinitely.

I worried for a minute that he was going to lecture me on the mathematical concept of infinity, but he went on impatiently. He gets to Ithaca in the poem. This is nothing more than a man-made screwup!

The next morning, as Daddy and I were sitting on our balcony, drinking our coffees in silence and staring at the choppy waters as the ship strained toward Athens, a steward knocked on the door of our cabin and handed me a note from the captain. He was aware, it began, that I had recently published a translation of the works of the Alexandrian Greek poet Constantine Cavafy. As I must know, Cavafy's poem "Ithaca" had gained a huge audience in the United States after it was read at the funeral of Jacqueline Kennedy Onassis, in 1994. Since our destination had suddenly "disappeared" (as the captain put it) and we now found ourselves with an entire day with no planned itinerary, would I consider filling the void a bit by giving a reading of Cavafy's poem and perhaps a small lecture about it? This way, although we would miss the real Ithaca, we would at least visit it metaphorically.

Of course I said yes; which is how it came to pass that, on the afternoon when we were supposed to go to Ithaca, I stood at a lectern in front of a small group of passengers talking about "Ithaca."

This captain is canny, I'd thought as I sent the steward back with my reply. For although it's named after the most famous destination in world literature, Cavafy's poem is about the virtues of not arriving.

Other poets before Cavafy, I began, had taken the *Odyssey*'s hero and refashioned him for their own purposes. In Dante's *Inferno*, for instance, Odysseus (here referred to by his Latin name, "Ulysses") makes an appearance among the False Counsellors—those who are damned for deceit—and madly sails over the edge of the world. But by the nineteenth century, the punishment had become a reward: the character's perpetual restlessness made him a hero to the Romantics. In 1833, the twenty-four-year-old Alfred Tennyson, who went on to become England's poet laureate and was a favorite of Queen Victoria's, wrote a poem called "Ulysses," a dramatic monologue seventy lines long narrated by the *Odyssey*'s hero. Tennyson's poem begins—a bit startlingly for those who have read the Homeric epic and have understood its themes of *nostos* and *homophrosynê*—with an aging Ulysses reflecting on a bitter irony: life back on Ithaca is not what he had hoped for during the long years of his homeward journey. The great adventurer has been reduced to an "idle king," bored by his royal duties and repelled by his people ("I mete and dole / Unequal laws unto a savage race"). Penelope he dismisses, rather cruelly, as "an aged wife"; Telemachus is dutiful but, we cannot help but feel, a bit dull ("blameless . . . decent . . . he works his work"). The longed-for destination has turned out to be unbearably disappointing—or, rather, the mere fact of having returned has been revealed as odious, symbolizing as it does an end to the adventuring wherein, he now realizes, the meaning of his life had lain. "How dull it is to pause, to make an end." As Tennyson's Ulysses looks around his island, his thoughts turn to those adventures, summed up in words that consciously echo those of the *Odyssey*'s opening lines:

Much have I seen and known—cities of men
And manners, climates, councils, governments,
Myself not least, but honoured of them all—
And drunk delight of battle with my peers,
Far on the ringing plains of windy Troy.
I am part of all that I have met . . .

But now, he says to his men, "You and I are old." The references to old age suggest that the ending that all that furious adventuring is meant to postpone is the one that awaits us all: "Death closes all; but something ere the end / Some work of noble note, may yet be done." And so, by the end of the poem, this Odysseus has decided to abandon the ending that Homer gave to him and return to sea, to the promise of more life:

My purpose holds
To sail beyond the sunset, and the baths
Of all the western stars, until I die.

In its much-quoted final line, "Ulysses" sums up the very spirit of travel, of adventure: "to strive, to seek, to find, and not to yield." A century after its publication, T. S. Eliot called Tennyson's work "a perfect poem."

Cavafy knew Tennyson's poem well—he cites it as an epigraph to an early version of "Ithaca," which he published in 1894, when he was in his early thirties, and in which he, too, dwells on the theme of the aging Odysseus' contempt for the destination to which he'd so long striven to return. ("He hated the air of dry land . . . Telemachus' affection, the faithfulness / of Penelope . . . they all bored him.") The Greek poet returned to this early work again and again over the next decade and a half, rethinking and reworking it, shaving off the material that was too clearly derived from Tennyson and arriving at something startlingly original. In its final version, which he published in 1911, when he was nearing fifty, he has abstracted the theme from the character; his poem nowhere mentions Odysseus' name, but instead refers obliquely to elements of the *Odyssey* while apparently addressing its hero directly:

> *As you set out on the way to Ithaca*
> *hope that the road is a long one,*
> *filled with adventures, filled with discoveries.*

Tennyson's poem, with its first-person rumination, gains drama by allowing us to overhear the hero's thoughts as they evolve, from his disgruntled survey of his realm to his impetuous decision to set out to sea again. But Cavafy's disembodied second-person address to Odysseus, which emanates from who knows what source, puts the hero on the same plane as the reader (we all read "you" as "us"), creating the eerie impression that we could be Odysseus ourselves: the heroes of our own journeys. The second stanza repeats the admonition "Hope that the road is a long one," as the poet moves on to catalog the riches that only travel can bring: harbors we have never seen before, fabulous riches from foreign ports, amber and ebony and coral, and exotic perfumes, and, best of all, encounters with wise strangers:

> *Many Egyptian cities may you visit*
> *that you may learn, and go on learning, from their sages.*

Of course we must remember our destination, the anonymous speaker admonishes, whatever that may be; but it becomes clear that life's meaning derives from our progress through it, and what we make of it:

> *Always in your mind keep Ithaca.*
> *To arrive there is your destiny.*
> *But do not hurry your trip in any way.*
> *Better that it last for many years;*

that you drop anchor at the island an old man,
rich with all you've gotten on the way,
not expecting Ithaca to make you rich.

Here we feel the breath of Tennyson's hero on our necks: Cavafy, like his British predecessor, understands that, as with so many things we anticipate for perhaps too long, the place we'd longed to see might not be quite what we expected:

And if you find her poor, Ithaca didn't deceive you.
As wise as you will have become, with so much experience,
you will understand, by then, these Ithacas; what they mean.

Cavafy's poem articulates, at an exquisitely high level of refinement, what has become a cliché of popular culture: that the journey is more important than the destination.

After the lecture was over, a few passengers milled around to talk more about the poems; I was happy to see that all of the regulars from our gatherings in the lounge were there. The Belgian and his daughter edged up.

Very nicely finessed, he declared with a foxy gleam in his eye. Not Ithaca, but "Ithaca"!

That evening, after dinner, my father and I started packing our bags. We'd be disembarking early the next morning.

Well, Daddy said, clichés are clichés for a reason. He'd spent the afternoon reading the Tennyson and the Cavafy on his iPad.

Do you believe it? I asked. That "the journey is more important than the destination"?

I think it's probably both, he replied after a moment. I mean, obviously I believe in results, in achieving things.

I shot him an amused look, which he chose not to notice.

So I guess that's what people mean by the "destination" part: getting where you want, fulfilling your goals. I'm not so sure I believe that that's not important. In life, you're judged by what you accomplish. There's no A for effort.

I'd heard this before.

But I can see the other side, too, he went on finally. You have to explore things, you have to *try* things . . . He grew quiet. I thought of our trips to Nino's house all those years before, of Nino describing his latest trip to Italy and saying, *But Jay, Jay! You should travel sometime!* and my father shaking his head and saying, *You don't understand.* I wondered how many things my father had wanted to try and hadn't, for one reason or another. Because Mother didn't like to travel; because of us.

Well, at least you're trying things now! My voice sounded brittle in my ears.

He looked mellow. Yeah, Dan, this has been great . . .

He seemed to be on the verge of saying something else, but in the end was quiet.

Now that I'm old, he said presently, I guess I can see the part about the importance of being out there and trying things even if you fail. You have to keep moving, at least. The worst thing is to go stale. Once that happens, you're *finished.*

He stood in front of the bed on which his suitcase lay open, preoccupied by some private thought. I recalled with a pang something Ralph, one of his Town Bagel buddies, had told me the previous summer, while I was home visiting my parents. He and Daddy had been playing golf, and Ralph stopped for a short visit after dropping Daddy off. (After all the years of tennis, my father's elbow had finally given out; in his late sixties, he decided he'd try golf.) When he saw me, Ralph took me aside. *Your father is a terrible golfer,* he said, *his swing is awful, his clothes are a mess! But I have to say this: not many people would take it up at his age. Or keep at it so hard.* He shook his head musingly and smiled gently. *I know he sometimes goes and plays alone. I've driven by the course and seen him playing in the rain, all by himself.*

When he said that, I'd pictured Daddy alone on a green hill, his gray hooded sweatshirt soaked through, swinging at an invisible ball. I could see the expression on his face, the upper teeth gnawing the lower lip in concentration, eyes narrowed. It was the look he'd worn when he'd taught himself how to do so many things.

So I guess I agree to some extent that the journey is something, too, he said as we packed our bags on the last day of the *Odyssey* cruise. If by "journey" they mean sticking in the game of life. That's something.

After a moment I said, Then you do agree with Tennyson and Cavafy. To arrive at the destination means it's all over, it's a . . . an end.

With a kind of embarrassment, I realized that I couldn't bring myself to say the word "death."

But he knew what I meant.

I think that they're saying that for these guys to return home is in some ways like dying. When they stop their travels and adventures, they're foreclosing the possibility that other things will ever happen to them. So being home in familiar surroundings rules something out from their lives.

He looked down at the bed.

There's no more . . . *uncertainty,* he said after a minute, almost as if to himself. There's nothing left to know.

"Uncertainty," I repeated. I was surprised to hear a note of admiration in his voice as he said the word. It wasn't one I'd have thought he approved of: What had his life been dedicated to, after all, but to certainty—to equations, formulas, the tools of quantification?

Uncertainty. I thought of his struggles over the past few years with ill health: a run-in with prostate cancer, with shingles, an emergency appendectomy the year before in the middle of the night (*Your father said it was just indigestion, but I knew there was something wrong and I made him drive to the ER*, Mother had said when telling the story, and indeed she had been right): afflictions that he'd endured so quietly that it had never occurred to me to wonder whether he had begun to be afraid of what might be next, of the uncertainty that lay ahead. Did he lie awake at night working out some algorithm, some way of calculating his own chances?

Daddy, I said.

What?

I took a breath. Are you afraid of dying?

I was surprised by how swiftly he answered. He frowned a little—not at me, but the way he did when confronted by some knotty problem, a crossword puzzle or a tax return or a set of instructions for assembling some piece of furniture that didn't make sense to him.

I'm not afraid of *being* dead, he said. At that point there's no consciousness. You're out of the woods.

I grinned.

But he was serious. It's the lead-up to dying that I'm . . .

His voice trailed off, and I realized he didn't like to say the word "afraid."

That I'm concerned about, he finally said. Falling apart, being diminished. Not being all there. You remember what my mother was like at the end.

I remembered. Nanny Kay had had Alzheimer's, although in the seventies people didn't have a name for it. But my father knew that whatever was wrong with her wasn't just "hardening of the arteries," as people said back then when their parents grew forgetful. I still remember the expression on his face when, during what would be his mother's last visit to us, she turned to him and said, And who are *your* parents?

I don't want to get like that, he said. Being dead itself can't be bad. It's just nothing. Zero. But what happened to your grandmother—that's worse, as far as I'm concerned. Worse than zero.

A negative number? I joked.

Yeah, he said, although he wasn't smiling. Then he said, So, yes, you want to keep going, keep doing things. But doing things as *yourself*, not as some kind of zombie.

He looked down again. I knew he was thinking about his mother, what people kept saying as her illness took its toll. *Kay had been so clever, Kay had been sharp! This isn't Kay, it's someone else. She's not herself anymore.*

We stood there for a while, not saying anything. Finally I cleared my throat. Anyway, I guess that's what I meant earlier today when the captain made the announcement and I said I liked the idea of not getting to actually see Odysseus' island—you know, the "infinitely receding horizon." It's *literally* poetic—it's the exact idea behind the Tennyson and Cavafy. By not getting to see Odysseus' home, we've kept the ending at bay. The story can go on and on. And how perfect is it that we substituted the poem "Ithaca" for the place Ithaca. It reenacts the whole point of the Cavafy.

After a pause he said, So I was right all along!

His voice was sly; the somber mood had evaporated.

Right about what?

The poem actually is more real than the place!

The next day, we flew home.

NOSTOS

(Homecoming)

———⊰∘∘⊱———

APRIL

νόστος, ὁ [*nostos*]: 1. *Return;* οἱ νόστοι [*nostoi*], *the return* of the heroes from Troy, the title of several poems now lost.

νόστιμος [*nostimos*, the adjective derived from *nostos*: "like a *nostos*"]: *essential, valuable, perfect, the best part of anything*

—E. A. SOPHOCLES, *Greek Lexicon of the Roman and Byzantine Periods (from* B.C. *146 to* A.D. *1100)*

The second half of the *Odyssey*—which, as Don Quixote Tom had observed once, feels half as long as the first, such is the momentum of its precipitous revenge plot— is structured around a series of reunions that escalate in emotional impact as they accumulate: Odysseus and his island, Odysseus and his loyal servants, Odysseus and his son, his wife, his father. But since the moment I encountered it when I read the *Odyssey* for the first time in high school, the reunion between Odysseus and Telemachus, in Book 16, has particularly moved me.

This is, in fact, the point at which the two narratives of the *Odyssey*, the one focused on Telemachus, the son, and the other on Odysseus, the father, finally converge. Books 13 and 14 focus on the father. The first describes the long-awaited moment of Odysseus' return, which is curiously anticlimactic: among other things, he is sound asleep when the Phaeacians finally deposit him on the Ithacan shore, along with the hoard of treasure they've given him, locked in the chest sealed with Circe's special knot. A moment of humor attends his awakening a little later on: because Athena has shrouded the coastline in a concealing mist, he doesn't recognize his home when he finally gets there. "Alas," he exclaims upon waking, "what kind of people have I stumbled upon this time—savage or civilized?" This is the first instance of the theme of disguise and recognition that becomes ever more complex as the second half of the epic proceeds. (Soon after Odysseus confronts Athena in Book 13, she gives him the appearance of a withered old man, a disguise that will allow him to stick to Agamemnon's advice to return home in secret.) In Book 14, on Athena's advice, the hero makes his way to the hut of a swineherd called Eumaeus, who, she assures him, is the most loyal of those servants whom he left behind; meanwhile, she'll fetch Telemachus back from Sparta.

Book 15 finally picks up a narrative thread that has been left dangling since the end of Book 4—Telemachus' visit to Helen and Menelaus in Sparta—and starts to twine it around the story of Odysseus' return to Ithaca. As this book opens, Athena appears to the young prince, whom "anxious care for his absent father" has kept awake all night after the banquet during which Menelaus and Helen had traded their stories about the Trojan War. Athena materializes before Odysseus' son and chides him for lingering so long in Sparta (never mind that it was she who sent him there in the first place); the news she proceeds to share with him suggests how urgent it is that he return. For the situation with the Suitors, she says, has become more dramatic: by this point Penelope's father and brothers, convinced that Odysseus is dead, have begun to urge her to marry Eurymachus, the suavest of the young men who court the queen. Electrified by this information, Telemachus attempts to extricate himself from Menelaus' hospitality. The Spartan king insists that there must be a grand farewell meal followed by the bestowal of lavish guest gifts, but Telemachus politely refuses, pleading the urgency of his mission home. (You have a strong sense in this charming scene that Menelaus' reluctance to let his old comrade's son leave stems in part from nostalgia for the old days, and perhaps even more from the fact that he's a little bit lonely in his opulent palace.) In the end, Menelaus does manage to press some choice presents on his restless guest; Telemachus, we realize—just like his father—will return home to Ithaca laden with valuables. After Telemachus leaves Sparta, he and Peisistratus return to Pylos; the two friends say their farewells and Telemachus boards a ship for home. The action then returns to Odysseus and the faithful swineherd, Eumaeus, sitting down to supper in the elderly servant's hut.

There is something almost cinematic about the way the action of Book 15 keeps cutting between Odysseus and his son, as if to pique our impatient eagerness for the two to meet, for the two threads to be tied together at last. Now, as Odysseus and Eumaeus break bread, the hero—his wily mind never at rest, his penchant for trickery by now curdling, it seems, into something more sinister, a reflexive inability to trust, to take anything at face value—decides to test Eumaeus' loyalty, despite Athena's earlier assurances that the old man has remained faithful to his absent master. Odysseus loudly declares that it's time for him to leave the hut and stop taking advantage of the swineherd's hospitality; he'll go down to town and try his luck begging at the royal palace, or offering his services as a household servant ("few men can vie with me in know-how!"). Eumaeus, aghast, won't hear of it—not least because the situation in the palace is so tense and the Suitors so cruel. "Or perhaps you're hell-bent on dying," he exclaims, "seeing that you want to head down there and mingle with the Suitors, whose arrogance and violence reach the iron sky!" Odysseus stays put, and the two men swap life stories over the firelight—although the one Odysseus shares is, of course, a tall tale: he still hasn't revealed his true identity. He pretends to be from Crete, a man of high birth who, after fighting at Troy, was subsequently ruined by the headlong foolishness of his ill-disciplined men, forced to throw himself on the mercy of a kindly king, kidnapped and imprisoned, and finally shipwrecked on Ithaca: a tale that borrows heavily from his own adventures. This is one of several so-called Cretan tales, elaborate lies that Odysseus tells to various characters upon his return home in order to wheedle or cajole or charm them into getting things that he needs.

Book 15 ends with a final glimpse of Telemachus, whose ship has reached Ithaca at last. Upon his return he, too, makes his way to the hut of the swineherd—who, Homer tells us, has been like a father to the lad during Odysseus' long absence.

In Book 16 the true father and his son finally meet.

On the mid-April morning when we discussed Book 16, Don Quixote Tom—who had asked me, recently, to call him Tommy ("it's what my parents call me")—raised his hand.

What I like about this book is how similar the father and son are by this point. It's interesting that both Telemachus and Odysseus do the very same things when they get back to Ithaca. They both come home with treasures. They both arrive in secrecy. They both go to the swineherd's hut. It's like there's a parallelism between them now. So I would say that *this* moment is really the end of the Telemachy. We see that the boy is now grown up. He's become a match for his father.

I paused to think about this. That's a great point, I said.

What *I* liked is the thing with the dogs in Book 16, Madeline said.

What she was referring to was this: At the beginning of Book 14, when Odysseus (who, following Athena's transformation of him, is to all appearances nothing more than a wizened old beggar) approaches Eumaeus' hut, he is nearly killed by the swineherd's snarling guard dogs, escaping only because he sinks down to the ground and drops his beggar's staff until he's rescued by Eumaeus, who tells him that he's lucky to be alive. "One moment more and these dogs would have torn you to pieces!" But when Telemachus makes his way to Eumaeus' hut at the beginning of Book 16, the hounds that had nearly killed his father simply fawn on him: "not a growl as he approached." The youth is known here, is welcome, in a way that his father, gone for so many years that this new generation of dogs does not know him, is not.

Madeline said, It's one of the things that reminds you that Odysseus has become a stranger in his own land.

As we discussed this scene, I couldn't help looking over at my father, who was wincing, as I knew he'd be. My siblings and I had long known where his fear of dogs came from, although I don't recall having ever bothered to learn the details of his famous childhood encounter with the rabid dog. It was just part of the background of his life, like the Bronx or the Mets or Mother; although for me, when I was young, the idea that he could ever have been a victim, or just a frightened little boy, was shocking, incomprehensible. Only quite recently did I actually bother to investigate the story, asking my siblings what they remembered about it. Perhaps because he was the oldest and had heard more long ago, Andrew said he remembered it very clearly: Daddy had been bitten by a rabid dog and had had to have those horrible shots with the long, long needles. Matt said he thought the whole thing might be apocryphal, that Daddy had just been afraid of dogs and that was that. (Had we been talking about Grandpa, my mother's father, I would have considered that possibility, but after all we were talking about Daddy, who didn't just make up stories about his life for the entertainment value.) Anyway, I always think of my father when I read the passages about Eumaeus' hounds and how differently they react to Odysseus and Telemachus, to the father and the son.

The dogs' failure to recognize Odysseus looks forward to, and is pointedly contrasted with, one of the best-known moments in the epic. In Book 17, Odysseus, accompanied by his loyal servant, finally makes his way to the gates of his palace, which he plans to infiltrate. As he passes by, a mangy dog lying on a dung heap outside the palace walls pricks up its ears: this, we are told, is the loyal hound Argos, which Odysseus had trained as a puppy and which now, like his master, has been made unrecognizable by the passing years—"an object of revulsion, his master long since gone." And yet the dog miraculously recognizes Odysseus:

> *But when he sensed that Odysseus was close by*
> *he wagged his tail and lay his ears down flat,*
> *but no longer had the strength to come to his Master . . .*

Constrained by his need to protect his disguise, Odysseus can't let on that he knows the dog: the sole, unbearably poignant sign of his repressed inner emotion is a single tear that trickles down his cheek, which he takes pains to conceal from Eumaeus. And just then, Homer says,

> *Death's darkness then took hold of Argos, who*
> *had seen Odysseus again, after twenty years.*

This moment of recognition, with its implication that there is some inner quality in Odysseus that has remained intact despite the passage of years and the hardships he's endured, in turn looks forward to his subsequent confrontations with Penelope, who will sense, in the beggar who has come to the palace, something familiar . . .

The three scenes with the dogs—the dogs that nearly attack Odysseus in Book 14; the dogs that fawn on their beloved master, Telemachus, in Book 16; and the wrenching telepathy between Argos and Odysseus in Book 17—are, in fact, designed to frame the recognition scene between Odysseus and his son in Book 16: to raise questions about how we recognize who someone is, and what true recognition means.

Athena carefully engineers this climactic encounter between the father and the son. Waiting for an opportune moment when Eumaeus is gone, she signals to Odysseus that she wishes to speak with him. Leaving Telemachus inside the hut, he comes into the yard where Athena is waiting, and there she announces that the time has come for his son to know him:

> *Godlike seed of Laertes, Odysseus of the many wiles,*
> *now at last the time has come to tell your son the truth;*
> *hold back no longer as you plan death and vengeance for the*
>   *Suitors . . .*

Waving her golden wand, the goddess makes Odysseus handsome and young and strong again: in fact, just the way he must have looked when he left his infant son to fight at Troy, beardless, tanned, and carefree. When he returns to the hut, Telemachus is terrified by the transformation. It's clear that the old beggar is no ordinary mortal—perhaps even a god in disguise. ("Be gracious . . . spare us!" the young man cries.) It is then that Odysseus reveals himself. "No god am I," he declares,

> *but your own father, because of whom*
> *you've had your share of tears, and suffered much,*
> *endured the outrages inflicted by grown men.*

At first, Telemachus recoils in disbelief when Odysseus declares who he is. This rejection reminds us of the vehemence with which, in the first few books of the epic, he had kept dismissing the notion that his father could still be alive:

> *No—you're not Odysseus, my father, but some spirit*
> *is bewitching me, that I may lament my woes more loudly.*
> *For no mortal man could ever contrive such tricks*
> *by his own devices, not unless some god came down*
> *intent on making him either young or old.*
> *Just now you were old and wrapped in rags,*
> *but now you look like the gods who rule the wide heavens.*

To this exclamation, Odysseus makes an oddly unsatisfying, almost legalistic reply. "No other Odysseus is ever going to come here," he tells his son, "but I am such a one as he." As for his transformation, that, he says, is indeed Athena's work; the gods can do anything, after all. It's at this point that Telemachus breaks down and embraces his father, who then dissolves in tears, too, the two of them "shrilly weeping," Homer says, like birds of prey whose nests have been plundered by farmers. It is a peculiar, even disturbing simile: the simultaneous characterization of them as both victims and predators points ahead to the murderous destruction that this touching father-son reunion sets in motion.

This stilted scene, the initial moment of resistance followed by the exaggeratedly hot tears and ending with that sinister simile, stands in stark contrast to the reunion with which, in fact, Book 16 had begun. For we are told that, when Telemachus first approached the hut, not only the hounds but Eumaeus himself had fawned on him affectionately:

> The swineherd started up,
> and dropped the bowls he'd been toiling over
> as he mixed the ruddy wine. He went to his master,
> and kissed his head and both his shining eyes,
> both his hands; and then he shed hot tears.
> Just as a father, brimming with love, might greet his son
> who's come home from distant lands after ten long years,
> his darling only child for whom he's suffered much;
> so then the beaming swineherd greeted godlike Telemachus,
> covering him with kisses, like someone saved from death.

It's just after this that Eumaeus and Telemachus enter the hut and the youth is introduced to the "beggar," who then sits quietly as his son and the swineherd talk at length. (His cool ability to contain himself at this first glimpse of the son he'd left behind twenty years later is another example of the unsettling, almost superhuman willpower that Odysseus is able to exert when necessary: hard experience has taught him not to show his hand too early.) Only after Eumaeus sets off for the palace to inform Penelope that her son has returned safely from his educational travels does Athena appear to reveal the father to his son.

A few hours after the previous class session ended I'd posted a question to the online discussion board asking the students to think about why the reunion between the father and son was the first in the series that structures the second half of the *Odyssey*. Why, I asked them, didn't it have a more climactic position? Why, indeed, would the father-son reunion come *before* Odysseus' reunion with his dog (which takes place in the next book, Book 17)? Not a single student had responded to my query online. In fact, none had commented on the reunion scene at all.

Still, when we discussed the two passages in class the next day, it was clear that they'd noticed a great deal.

Madeline said, The emotion is so *real* here. It shows that Eumaeus has been a father figure to Telemachus his whole life. You can tell that *he's* been the real mentor figure, way before Athena comes to Ithaca in Book 1 as Mentes, and then later as Mentor.

Brendan said, Homer pretty much tells you how to interpret the whole book. When Telemachus comes to Eumaeus, it's a real homecoming, and the simile compares him to an actual father, but when he's reunited with Odysseus he's compared to a bird of prey.

Trisha looked up. There's a kind of hysteria in the scene between the biological father and son, she said. It's almost like they're overcompensating.

I was impressed.

Overcompensating for what, do you think?

She said, For the fact that the emotion between them is sort of . . . abstract. It's what fathers and sons *should* feel. But with Eumaeus, it's real.

That's a really great observation, I said. So now take that idea and push it one step further, so you can answer the question I asked last week: Why is the Odysseus-Telemachus reunion the first reunion in the poem, the least emphasized?

Jack raised his hand.

No jokes! I said.

No, I promise, he said. I think it's because you sort of have to take it all on faith. They've never really known each other, Telemachus was just a baby when he left. So . . .

He stopped then, looking sheepish.

So *what*? I said. Yes, the emotion in the scene is abstract; yes, Telemachus has to take Odysseus on faith. What does it add up to?

I looked around the room.

It was Brendan who broke the silence, and the point he went on to make forced me to wonder—not for the first time since he'd speculated, during our discussion of Book 3, that maybe Telemachus was unconsciously hoping that Odysseus was dead—what his relationship with his father was like. Brendan said, If you never knew your father to begin with, there's actually nothing to *recognize*.

My father had been curiously quiet through all of this, and he remained quiet as the kids collected their books and backpacks and filtered out of the room. That morning, as we were having coffee at my place, I'd asked him if he wanted to stay over that evening, but he said he'd already bought his ticket for the two o'clock train down to New York. Again I thought how odd it was that he was suddenly so eager to take the train. Now, as the crowd of students in the seminar room thinned out, I noticed Madeline hanging back, as if she wanted to talk to me. So I was surprised when it turned out she was waiting to talk to my father.

She looked at both of us and then turned to him. I'll pick you up at Professor Mendelsohn's house at one-thirty?

She'd cut her hair, I noticed; the shimmering curtain had become a sporty bob. She looks older, I thought.

Yup, my father said. Thanks!

I looked from my father to Madeline.

She blushed. I ran into your father last week on the train, she said. I go down on Fridays to have my cello lessons in the city. So I said I'd take him to the station if he wanted to. I figured it'd save you a trip?

My father hadn't mentioned it.

Fine with me! I said. Thanks, Madeline. You know where my place is?

Yeah, she said, your dad told me.

See you in about an hour, my father said. He was jaunty.

I gathered up my books, and we walked to the faculty parking lot.

As I mentioned, my father had said little in class that day about the reunion between Odysseus and Telemachus. But we had talked about it at length the evening before, over dinner at Flatiron.

I'm looking forward to tomorrow, I'd said. Book 16 is one of my favorite books. What did *you* think? The reunion scene?

At that moment, he spit the piece of steak he'd been chewing onto the side of the plate.

Oh, come *on*, Daddy, I sputtered. Jesus. *Really.*

What? he barked, halfway between defensive and irritated. It was all gristle! He glared at me.

My father's heedless table manners were a perennial embarrassment to my mother and us. But what could we do? As he slurped his soup or coffee, making the *zhupping* noise my mother had stopped bothering to complain about years ago, we would groan, *Daaaaad!!!* But he wouldn't reply. Instead, he would tuck his head deeper into his collar, turtlelike, making you feel slightly girlish for noticing things like *table manners*. When I was at college in the South, I was particularly embarrassed by my father's manners, which would be hard to conceal on those occasions when my parents and I would join my roommates and their families for meals at local country clubs or in expensive restaurants, meals that would be hosted by my Southern roommates' fathers, the broad-faced drawling lawyers from Memphis or the seersuckered department-store owners from Chattanooga, the foxily elegant businessmen from Savannah whose families were "in shipping"—men to whom, with their neat creases and suave manners and exaggerated politeness to my mother, whose beauty they would flirtatiously remark on, I would gravitate. Of these I was drawn to one in particular: the heavy-browed father of a roommate from Houston, a successful architect who, every time he and his wife would come to Virginia to visit their son, loved to take eight or ten of us undergraduates to dinner at the most expensive restaurant in town, quizzing us about the courses we were taking with an exaggerated self-deprecation, as if to say that our studies were way above his capacity to understand, regaling us with amusing Faulknerian stories of his childhood in Mississippi, tales that suggested that he himself was a bit dazzled by the life he had ended up having, although the thing I secretly envied was not the opera or the Petroleum Club or the ocean liners but the easy relationship he had with his handsome son, my friend. This man, to whom I eventually grew very close, would become the most recent in a line of mentors to whom I felt an urgent need to attach myself: men who, it seemed to me, were far more appropriate candidates to father me, with my strange enthusiasms and exotic hobbies, the Fabergé eggs and the hieroglyphics, than my own father had ever been, tinkering endlessly with the transmissions of his failing cars, making the repeated trips to Radio Shack in order to keep the clock radio, with its bisected numerals flicking every minute like shutters, alive for a few months longer.

And so I had found, again and again, alternatives to my father; had found mentors. There was the high-school music teacher who, when I was fourteen, thought nothing of driving me three hours to listen to a concert of the early music that I loved at that point in my life. There was, a bit later, another music teacher who, in his time off from school, directed the choir of a nearby church, which he cajoled me into joining. Sometimes, after rehearsals, this man used to take me to the only French restaurant, I suppose, in the whole county, where he would impress me by ordering in French. My parents cultivated this man as a friend, I suspect to make a show of how much they trusted him, since back then it was not necessarily the case that parents would let their adolescent children spend unsupervised days with music teachers who were known to have "roommates." When he came to our house, he would sit down on the floor of my mother's living room and caress the wall-to-wall carpet and say, *There's nothing like wool,* and my mother flushed with pleasure at his connoisseur's appreciation of her otherwise-underappreciated decor.

Best of all was the fine-boned, olive-skinned, cigarette-voiced German teacher who took me under his wing when I was in my mid-teens and had moved from the junior high school to the high school. *Fred.* On weekends when he took me sailing out of Huntington Harbor on the big wooden boat captained by his "cousin," Horst, the two of them blasting Wagner from an onboard Bang & Olufsen stereo, Fred would sometimes hand me a glass of Burgundy or an old brandy. *Can you smell that dark sweetness at the center?* he would say, watching intently as I sipped, and I would say, embarrassed by my ignorance, *Like a berry?* and his dour grayish features would relax into a weary smile and he would raise both hands heavenward, like someone giving thanks to heaven for some unexpected reprieve from a cruel fate, and say, Ah, *Mr. Mendelsohn, there is hope for you yet!* And I suppose there was. From him I learned most of the rudiments of what I know about opera, music, dance, and literature, not least because after I turned fifteen and had, I suppose, showed myself an apt pupil, Fred and Horst quietly added me to their subscriptions to the New York City Opera, the Metropolitan Opera, the Philharmonic, the New York City Ballet, the Lincoln Center Theater. With a secret thrill I would linger on certain afternoons, after classes had ended, in front of the entrance of the high school until Fred and Horst roared up in their pale bronze-colored Volvo sports car. We would tear into Manhattan, hydroplaning past the acres of cemeteries that extended as far as you could see on either side of the Long Island Expressway in Queens, rattling across the Queensboro Bridge, coming to a screeching halt in the garage under Lincoln Center, into which we would finally ascend, the three of us, to see the opera or the theater, which are, not coincidentally, things I now write about.

It was from Fred that I understood that beauty and pleasure are at the center of teaching. For the best teacher is the one who wants you to find meaning in the things that have given him pleasure, too, so that the appreciation of their beauty will outlive him. In this way—because it arises from an acceptance of the inevitability of death—good teaching is like good parenting.

It never occurred to me when I was young, first in my teens and then in my twenties and even into my early thirties, that my fierce attachments to these other, more sophisticated father figures, the evident pleasure with which I went off with Fred and Horst and the others, the constant references, when I was in college, to my roommate's architect father, might have any emotional effect on my own father—perhaps because I was accustomed to the idea that my father wasn't very emotional about anything. His seeming coldness, I told myself at the time, was indeed

one of the many reasons I needed these other, warmer, more demonstrative men; another of those reasons being my father's lack of finesse,
for instance the atrocious table manners of which I had always been
ashamed.

At Flatiron that night, the night before we discussed Telemachus'
reunions with Eumaeus and with Odysseus, the night before Brendan
made his *scathingly brilliant* point about why a reunion with a family
member you don't actually know that well can't really be a recognition,
my father noisily chewed his next mouthful of steak. Finally I mastered
my irritation and asked him again what he'd thought about Book 16.

Well, as you *know*, I'm not a big fan of Odysseus. But I have to say that
this time, I was impressed by his self-control.

"Self-control"? You mean, in the scene with Telemachus?

I assumed he was referring to how Odysseus keeps his cool in the
face of Telemachus' initial rejection, once he has revealed his identity. I
thought, Typical of Daddy to focus on *that*.

No, *no*, he said. Earlier. *Before* he tells his son.

I couldn't think what he was talking about.

Before, my father repeated. When he's still in disguise and the son
walks in and has the big reunion with the peasant guy.

The swineherd, I corrected him reflexively.

The swineherd. Whatever, he's a peasant, you know what I *mean*.

He was quiet for a minute and then said, slowly, Anyway, I thought
that was admirable.

"Admirable"?

My father looked at his plate. He said, It must have been hard for him
to have to sit there watching while his own son acted like that other guy
was his real father.

As the action of the *Odyssey* begins to move toward its conclusion, Homer's plot and Odysseus' plotting become inseparable.

After the reunion with Telemachus, Odysseus and the loyal swineherd (who still doesn't know who his guest really is) make their way
from the countryside into the center of town, where, at the beginning of
Book 17, Odysseus sets about infiltrating his own palace. Gaining access
to the royal hall by pretending to be an itinerant beggar, he finally wit-
nesses firsthand the outrages that have fallen on his home and family for
so long: the gluttonous Suitors dining uproariously in his hall, treating
his young son with patronizing disdain; his besieged wife hiding upstairs
in her rooms. Once he has insinuated himself into the banquet hall,
Athena urges him to make the rounds of the Suitors, begging each for a
crust of bread, "to see which ones are respectful, and which are wicked."
Some, indeed, are kind, giving him scraps from the table; but Antinoüs,
their leader, reacts to the presence of the beggar whom Eumaeus has
brought into the great hall with alarming condescension and contempt:

> *Listen, Milord Swineherd—why have you brought this . . .*
> *thing into town? Haven't we enough of beggars, then,*
> *irritating moochers who lay waste to every meal?*
> *It's not enough they gather here and eat*
> *your absent master out of house and home—you have*
> *to go and ask another to join in?*

Just as Antinoüs' name means "anti-mind," so do his actions mark
him as "anti-hospitality": an emblem of the worst extremes of the Suitors'
blasphemous disregard for the laws of guest-host relations. That this is so
becomes clear in the retort the swineherd Eumaeus—whom Antinoüs
has jeeringly referred to with a sarcastic "milord"—makes: "Antinoüs,
you who are so wellborn have spoken ill." He acts ill, too: when Odysseus
reaches Antinoüs and begs a scrap of food from him, the haughty Suitor
throws a footstool at him. (Homer tells us that, despite the pain, Odysseus "just stood there like a rock, silently shaking his head / and churning
bloody deeds within his mind.") Even some of the Suitors are shocked

by the behavior of Antinoüs, whom they remind that sometimes the gods themselves descend to earth disguised as beggars in order to test men's character.

Odysseus' testing of the Suitors inspired a small debate when we discussed Books 17 and 18 on an unseasonably chilly morning toward the end of April. After the contretemps with Antinoüs, Odysseus is comforted by a Suitor named Amphinomus, the kindest of the young men courting Penelope and the one who, Homer says, "pleased Penelope best"—perhaps because of certain things he has in common with Odysseus. ("She liked his words—a man who had his wits about him.") In an extraordinary moment, Odysseus takes this Amphinomus aside and tries to warn him to leave the palace and abandon the arrogant men who have ravaged the household and insulted the wife of a great hero—who, he declares, will soon be returning home:

> *May some Power*
> *spirit you home, save you from encountering him*
> *when he returns at last to his dear fatherland:*
> *for I doubt that he and all of you will part company*
> *bloodlessly, once he's home again.*

It's a measure of the urgency Odysseus feels in warning the kindly young man that he nearly gives his disguise away: when he first approaches Amphinomus, he tells the young Suitor that he looks like a sensible man, "just like your father"—a gaffe he swiftly covers up ("or so I have heard him praised"). Although Amphinomus is deeply disturbed by the old beggar's words, he cannot bring himself to leave the room. For by now, the poet darkly tells us, "Athena had already fettered him to his fate"—doomed, Homer reveals, to be killed by Telemachus during the imminent slaughter.

Brendan was puzzled by all this.

We know that Amphinomus is the best of the Suitors, and even Odysseus tries to save him. But it's like he can't get away from his fate because of Athena. If it weren't for her, Amphinomus would have fled the palace and been spared. So why would Athena prevent his escape? Are we supposed to think that Amphinomus, even though we're told he's so nice, has already crossed far beyond some "point of no return" just because he was using up the livestock and wine in Odysseus' palace?

I looked down the long seminar table and said, Okay, now I *promise* I'm not trying to push you toward my conclusions here, but Brendan is on the verge of something I think is really important. Can I just *nudge* you a little?

There were some chuckles. Good, I thought, at least we're over that.

I said, Okay, now, Brendan is wondering why Amphinomus, who's otherwise characterized as the "nice" Suitor, is punished along with the others "just" because he's party to the Suitors' ravaging of Odysseus' household. I want to question his use of the word "just" here. In fact, haven't we been given information from day one that this is a big deal?

Jack said, "Day one"?

Yes, I said. Think of the proem.

Madeline thrust her hand in the air. Oh, I *get* it!

I said, Go on.

The Cattle of the Sun! Madeline said loudly. You keep talking about how it's the only one of Odysseus' adventures to be mentioned in the proem, how they ate the cows and sheep, and they all had to die. So we know it's important—you know from the start that this is a big deal, how eating something you've been told not to eat gets this really vicious punishment. So it's like what happens to the Suitors, that they all have to be killed, even the nice ones, is foreshadowed all along.

Jack said, I still think it's pretty harsh.

My father suddenly chimed in from his corner. No. A crime is a crime. If you've done wrong, you've done wrong. There's no gradations (his voice soured on the word *gradations*, and I knew what he was thinking: moral gradations were like sloppy arithmetic, that it was a contradiction in terms)—there's no gradations in breaking the law. It's either not broken or it's broken! That's what justice is.

Jack looked over at my father. Rough justice!

My father looked at him and grunted. It's a rough world, he said.

Some of the kids found this funny, although I was struck once more by how greatly he cherished the notion that the world was rough, by the bitter satisfaction with which he would flourish the story of some "little guy" who'd been broken by life, or fate, or bad luck. The roughness of the world, I knew, was what justified his own rough justice: the inflexible application of severe standards of honesty and of intellectual performance to himself, to his friends, to us. You had to be tough. The world didn't compromise, after all, so why should you?

All of this came up recently when I was talking about my father with Andrew, who had come out to New York from California with Ginny and their kids. It was high summer, and we were all sitting outside my house on the edge of the Bard campus, drinking white wine. At some point we'd been chatting about our brother Matt, who more than any of the rest of us shares my father's outraged sensitivity to injustice, as if it were a trait transmitted by a gene. We like to tease Matt about his Facebook page, for instance, the postings that oscillate between indignant denunciations of corrupt world leaders, violent cops, or indifferent fellow citizens and links to wrenching stories of heartbreak or stoicism, stranded pets and improbable rescues. Often, as I read Matt's posts about the decline of the national character, it's my father's voice that I hear in my head.

So Andrew and I were talking about Matt, which, because he resembles our father so greatly in certain respects, soon led us to reminisce about Daddy, too.

It's hilarious, I said at one point. Daddy had that same thing—justice! Unfairness! The oppressed little guy!

Ginny brushed back a lock of bright red hair. Your father did have that, she said in her clear voice. Outrage for the downtrodden!

Yeah, Andrew said a little sourly. And then he added, Well, no wonder.

No wonder what? I said.

No wonder he was always so outraged by that stuff, Andrew said. It all goes back to the thing with the dog.

The thing with the *dog*? I stared at him. What the fuck are you talking about?

You know! The dog, the rabid dog. You know that story.

He held up his glass appraisingly. Andrew knows a lot about wines. Like the rest of us, in our different ways, he has benefited from my father's conviction that the world is available to anyone who does the work to know and learn it—although, since nothing about my father's childhood could have suggested that the world would be an easy place for him to know and learn, in his case that conviction was really nothing more than blind hope. Sometimes when I think about my father's early years, about his fanatical pursuit of education, I imagine him as a ship-wrecked man who swims wildly in the direction of a shore that, he must believe, is out there somewhere. The confidence we have in our ability to enjoy what is in the world, country music and oenophilia, species rhododendra and Shelley teacups, Jewish genealogy and Greek syntax, vintage posters and Jacques Demy, is, I now see, a kind of ironic birthright from our father, who showed us that it could be thus, as his own father had not done for him.

You know, Andrew said again. The rabid dog.

I said, All I ever heard was that Daddy was bitten by a rabid dog when he was little and had to have those horrible shots in his stomach, and that's why he was afraid of dogs. But how on earth is that connected to his thing about unfairness?

I paused, then added, Anyway, Matt said he thought it was all a myth.

Andrew shook his head impatiently. I couldn't be sure whether he was irritated with me, for not having faith that the story was true, or with Matt, for having suggested it wasn't.

No, *no,* he said, it's true. Dad told me the whole story once. He was little and some neighbor's dog bit him really badly, and so Nanny Kay had to take him on, like, three different buses to a hospital. And then when they got to the hospital, the doctors wanted to know if they knew the dog and who it belonged to, and Daddy said, sure he knew whose dog it was. So they had a couple of cops contact the neighbor, the one whose dog had bitten him, but when they confronted her she lied and said she didn't have a dog and didn't know what they were talking about! Dad being a little kid, of course they believed the neighbor. And because the doctors at the hospital couldn't officially ascertain the identity of the dog, they had to go on the presumption that it was rabid, just in case. *That's why he had to get the shots in his stomach.* He said it was every other day for two weeks, something like that.

It was late afternoon. Around us, insects hummed and buzzed.

Dad said the needles were really long, Andrew went on. And he told me that the whole time this was going on he was crying. *Not because of the pain*—

(when Andrew said "not because of the pain" I knew he was quoting my father verbatim)

—but because he knew for a fact whose dog it was. But the neighbor lied and so nobody believed him.

He paused.

You can imagine the effect that had on him. The outrage! The injustice! The—well, you know Dad.

Yeah, I said. I know Dad.

Andrew looked at me. You didn't know that story?

Nope. I never heard it until now.

He looked noncommittal. Hmmm, he finally said. I guess he must have just told me.

Yeah, I said. I guess so.

A week after my father had observed, in response to Jack's complaint that the slaughter of the Suitors was "rough justice," that it was, after all, *a rough world*, we were discussing one of the major climaxes of the *Odyssey*: the scene in Book 19 when the faithful old nurse, Eurycleia, recognizes that the beggar is really Odysseus, having seen the telltale scar on his leg while bathing him. It was the last Friday in April, a beautiful warm morning. I was ebullient as my father and I walked into the classroom; we were, at last, going to be talking about this famous moment, which circles back from Odysseus' scar to a crucial history of his early days in the epic's most elaborate and significant example of "ring composition."

Penelope's growing sympathy for the beggar who has come to the palace sets this great scene in motion. By the end of Book 17, rumors about the unusual vagrant, together with reports of Antinoüs' disgraceful treatment of him, have reached the queen's ears, and she summons him to her chambers. The two finally meet at the beginning of Book 19. (Odysseus' encounters with the various Suitors and his exchanges with the villain Antinoüs and the doomed Amphinomus take up most of Book 18. Penelope shrewdly insists on meeting with the beggar later that evening in secret, after the Suitors and their henchmen have gone to bed.) The beggar and the queen talk late into the night. Pretending to be a Cretan prince down on his luck after the Trojan War—another of his Cretan tales, which so confusingly blur the boundaries between fact and fiction; Odysseus himself, as we know, being a king who's been down on his luck since the Trojan War—Odysseus insists to the queen that he has recently seen her long-lost husband, and that he is not only alive but about to return to Ithaca at long last. Since many travelers and guests have passed through Ithaca's palace over the years claiming to have news of Odysseus, he demonstrates his bona fides by describing a certain brooch that, he tells Penelope, Odysseus was wearing when they met. Of course the description is accurate, and on hearing it the queen dissolves in tears. Collecting herself at last, she declares to her maidservants that the beggar must be bathed and given decent clothes and a comfortable bed. He refuses at first, claiming that he's no longer accustomed to such luxuries and prefers to sleep on the floor, but he finally relents and allows the elderly nurse, Eurycleia, to bathe his feet. After remarking on the similarity between this stranger and her absent master—here Homer is winking at his audience, who know of course that the two men are one and the same—Eurycleia sets about her task. While doing so, she notices, with a start, a distinctive scar on the beggar's thigh—a scar that, she well knows, marks him as none other than Odysseus, and which he has forgotten to conceal.

At this suspenseful moment, the poet, rather than indulging his audience by providing an emotional scene of reunion between Odysseus and the nurse (who had, as we soon learn, been his childhood nurse) pauses the narrative and circles back in time to a series of flashbacks from Odysseus' early years. First he mentions how Odysseus got the scar. When he was a youth newly grown to manhood, he was wounded during a boar hunt that he participated in while visiting his mother's father, a notorious thief and trickster called Autolycus. (The name means something like "lone wolf.") Then, in order to explain why the young Odysseus happened to be visiting his grandfather in the first place, the narrator delves even further back in time to a moment long before the boar hunt: in fact, to the moment just after Odysseus' birth. Autolycus, we learn, had paid a visit to his daughter and her husband soon after the birth, and it was during this visit that the baby's young nurse—the very woman who, in the "now" of the *Odyssey*'s narrative, recognizes the grown man as he sits in the bath—insisted that Autolycus, an infamous "master of thievery and oaths," give the newborn a name. This is how it came to pass that this dishonest trickster of a grandfather, who had caused so much pain to others, became the author of Odysseus' strange name. In a fit of narcissistic preening, to which some grandfathers can indeed be prone, he gave his daughter's infant son a name best suited to himself: "the man of pain."

From this narrative ground zero, the crucial moment in the remote past that recalls how the hero's identity was first established, the story begins to climb gradually back to the surface again: to the moment when the now-elderly nurse recognizes the scar on the thigh of the beggar in the palace at Ithaca. And yet before arriving there, the narrator pauses to relate in greater detail the story of the boar hunt. Only after the extended description of the hunt do we finally reach once again the moment with which we began, when Eurycleia first recognizes the scar: a moment that by now has taken on a special burnish, has much greater significance than we might have thought possible, because we now have the history of the scar, and its owner, and his name.

On this warm late-April morning when we were to discuss Books 19 and 20, I was eager to get to the scar of Odysseus, which twines together so many of the *Odyssey*'s core themes: disguise and recognition, identity and suffering, narration and the passage of time. But once again it became clear to me how greatly the students' interests could differ from mine. Only Damien, the Belgian boy, had posted about Odysseus' scar. Perhaps, I thought, the fascination of the scene was greater for me, a writer, than it could be for them: ring composition, after all, being one elegant solution to a technical challenge facing anyone who wants to weave the distant past seamlessly into a narrative about the present. They were so young, I thought ruefully, their past was still so close to their present that there was no pressing need to figure out a way to reconnect them.

What they wanted to talk about was something that I don't even recall reacting to when I was their age, perhaps because it came under the heading of what I then dismissed as the "romantic" aspect of the epic. What the students wanted to talk about that morning was this: the fact that during his long conversation with his wife, the disguised Odysseus betrays little emotion at being so close to the woman he has spent twenty years trying to return to.

His unsettling reticence is already evident in Book 18. Just after Odysseus' fraught exchange with the doomed Amphinomus, Athena inspires Penelope to make an appearance before the Suitors

> *that she might fan a flutter in the Suitors' hearts*
> *and make herself more worthy in her husband's eyes,*
> *and in her son's, than she had been before.*

Before the queen goes downstairs, the goddess wafts a deep, reju-venating sleep over her, beautifying her, making her appear younger, causing her limbs to look "whiter than ivory." When the queen awakens, she dons her finest clothes and jewels and goes down to the great hall in order to display her renewed beauty to the Suitors—to show herself as a worthy potential bride. Dazzled—Homer tells us that they go "weak in the knees, as desire had bewitched them"—the Suitors shower her with gifts and compliments. To the glib praises of Eurymachus—"you surpass all women!"—Penelope modestly demurs, "the immortals took away my beauty, my form, when the Greeks set sail for Troy, and Odysseus with them . . ." She withdraws soon after to her chamber upstairs, her maids following her, bearing the fabulous jewels and robes the Suitors have given her.

Now Odysseus, we must remember, is witnessing all this. What does he feel when he glimpses her—what are his emotions on seeing the woman he has suffered so much to return to, for whom he rejected Calypso's offer of immortality? Is his heart bursting, breaking?

Homer doesn't say.

All that the poet tells us is that the disguised hero is thrilled to see his wife manipulating the Suitors into giving her presents:

> . . . *much-suffering, godlike Odysseus exulted*
> *since she'd wheedled gifts from them, charmed their hearts*
> *with her honeyed words; and meantime he was pondering other deeds.*

It may not be the reaction we expect, but it is, in fact, wholly in keep-ing with the poet's ongoing emphasis on a trait of Odysseus' that is of paramount importance to the plot of his epic: the hero's ability to keep his emotions in check in the pursuit of his larger goal. Had he erupted in tears, run toward his wife, he'd have betrayed his disguise and sacrificed the success of his mission. Another theme that this strange scene under-scores is that of *homophrosynê*. For in finagling the gifts out of the Suitors,

Penelope displays the same wiles practiced so often by her husband, the man who'd managed to end his sojourn among the Phaeacians loaded down with gifts, he who'd arrived on their island naked, a nobody. However much it may disappoint modern expectations of this fraught encounter, the scene of Odysseus' first glimpse of his wife reminds us of what has motivated this couple's actions for so long: they are a perfect match.

And now, in Book 19, Odysseus once again manages to remain in Penelope's presence—much closer, this time, as the two sit talking into the night—without betraying a flicker of emotion. At the moment when the "beggar" describes the brooch Odysseus was wearing when he saw him last, thereby proving that his tale is true and that, at least until recently, the hero was still alive, Penelope bursts into tears of despair, which run, Homer says, "like snows that melt from high-up mountain crags / snow heaped up by the cold West Wind and thawed out by the East . . ." But in contrast to her emotionality, Odysseus reveals nothing. Inwardly, Homer tells us, he grieves for his distraught wife, but "his eyes were as motionless beneath their lids / as if they'd been carved from horn or iron."

Here again, the supreme self-control.

It's after this conversation that Penelope insists the stranger be treated honorably, given a bath and a luxurious bed, leading to the scene with Eurycleia, the ring composition, and the scar. But the kids didn't want to talk about any of that; they wanted to talk about this scene, the scene before, the odd contrast between the curious atmosphere of nocturnal intimacy and Odysseus' refusal to be truly intimate when the moment seemed so right. Why, they wanted to know, couldn't he be more emotional?

I think it's inhuman, Jack blurted out that morning. There's this totally romantic setup, it's nighttime, the fire is burning, they're sitting *this* far apart—he held up his hand, thumb and forefinger an inch apart—and he does absolutely nothing. It's like he's made of stone! It was a real turnoff for me.

Nina smiled from under her dark bangs. Not made of *stone*, she said. "Horn or iron." It tells you right there.

My father said, He's doing what he has to do.

How? I asked. What does he have to do?

He has to see for himself that she's still faithful.

He looked over at Jack. I'm not so sure I would agree that the setting is so romantic. Or maybe it is for her, but not for him. For him it's an interview. He's testing her. He has to be careful.

I hesitated to reply. It's true that Odysseus—like us—is ever mindful of the fate of his comrade Agamemnon, slaughtered by his unfaithful wife upon his return. And yet by this point in the poem many readers will wonder just why he has to be so stony, so cautious. His testing of Penelope here—whose sly manipulation of the Suitors he has just delightedly witnessed, after all—begins to seem as superfluous as his testing of Eumaeus was in Book 14, after Athena herself had assured him of the swineherd's loyalty.

The emphasis in the first part of Book 19 on the hero's maniacal need to hold back, his off-putting ability to keep normal human impulses in check—the characteristic the students were so eager to condemn that day—is, in fact, cunningly connected to the story of the scar that dominates the latter part of this book, the part the students had no interest in. The scar, we remember, is the telltale sign that identifies Odysseus to Eurycleia, and its history deeply entwines the poem's themes of pain and identity: the hero's strange name, "the man of pain," is given to him at birth by Autolycus, the lone-wolf grandfather who'd caused so many people so much pain, and it is while visiting this same grandfather that he goes on the boar hunt during which he receives the wound that will become the scar. Which is to say, both of the things that identify Odysseus, the markers of who he is, his name and his scar, are connected to pain.

What's interesting is how he got the scar. Homer goes out of his way to emphasize how the youthful Odysseus behaved during the hunt—how, while the rest of the hunting party (his uncles, Autolycus' sons) hung back, he went ahead with the hounds:

> *The beaters reached a wooded combe; in front of them*
> *the hounds, who had the scent, raced on, but the sons*
> *of Autolycus hung back, godlike Odysseus nearby*
> *but closer to the dogs, wielding his shadow-casting spear . . .*

And when the boar lunges forth from his lair, the adolescent Odysseus rushes to meet him:

> *But Odysseus was by far the first*
> *to lunge, waving the long spear with his sturdy hand,*
> *desperate to score a hit; but the boar struck first . . .*

The great irony of Book 19, then, is that the scar that identifies Odysseus in such a memorable way, that proves who he is, is the visual symbol of a youthful act that is *not* typical of his adult behavior: the excessive caution, the guardedness, the willed reserve. Hence it identifies him (the scar proves that he is Odysseus, the person who went on the boar hunt and got himself wounded) while being, at the same time, a false identifier, the marker of a behavior that is no longer characteristic of him.

Do you see how great this is? I said excitedly to the kids that day. This is why the ring composition that spirals out from the bath and the scar isn't just some digression. It's crucial. If he got the wound by leading the pack when he was a teenager, but now, as we know, he likes to hang behind and suss out every situation before he gets into it, what does that mean?

My father didn't bother raising a hand. He simply called out, It means that in his life he's learned something.

Yes, I said. In his life, he does learn something, and this is the moment when we realize it. What does his having learned something mean for the poem as a whole?

Madeline didn't raise her hand, either. Tossing her head to the side so that her new red bob flipped a bit, she said, It means that Odysseus was once like Telemachus. Through the scar flashback, the *Odyssey* can be about the father's education, not just the son's.

Yes, I said again. Wonderful. Everything you've all said today is great.

Then I turned toward my father's corner and declared, See? Fathers can learn something, too.

They laughed.

In his life, he learned something.

Six months after we talked about Odysseus' scar in Book 19 and what it revealed about the hero's education, this phrase cropped up during a conversation I was having with Uncle Howard. During those months, I'd decided that I would seek out the two men to whom Daddy had been so close at one point or another: Howard and Nino. There were things I wanted to know about the past, not least things about my father's education; things I thought these two men in particular could tell me.

The living room of Howard's apartment in Queens was shadowy, the curtains drawn. It was October. A half-hearted drizzle had been misting the air as the express bus from midtown Manhattan made its way out to Queens, east along the gray parkways, past the airports and the cemeteries. His apartment was in a modest brick building on a major thoroughfare which, Howard had assured me when I was making the plans to visit that day, would be very easy to reach, and as he was explaining to me that *nothing could be easier!* and that the bus stopped *right in front of their entry!* I had a sudden sharp recollection of Claire talking excitedly about this very apartment building on the day thirty years before when she and Howard came over to announce that they were selling their house in the suburbs—the one to which I'd bicycled so many times in order to sit and listen to Segovia albums with Howard and drink Claire's potion-like "Spanish" coffee—in order to be closer to "the city." *Queens!* she had rasped that day, inhaling deeply on an extra-long cigarette, sitting with Howard on my mother's delicately flowered living room sofa, indifferently sipping pale brownish decaf out of blue-and-white mugs while my parents and brothers and I took in the news. *Queens!* Claire repeated.

It's perfect! We have the city in our front yard and the country in our back-yard! We all made approving noises, but none of us could really muster much enthusiasm: Queens was the borough I associated with my grand-parents and their siblings, the old people who would shuffle to their front doors when we visited from the suburbs, the one watery eye that they would press against the peephole until the doors opened and we were admitted to the dark, cavelike interiors.

So it was to Queens that I went that day. Howard opened the door. He was ninety-two and, not for the first time, he surprised me with his vigor, his nattiness. On this cool morning he was wearing a blue sports coat, a gray V-neck sweater over a button-down shirt, and a striped tie. His Errol Flynn mustache was neatly trimmed. Like my father, he had a habit of looking away, slightly downward, when you greeted him. We hugged awkwardly, and with a little sweeping movement of his left arm he indicated that I should pass through into the living room. The cur-tains were drawn, and the velvety darkness reminded me of the house I had known years before, when they lived so close to my parents. Claire had died a few months before; I'd gone to the funeral. *It's a good thing you didn't see her in the last couple of years,* Howard had said as we rode in the limo to the cemetery. *You wouldn't have recognized her . . . That wasn't her,* he'd added, shaking his head sadly. I walked past him into the shadowy apartment. In a little dining area off to the left at the far end of the living room there was a round table on which he had placed stacks of sandwiches and little plastic bowls of pickles, all sealed with tinted Saran Wrap. He must have gotten them from the deli. The olives had been speared with frilly toothpicks.

It was the only time I'd been here, apart from the morning of Claire's funeral. By the time she and Howard settled here, Daddy had stopped speaking to his brother. This was surprising, but not nearly as shocking as the fact that at the very moment my father ceased communicating with this gentle eldest brother, the only uncle we'd ever known, he had started speaking again to Bobby, whom he hadn't spoken to since we

were children. The polio had come back, my father said, as if this were
an explanation. In that family (my siblings and I would say soon after,
making the inevitable mathematics-themed joke) fraternal affection was
a zero-sum commodity.

But that was long since. Now I sat in the murky apartment talking
about Daddy, a conversation during which I heard some things I hadn't
known.

I asked Howard about their childhood, what he had been like. Where,
I began, had he gotten his notorious aversion to displays of physical affection from? Had their parents been like that—had Poppy Al been cold,
had Nanny Kay been aloof? Were they physically affectionate with each
other? Laughing, I remarked that I didn't think I'd ever seen my father
kiss my mother, or for that matter use any kind of endearment. The husbands of her best friends, the Gang of Four, were always calling their
wives "darling" and "hon" and "dear"; my father always addressed Mother
as "Marl." I never heard him say *I love you* to her—nor to any of us, for
that matter. I once asked him about this, and he said, Oh, *you* know I
don't go in for that stuff; which is why, I suppose, I go out of my way to say
those words to my own boys, at the end of phone calls or e-mails or texts,
in the way that children become the parents they wish they'd had . . .
Making a virtue of necessity, my mother turned the fact that my father
was, as she liked to say with a roll of her blue eyes, *undemonstrative* into
a source of humor—much as her father, the great raconteur and jokester,
might have done. Sometimes, when I was a teenager, she would position
herself at the top of the stairs just as my father got home from work and,
at the moment when he had trudged up the stairs and was passing by
her on the way to their bedroom without embracing her, she would cry
out stagily, as if fending off an amorous attack, *Jay, no! Not in front of
the children!* which would crack us up. He'd smile a tiny weary smile as
he headed to their room where the mail and bills were waiting for him
on the little wooden desk. Later on, when she had returned to teaching
elementary school, my mother would make a joke of excitedly asking her

colleagues each week if today were Tuesday. *Why do you want to know if it's Tuesday?* would come their reply, and Mother would say, *Because Jay lets me kiss him on Tuesdays!* Over time, my father's unwillingness or inability to display affection to my mother paradoxically became the vehicle for demonstrating his affection for her, his forgiveness for her needing signs of affection: one of those small jokes, indecipherable to others, that couples have, the symbols of a deep and secret intimacy. *In the afternoon I would go into his office where he was working on his computer and say to him, "Jay, my dearest darling, who is your greatest love?" and your father would answer, still looking at the computer screen, "Get the fuck out of here!"* My mother loved to repeat that anecdote.

I told Howard about my theory that Daddy's aversion to touching was the result of his claustrophobic childhood: the tiny room, the three young men, the shared foldout bed, above all the forced intimacy with Bobby and his illness. *I remember the sound his iron leg clamps made when he leaned them against the radiator.*

Howard listened patiently. When I finished, he said, Nah. No one was cramped. This thing is, your father was all alone in that apartment.

I blinked and said, But I thought you were all crowded into

No. Howard slowly shook his head, smiling the kindly, vaguely apologetic smile he'd smile when you erred about this or that, so different from the impatient grimace that would twist my father's features when you were wrong.

Remember, Howard said, I was already out of the house when your father was still a little boy. I was born in 1920 and I joined the armed forces in 1938. Your father was only nine or ten!

Nine, I said.

His voice trailed off a little sadly. Then he said, And of course my mother and father weren't there—

"Weren't there"? This was news to me. Why not?

Howard looked at me, surprised, I suppose, that I didn't know any of this: I, the family historian.

My father was an electrician, you know that.

I nodded. Of course I knew that. *Stop running around the house, you'll hurt the wiring!*

He was a union electrician, Howard went on, he wired the George Washington Bridge! He smiled again, more to himself than to me, and I had an obscure sense that this sentence had been a refrain of sorts at certain occasions a long time ago, much repeated in the kitchens of the Bronx.

But even before the start of the war, Howard continued, my father was out of the house a lot working on long-term jobs. For one thing, he went to Washington to work on the Pentagon, I think it was very soon after Pearl Harbor or maybe just before, and he was down there throughout the whole war. So he was out of the apartment. And I was gone, too.

He looked across the table. You didn't know that?

I shook my head. *No.*

And Mother, Howard went on, she worked in a factory, an armament plant somewhere uptown, in Washington Heights, I think it was.

His narrow face lightened.

My mother was a very intelligent woman, you know. She had no education, but she had a *brain.* She was very clever at all kinds of games, cards, rummy, mah-jongg, things like that. I think that's where your father got his mathematical brain from, frankly.

It was as if he were talking to himself, not to me.

So she wasn't in the apartment, either. And Bobby—your uncle Bob—he liked to be out in the street, loafing around on the corner with the neighborhood kids. He was crippled with the polio, of course, but he was very outgoing, very popular, not like your father. Your father, he liked to read, to study, even as a kid.

I thought about all this and then I said, So he was alone.

And Howard looked at me and said, Yeah. Most of the time, he was all by himself.

He shook his head. Then, as if he were offering some kind of amends for the loneliness that, we both simultaneously realized as he spoke, my father must have lived with throughout his childhood, he said, But he had all that time to *read*. I'll say this about your father: all that reading did him good. He learned something, in his life.

In his life, he learned something.

It was, perhaps, to exculpate himself, to indicate that he hadn't been responsible for my father's solitude as a child, that Uncle Howard let slip the second piece of information that I hadn't known about Daddy.

Remember, your father was nearly ten years younger than me, he said again a little later on, so I wasn't around much when he was in school. But I know he always got very good marks, all the way through high school. Of course I was long gone by then.

About my father's high-school experience I knew something, of course: the Latin, *Oh-vid*, the refusal to go on with the Latin. Getting into Bronx Science but going to that other school. I was about to ask Howard if he knew why Daddy hadn't gone to the very *best* school when he interrupted my thoughts.

Even in the army, he was the smartest.

I smiled, remembering my father's sour little joke about the dreary service he had endured in order to go to college. The potato peeling, the GI Bill.

Oh yes, Howard went on, in the army. When your father was in the army, he was so smart they wanted to send him to West Point.

I sat up. Really? I said. Daddy never told us that, he never—

Howard, avoiding my eyes, gave a tight laugh and said, Oh yes. But he didn't want to go.

I stayed silent.

Yeah, Howard said, oh yeah. Jay went into the army after the war so he could get a GI scholarship and go to college. His commanding officer felt that he was so outstanding that he wanted him to go to West Point and become an officer. An officer! The commanding officer said he'd be happy to write the recommendation himself.

When he said the words "commanding officer," his voice stiffened; it was hard for me, sometimes—because of his gentleness, perhaps, the hours on the velvet sofa nodding happily as we listened to the Segovia albums, his easy acquiescence to Claire's schemes and projects—it was hard for me, sometimes, to remember that my uncle had spent most of his life in the military. *Commanding officer.* He looked down at the lino-leum and moved his head from side to side, making the same rueful grin I'd often seen on my father's face: the expression of the *little man*, maybe, as he yields to forces he'll never understand. Then my uncle looked up at me again.

Your father told me about it only years later. I never understood it. He could have had a West Point appointment!

He looked down at the floor again, bemused.

I was perplexed, too. I thought of my father, of his obsession with edu-cation, with finishing the degree, with achieving, with rising to the top; thought, indeed, of how he had pushed me to investigate the possibility of joining the ROTC, back when I was about to go off to college. *You'd be an officer,* he had told me, *they'll pay for everything, and then all you have to do is work it off with a few years in the service!* And now I knew that he himself had turned down the very course that he would recommend for me thirty years later; knew that he'd been a candidate for top honors, for a supremely elite position, but for some reason had turned it down. This wasn't like his failure to finish his dissertation, which, we knew, had been because of economic necessity, because my mother became pregnant with Andrew. So why had he turned down a chance for success?

As I turned this over in my mind, it occurred to me further that what-ever pleasure my father had felt over the years as his children went to uni-versity and then on to graduate school—finished the degrees he hadn't been able to finish, earned the titles he hadn't been able to earn—it must have been complicated. The pride he took in our success must have made him feel all the more poignantly the memory of his own failures, the roads he had not been able to take—and, as I now knew, those he had, for whatever unknowable reason, chosen not to take.

This endless tug-of-war between fathers and sons, successes and fail-ures: I sometimes wondered what Homer's father was like, if there had ever been a Homer. "Few men resemble their fathers. Few sons are better, most are worse . . ." But then, this has to be the case for the *Odyssey* to work. After all, if Telemachus were his father's equal all along—if he were able to kill the Suitors, marry off his mother, take charge of Ithaca— there'd be no reason for Odysseus to come home; there'd be no *Odyssey*. Whatever its emphasis on Telemachus' education, the *Odyssey* can't really let him—so to speak—*graduate*.

I thought briefly of this as I sat in Howard's darkened living room, absorbing these facts about my father that I hadn't known before. It's a little awkward to interview people you know—to shed the familiarity and treat them, suddenly, as sources of information. I sat there staring at the red light on my tape recorder, thinking of how to bring our conversation to an end, to return to normalcy. Finally I said, If you had one word to describe my father, what would it be?

I was expecting him, almost wanting him, to say "lonely." I wanted him to say it because that adjective would have so conveniently explained so much about Daddy: his awkwardnesses, why he was so prickly, so undemonstrative. All of it.

But the facts often resist the meanings we want to give them. After thinking for a few moments, Howard replied

He said, Your father was brilliant. He didn't start out with much, but he learned a lot.

ANAGNORISIS

(Recognition)

———◦◦◦◦———

MAY

A "recognition," as the term itself implies, is a change from ignorance to knowledge ... recognition is most effective when it coincides with a reversal of fortune.

—ARISTOTLE, *Poetics*

One of the strange things about teaching is that you can never know what your effect will be on others; can never know, if you have something to teach, who your real students will be, the ones who will take what you have to give and make it their own—"what you have to give" being, in no small part, what you yourself learned from some other teacher, someone who wondered whether you would absorb what she had to give, someone who is, by the time you're old enough to write about the experience, as old as your parents, perhaps even dead—can never really know which of the young people clustered around the seminar table is someone whom the teacher or the text has touched so deeply, for whatever reason, that the lesson will live beyond the class-room, beyond you.

But then, the process of education, of pedagogy, of *leading a child into knowledge*, is a delicate and unpredictable one, its mechanisms and effects often mysterious to student and teacher alike.

For instance:

On the mild day in mid-May when Classics 125: The *Odyssey* of Homer ended, I was convinced that this experiment—having my father sit in on the seminar, an idea that so many of my and my parents' friends had found so charming, so amusing—had borne no fruit. By the time we got to that fine spring day, so long after the January morning on which my father pulled up to my house in the snow, grimacing, after the bitter month of February in which we talked about the Telemachy and what it told us about the "harmonious molding" of that young character's soul, after the wet month of March when we talked about Odysseus' sojourn among the Phaeacians, filled as it is with stories and lies, with the hero's narration of his fabulous adventures, the Apologoi; after that freakishly cold April when we analyzed the series of recognitions that marked the hero's return to his home and his true identity—by then, I'd become convinced that I had failed to teach my father. I had never found a way to persuade him of the beauty and usefulness of this great work, whose hero he still didn't find very heroic, whose structural ingenuities left him cold, whose famously fascinating protagonist had failed to fascinate him. And indeed, at a certain point after that semester ended I forced myself to acknowledge that, in precisely the way that I had been mortified many years earlier by my father's rough table manners, had felt the compli- cated shame that eventually pushed me when I was a teenager toward all those mentors, some of whom were exemplary teachers and some of whom were not, I had been slightly embarrassed by my father. I wor- ried that my students had, in the end, been put off by his gruff attitude toward the text and confused by his evident disdain for my teaching of it. I squirmed inwardly when I thought of what they must have made of the bald and withered old man hunched in the corner each week, his baggy white sweater only emphasizing how shrunken his limbs were, as he grumbled and argued and contested the points I was eager for them to absorb.

During the course of the semester, there had been only one occasion on which my father had charmed the class in the way that, so effortlessly and surprisingly, he would charm the passengers on the *Odyssey* cruise just weeks after the course ended; only one moment between January and May when he revealed one of those sudden and unexpected softenings that, when I was a child, I used to wish would come more frequently— as on those nights when, instead of staying bent over the small wooden desk in the hours after dinner, muttering at the bills, he would stand up with a sigh and walk across the narrow hallway into my room and then, after doing a *super-duper-tucker-inner,* would sit at the edge of the sturdy wooden bed that he had built and read *Winnie-the-Pooh* aloud to me. I would lie there in bliss, cocooned like a mummy, unable to move my arms but nonetheless feeling safe, as his high nasal baritone wrapped itself around the short, straightforward sentences that, many years later, he would try and fail to pick his way through during one of his periodic attempts to revive the Latin he had once forsaken.

Winnie ille Pu.

There was only one time during the spring semester of 2011 when my father revealed this other face, which I would see so much more often, so unexpectedly, during the *Odyssey* cruise. This strange moment occurred on the second Friday in May—the final meeting of the seminar, when we were talking about the culminating reunion between Odysseus and Penelope, which takes place immediately after his vengeful slaughter of the Suitors. For weeks I had been preparing the students for this climax, which is also the climax of the epic's ongoing preoccupation with identity and recognition. The Greek word for "recognition" is *anagnorisis,* I'd told them, explaining that this is a key term in the vocabulary classicists use when talking about how plot works. Aristotle in his *Poetics,* for instance, says that certain plots in tragic drama pivot on a moment of *anagnorisis,* and others pivot on a sudden and total change of fortune, or *metabasis;* but the best kind of plot, Aristotle says, is the kind in which the moment of recognition is also, simultaneously, the moment of reversal of fortune. For Aristotle, Sophocles' *Oedipus Rex* is the ideal play in part because it effects this double plot: Oedipus' recognition that his wife is really his mother is also the moment of his downfall. But this twinning of recognition and reversal happens in the *Odyssey,* too, although there the outcome is a happy one: the moment when Odysseus' true identity is recognized is also when his fortunes are restored and he wins back his wife, his family, his household, his kingdom.

The recognition scene between Odysseus and Penelope is also the culmination of another of the epic's ongoing themes. I reminded them of all the other females who had enticed Odysseus during the course of his long journey home, mortal and immortal: of Calypso and Nausicaa and Circe, all of whom were alluring alternatives to Penelope, alternatives that, in the end, he rejected. I had reminded them of Odysseus' pointed use of the word *homophrosynê*, the "like-mindedness" that he recommends in Book 6 to the Phaeacian princess as the hallmark of an authentic relationship, a true marriage, the very quality that was lacking in his entanglements with the goddesses with whose beauty Penelope could never hope to compete. I reminded them of the many physical transformations that had been effected throughout the poem, starting with Athena's transformations, first into Mentes and then into Mentor, continuing with the disguise that Odysseus uses to sneak into Troy during the escapade that Helen recalls in Book 4, going on to include the way that Athena beautifies Odysseus in order to impress the Phaeacians in Book 6 and the way in which she makes him wizened and ugly once he returns to Ithaca, in Book 13, the better to deceive the Suitors, who are indeed fooled by the appearance of the bald, shriveled old man in their midst, a great hero in disguise. I had reminded them of all those transformations, metamorphoses that, whatever their charm or their value for the plot, force the reader of the *Odyssey*, in the end, to wrestle with the question of just how it is we know who someone is when outward appearances can no longer be relied on.

And now here we were, in May, at the end of the semester, discussing the long-awaited reunion between the husband and the wife. This tender scene follows, with almost jarring swiftness, the slaughter of the Suitors, the two moments grotesquely twined into a double climax reflecting the poem's ongoing, paired concerns, the ethical and the emotional, the public and the personal: the Suitors' blasphemous insult to the laws of hospitality, on the one hand, and the status of Odysseus' marriage, on the other, the question of whether husband and wife will be able to know each other again.

The close relationship between the vengeance narrative and the recognition theme is evident in the fact that the slaughter of the Suitors results from an idea that Penelope comes up with. At the end of Book 19, following the queen's long and emotional conversation with the beggar and after Eurycleia's recognition of Odysseus' scar (the old nurse wants to alert Penelope, but Odysseus swears her to silence), Penelope declares that the next day will decide her fate at last. For on that day she will set a contest for the Suitors—a test of skill whose winner, she says, she will be happy to marry. The contest is in fact designed to ensure that whoever wins will have at least some of her husband's remarkable qualities, since it involves accomplishing a tricky feat that Odysseus liked to perform in days gone by: to shoot an arrow through a series of twelve ax-heads lined up in a row. Since merely to string the mighty horn bow requires enormous physical strength, Penelope's future husband will not, at least, be a weakling.

Penelope announces the contest to the Suitors in Book 21, and it soon becomes clear that, whether consciously or unconsciously, she has devised a way to put a weapon into the real Odysseus' hand. Odysseus, for his part, has been conniving to better his chances against the Suitors for some time now, seeing how vastly outnumbered he and his son and their pathetically few allies are—the loyal Eumaeus, to whom he at last reveals himself, another old farmhand, a cowherd named Philoetius, and of course the devoted Eurycleia. Soon after his reunion with Telemachus, he orders his son to lock away the Suitors' weapons in an upper storeroom while keeping his own arms at the ready; now, as the time for Penelope's contest draws near, he instructs Eurycleia to lock herself and the other womenfolk in their quarters and tells the cowherd to slip outside and bolt the palace gates so no one can get in or out. But how to get weapons into his own hands? The contest of the bow at last provides a pretext.

Like Cinderella's sisters trying on the glass slipper, one Suitor after another tries to string the bow and fails. Finally, the "beggar" offers to have a try, much to the derision of the Suitors. Antinoüs wheels on him: how outrageous for someone as lowly as he to insert himself into the proceedings! Here Penelope herself slyly intervenes—suggesting, at least to some readers, that she has known all along that the beggar is her husband. Does Antinoüs really think, she laughingly declares, that she'd marry the old drifter if he wins? Certainly not. But since everyone else has failed, could it really hurt to let the old man have a go? Despite the mutterings and imprecations of the disgruntled Suitors, loyal Eumaeus takes the great weapon and carries it across the crowded room to the beggar, into whose hands he places it. Odysseus picks up the weapon, testing it to see whether "the worms have been at the horn in its master's absence." Then, finding it sound, in one fluid motion—as graceful, Homer says, as a bard stringing his lyre—he strings it. At which point,

> *from the Suitors there rose up a mighty groan, their skin*
> *turned white; and Zeus let crash a mighty thunder-sign,*
> *while much-enduring, godlike Odysseus rejoiced*
> *that wily Cronus' child had sent this portent.*
> *An arrow lay there on the table—he took and let it fly;*
> *the others, still within the quiver, the Achaeans soon would taste.*

And then the mayhem begins.

The jarring reference to the Suitors as "Achaeans"—the word Homer uses to refer to the Greek allies in the *Iliad*—prepares us for the fact that, however much the *Odyssey* has been preoccupied till now with its hero's ability to use his wits to conquer his enemies, the climactic act of vengeance for which he has waited so long will be characterized by the kind of violence we associate with this poem's great predecessor. After stripping off his rags and declaring to the astonished Suitors his true identity, he takes aim first at the loathsome Antinoüs; the arrow he shoots catches the leader of the Suitors in the throat just as he's downing a cup of wine—a fitting ending to the character who, more than any other, emblematized the Suitors' arrogance and impiety in defying the laws of hospitality. "You dogs," Odysseus explodes at last,

> *you never thought that I'd be home again*
> *from Troy! And so you ate my household up,*

forced yourself upon the servant girls,
courted the wife of a man who was still alive,
outraging the gods who hold up the wide heavens
as if no one would ever take revenge:
now dire destruction waits for all of you!

Eurymachus dies next, after trying to smooth-talk his way out of his predicament (he blames everything on Antinoüs), and then poor Amphinomus, speared through the back by Telemachus as he tries to flee the hall. But the vengeance that ensues doesn't, at first, go quite as Odysseus had planned. In a final nod to the theme of Telemachus' education, Homer tells us that the youth has made a near-fatal mistake at this critical moment: he's left the door to the storeroom where he'd stashed away the Suitors' arms wide open, and for this reason they eventually manage to don their armor and defend themselves from Odysseus' onslaught. When Odysseus learns of this deadly error, he assumes he has been betrayed by one of the Suitors' allies among the servants; but Telemachus admits that the mistake was his. Interestingly, Homer cuts away at this moment, and so we never know what his father's reaction to the news of his son's error is. On the first Friday in May, when we discussed this passage in class, my father raised his hand.

So Telemachus nearly ruins it all, he began.

Oh, God, I thought, here it comes.

But then he said, It's *very* impressive that he admits it was his fault. He could have gotten out of it and let his father think it was the servants' fault, but he owned it. So maybe this is really the culmination of the theme of his education. He proves he's a grown-up by taking responsibility.

Tommy cut in before I could reply.

Well, he said, I think it's just as interesting that Odysseus seems to let him off the hook—he doesn't say anything, doesn't scold him. So maybe he's learned something, too.

Whatever its significance for the father-son theme, Telemachus' mistake makes possible a genuine battle scene straight out of the *Iliad;* the

bloodshed continues for the next two hundred lines, with a few key inter-
ventions by Athena to keep the odds on her favorite mortal's side. (You
see? my father cried for the last time that semester. He only wins because
he gets help from the *gods!*) Finally, Odysseus scans the carnage to see
whether any Suitors are left breathing. But no; all are dead, lying in the
gore like

> *fishes that the fishermen have hauled*
> *from the iron-gray sea onto the winding shore*
> *meshed in the intricate nets; and they, the fish,*
> *lie there on the sand, croaking for the salty waves,*
> *but the blazing Sun beats the life from them . . .*

An undignified simile for an unworthy group of men.

It is only after the gore has been cleaned up and the palace ritually puri-
fied that Odysseus encounters his wife once more and finally reveals his
identity to her.

And yet, as with the scene in Book 16 that reunites the father and his
son, the reunion between husband and wife in Book 23 starts off with a
disconcerting anticlimax. Penelope, we are told, has slept through the
mayhem; now she is waked by Eurycleia, who announces the great news
to her mistress—Odysseus has returned and killed the Suitors! But to the
nurse's bewilderment and to the stupefaction of Telemachus, the queen
doesn't believe a word of it. Indeed, she turns out to be as suspicious and
wary now as her husband has been throughout the poem. Her cautiousness in this scene, so like Odysseus', is simultaneously a marker of the
couple's genuine like-mindedness, *homophrosynê*, and a frustration for
Odysseus, that notorious deceiver and trickster, who finds himself in the
odd position of not being believed when he finally wants to be—when he
is finally telling the truth.

So here again, I said to the class that day, the great question of identity is raised. Exactly how are these two going to prove to each other who they are? After all, so much time has passed, twenty years, difficult years, years of hardship and shame and tribulation. The magical transformations effected by the gods, I suggested, are merely supernatural parallels to the force that really does transform our faces and bodies, withering us, making us bald and wrinkled: Time. When the exterior, the face and body, have changed beyond recognition, what remains? Is there an inner "I" that survives time?

They were quiet.

This isn't some hypothetical literary issue, I went on after a moment, looking around the room. This is a question that people have to deal with in real life!

They were looking listless. The previous Friday, when we'd discussed the slaughter of the Suitors, the viciousness of which had stunned them despite our discussion of why Zeus' "rough justice" was appropriate, had been a warm day with brilliant skies; I'd taken the class to a grassy spot outside, where we basked in the strong May sun and talked about murder. But today was unseasonably cold, and we were inside again. They seemed restless, glum. To relax them, I repeated a funny exchange I'd had a few weeks earlier with my mother, who'd just turned eighty.

So the other day I asked my mom, How does it feel to be so old? And she said, It's so *strange*. Every morning I look in the mirror and think, Who is this old woman staring at me? Inside, I'm still sixteen!

The kids laughed. I didn't share with them the rest of the conversation. Are you afraid of getting very old? I'd said that day, taking advantage of her light mood. Are you worried about getting sick and falling apart? My mother grew serious and looked at me and said, I'm only afraid of being without your father.

You see? I said to the class after telling them about my mother's remark. This is a question that faces real people. How you look and how you feel, the inside and the outside, what you see and what others see. It's a totally Odyssean issue. *This* is why this recognition scene has to play out the way it does.

But they weren't reacting, weren't taking my thought and making anything of it. I thought back to the first day of class, how sluggish they'd been.

What a way to end, I said to myself.

The recognition scene in Book 23, which many scholars and critics see as the climax of the *Odyssey*, plays out around a bed: a bed of very special construction, a bed with a secret. After Penelope awakens, she goes downstairs to confront Odysseus, who sits waiting for his wife in the great hall. The queen takes a seat on the opposite end of the room and the two sit looking at each other. After the furious Telemachus berates her for being so "cold," her heart as "hard as flint"—for, in other words, acting very much as Odysseus has acted in tricky situations—Penelope declares that she will test the man who claims to be her husband:

> *. . . for if truly*
> *it is Odysseus and he has come home, then we*
> *shall surely know each other, better than anyone:*
> *for there are certain signs, secret from all others, that are known to us.*

After a brief interlude during which Odysseus is bathed by a servant woman and beautified by Athena, he returns to his seat opposite his wife and chides her for her coldness, as his son had just done. Claiming to be confounded by her stubbornness, he turns to Eurycleia and instructs her to make up a bed for him. This request, it so happens, gives Penelope an idea for the best way to test the stranger—who, she must admit, does in fact look uncannily like her husband. Turning to Eurycleia, she, too, tells the maid to make up a bed—not any bed, she says, but Odysseus' own bed, which she orders the servant to move into the hallway outside the royal bedchamber and prepare for the stranger.

Here her trap springs shut: for, on hearing her instructions, Odysseus for the last time loses control of himself; for the last time gives himself away, as he had once done so fatefully after his triumph over the Cyclops. Outraged, he reveals that the bed, because of a unique feature of its design, would be virtually impossible to move, "unless a god himself came down, minded to move it elsewhere":

> No mortal man, even in the prime of life,
> could crowbar it aside; since this great secret sign
> is wrought into the bed itself, which I made—no one else.
> A tree of spear-leafed olive grew inside the lot,
> full-grown, thriving; as massive as a pillar.
> I planned the room around it . . .
> sheared off the crown of spear-shaped leaves,
> planed the stump from the roots on up, expertly,
> using the line to make sure all was plumb;
> and wrought from it the bedpost, drilled all the holes,
> and went on from there to fashion the whole bed, my design,
> inlaying it with gold and silver and ivory;
> and from those posts stretched crimson ox-hide thongs.
> I say to you clearly that this is our sign . . .

The "sign" is received and understood: now, at last, Penelope recognizes that the stranger is truly Odysseus. For the secret of the bed's special design, knowledge of which went deeper than any physical marking, was shared by one man: her husband, the only man who had ever had access to her bedchamber and her bed. The bed is, therefore, a dual marker: a sign of Odysseus' identity and a symbol of Penelope's fidelity. The queen, "her knees and heart gone slack," throws herself weeping into her husband's arms; he weeps, too. The sight of him, Homer says at this moment, is as welcome to Penelope as the sight of dry land is to men swimming away from a shipwreck: a simile that not only suggests, once again, how alike this husband and wife are, but implies that Penelope's years at home have constituted an "adventure" every bit as harrowing as the ones her husband has had. Only now does the couple retire to the great bed for their first night together in twenty years—a night that, in one of the poem's loveliest touches, Athena extends, restraining Dawn so as to give the couple more time for their reunion. First they make love; then, the poet tells us, each narrates to the other at length everything that has happened over the past two decades.

To my delight, the students perked up a little as we started talking about the scene.

I think it's very fitting that Penelope's final test for Odysseus is so clever, Tommy said. She doesn't ask for a sign, but instead tries to trick him. It's very Odysseus-like, and a perfect example of their compatibility. So in the end, *homophrosynê* is the only thing that can see through disguises.

Penelope's test in Book 23 is *perfect*, Nina said. The fact that the whole palace is centered around the bedroom is a nice metaphor for the bond Odysseus and Penelope share.

Jack looked at her, then at me. Don't you think it's kind of funny, even inappropriate, that the fact that they share such a strong bond is based on something as superficial as sex?

Sex? I said.

Well, he said, that's what happens in the bed!

Nina gave him an exasperated look.

I think, she said, that when Odysseus talks about the immovability of the bed he's really referring to his unwavering faith and love for his wife.

Tommy offered what I thought was the most interesting observation anyone made that day.

Actually, the sex isn't the most important part of the reunion. Talking is. I thought it was interesting that they make love first but then they spend the rest of the night telling stories to each other before they sleep. It's like they need to emotionally process what they've been through, and the way they do that is through storytelling. The real emphasis is on communicating, you could say. It's like the Cyclops story. In the end, it all comes back to language.

Yes, I said. Remember, we were just saying that bodies are unreliable, that outward appearances can be altered, whereas the inner self remains—

Well, *I* can tell you something about this, my father suddenly said, rather loudly.

I looked over at him. He'd sat up in his chair and was leaning forward a bit.

I know something about this, he repeated, clearing his throat bossily. As with *You can't believe the traffic* or *Don't tell me what to do*, these words had become part of the repertoire of stock phrases that, like a spell or an incantation, can now summon up my father vividly, the way certain aspects of his physical presence can evoke him: the hearty aroma of the Old Spice cologne that he'd slap on his sunken cheeks and throat after shaving, a smell as synthetic as that of dry-cleaning fluid, or the oddly satisfying scraping noise made by the preposterously jazzy quadruple-blade razor he used against the whiskers of the wattles on his throat. (But it was my mother who taught me how to shave. This was in the early 1970s, when my father was away two weeks out of each month working on the artificial heart project, and at a certain point, when the soft dark tufts on my cheeks and chin had become impossible to ignore, my mother took me into the bathroom and said, *Come, I'm going to show you how, I know, I used to watch Grandpa,* and then she wet my face and lathered it and went to work, pulling the razor down along my throat and then upward along my cheeks. For years afterward I assumed that the permanent rash on my cheeks and neck was acne until one Sunday afternoon when we were all at Uncle Howard and Aunt Claire's and suddenly Claire took my face into one white hand, the way you might hold the snout of a dog, and said, *Boychik, you have terrible razor burn, you're shaving against the grain but you should be shaving with the grain. Who taught you how to shave?*) . . . At the moment in class when we were talking about Penelope and Odysseus and my father said *I know something about this*, a phrase that summons him now as vividly as the smell of Old Spice aftershave, I had a sudden jabbing memory of him saying the same words when, during spring break of my junior year at the university he'd urged me so strongly to attend, convinced that it would be a *better place for me*, I confronted my parents and tearfully blurted out the secret I'd been keeping from them all those years. I was gay, I said, sitting on the corner of the bed and staring stupidly at the pattern on the bedspread, and my father said, in what was the most surprising of his rare softenings, *I know something about this, Marlene. Let me talk to him.*

That particular corner of the bed was the last place he would ever sit in our house. On a Friday in January 2012—a year to the day after he had first sat in the classroom at Bard to take my *Odyssey* seminar—my father rose from a table in a restaurant where he'd been having lunch with some former colleagues and (one of the friends later told us) began walking around the restaurant in circles, looking confusedly for the front door. This alarmed some of those friends at the time but would not have come as a surprise to a neurosurgeon, since spatial and directional confusion is, as we later learned, one of the first signs of a certain kind of cerebral hemorrhage, a so-called wet hemorrhage, in which the blood leaks out of the vessels in the front lobe of the brain, thereby affecting the stroke victim's ability to gauge distances and angles and spatial relations—to, in a word, navigate. When I heard about this later that afternoon, after my mother called me and told me I had to get on a train and come *quickly,* when I heard about my father wandering around the restaurant unable to find his way to the door I was struck with a kind of shamed horror, because one of the things my father was famous for was his uncanny sense of direction, his ability to find his way around. I remembered the relish with which, in those pre-Internet days, he would study road atlases and plot his routes when we went on long car trips; and I recalled his contemptuous disdain for people who "asked directions." *If you can read a map, you don't need to ask directions!* This failure of navigational ability was to repeat itself on a smaller scale some twenty or so minutes after my father was finally led to the door of the restaurant by one of his anxious friends, who then drove him home and, as he dropped my father off, mentioned to my mother that Daddy was "acting funny." Then she watched Daddy disappear into the small bedroom that he had shared with her for fifty-one years, the room which, on that January morning, he would enter and leave for the last time, and once in that room (we can assume, based on

what she later saw) he sat down on the corner of the full-size bed and
tried, and kept on trying, to plug the power cord into his iPad. But he
couldn't navigate even that small distance. He sat there on the bed where
my three younger siblings had been conceived and kept holding the cord
in one hand, trying to direct the male lead fruitlessly toward the female
receptor on the device, but kept missing it, like a drunkard with a key,
and we know that this is how he passed those minutes, the last that he
would ever spend dressed in his own clothes and surrounded by his own
familiar things: the sleek midcentury dresser against which I had once
fallen in a dead faint when I was eleven or so, only to wake to the terrifying realization that I couldn't remember who I was; the narrow mirror,
screwed to the inside of the closet door, at which he gazed every morning
of his working life as he straightened his narrow ties; the desk at which
he did his work and paid his bills and toward which I would reluctantly
tiptoe when I had a question about my math homework. On the corner
of this bed, surrounded by those familiar objects which were about to
become terribly unfamiliar, he was still sitting when my mother, who'd
decided she wanted to check on him because she was a little unsettled
by what Geoff had told her about Daddy not being able to find the front
door of the Applebee's, came in and found him. *He was sitting on the bed
trying to plug in his iPad and he couldn't do it,* my mother told me that
night, when I met her in the ER of the local hospital. *He kept saying,
"I've done this a million times, I don't get it," and that's when I called 911.*

When this happened he was sitting in the exact spot where I had
once sat and told them who I was, and he'd responded with such surprising tenderness. *I know something about this.*

Now, in May 2011, on the last day of the *Odyssey* course at Bard,
my father was sitting against the wall beneath the window, in the same
seat he'd taken fifteen weeks earlier, that cold January morning when I'd
looked over this unknown crew of teenagers for the first time, and was
saying again, *I know something about this.*

The students were looking at him.

And then he went on. Face it! I'm the only one here who knows what it's like to be with someone so long that they don't look anything like the person you started out with.

Of course he was right. They were eighteen, maybe nineteen. I couldn't imagine, on this May day when my father started speaking about what it was like to watch as someone you knew long and well grew unrecognizably old, someone whom the habits of love and intimacy had grooved into your body and your soul the way that ivy will incise itself into the bark of a tree—I couldn't imagine how old eighty-one must seem to these kids. As he began to speak I imagined the students silently studying his lined face, the age spots, the thin fluff clinging to his taut scalp. I looked at him, too, and suddenly I thought, This is what Athena makes Odysseus look like when she waves her wand at him in Book 13. "The skin withered on his curved limbs / the flaxen hair vanished from his head, and round / all his limbs she fixed an old man's skin / and the light went out of his eyes, which were once so lovely."

I know about this, Daddy was saying. *His mother*, he went on, shaking his head and staring down at the floor, his mother was the most beautiful girl. Not pretty—*beautiful*.

As I had done once many years before, when I was in high school and he was telling a neighbor how terrific my mother had looked at some event, a bar mitzvah or wedding, I thought, Why doesn't he ever tell *her* that?

But of course I didn't say that now. Like the students, I remained quiet and let my father talk.

And it's funny, he went on, regaining his composure and squeezing his eyes tightly shut as he spoke, nodding up and down as if he were talking to himself, just as he did when he was trying to remember some bit of trivia, the name of some character actor in an old movie, the batting average of a baseball star from his childhood, some fact that would prove to you that he was still as sharp as ever, *It's funny*, my father said, but I think this part of the poem is very true. There are these things you have with someone, not physical things, but private jokes and memories you gather over time, little things that nobody else knows about.

He looked up and saw the kids staring at him. A bit sheepish, suddenly, he tried to lighten the mood. Well, *sometimes* it's physical things! he said.

I was too startled to say anything. But I was realizing not only that he was right but how deeply right he was. I was realizing, for the first time, how much the *Odyssey* knew about this ostensibly trivial but profound real-life phenomenon, the way that small things between people can be the foundation of the greatest intimacy. And not just between husbands and wives, or lovers. I thought about "Daddy Loopy." I thought about the bed upstairs in my study, with the silly secret of its construction.

When my father said, "Well, *sometimes* it's physical things," I expected the students to react, perhaps to laugh. But they were rapt. Nobody said a word.

He went on.

Like I said, I think the poem is right about this. When you have those things, those things that couples have, they keep you connected long after everything else becomes unrecognizable.

He looked over at me, as if to see whether I'd registered that he was using this key word from our weeks of conversations about the *Odyssey*.

Those are the things that you hang on to, he said, suddenly self conscious. It's why you stick with this . . . this thing in the first place.

He sat up straighter in the chair and gave his head a little shake then, as if to dispel the mood he'd created.

Anyway, trust me, his mother was beautiful.

He jerked his head in my direction and then shrank back into his chair.

The students stayed quiet. Well, what could they say? My parents' marriage had lasted three times as long as their entire lives. I could tell from their solemn faces as they stared across the room at him that they were impressed. I had the sudden sense that they were looking up to him.

And then, as I glanced around the table and felt their silence, I realized that this is what those magical transformations in the *Odyssey* really are. It isn't magic at all. Something happens, someone speaks heatedly or

with authority—with "wingèd words," as Homer puts it, *epê pteroenta*—
and you suddenly see things differently: the person actually looks different. At the moment my father pushed himself back in the chair after
admitting that the *Odyssey* had gotten something right, that between
couples there are secrets that serve, in the end, as the bedrock of marriage, secrets unknown even to the children of that marriage—at that
moment it occurred to me that he looked bigger and more impressive,
somehow, the way that Odysseus looks taller and more beautiful when
Athena needs him to succeed, to impress some stranger in whose hands
his fate hangs. On that May day toward the end of the seminar, my father
had succeeded, too. With this fleeting display of tenderness, before an
audience of children too young to understand what they were witnessing,
he had, for a moment, been transformed.

I didn't tell my mother about this incident at the time, and then everything else happened, so I forgot. But when I was visiting her one spring
afternoon, a year after that final day of class, I brought it up. I'd come out
to Long Island to help her with some financial papers, but of course we
ended up talking about Daddy.

He said I was *beautiful?* We were sitting at the smooth white table in
her spotless kitchen. On the far wall there hung, artfully arranged, the
old-fashioned cooking implements that had been her mother's: eggbeat-
ers and sieves and chipped white enamel colanders. She'd once shown
me the diagram she'd made on a piece of lined notebook paper, indicating where each item belonged. *That way, when I take them down to clean
them, I know where everything goes.* Every object she'd outlined was rec-
ognizable to me, although because of the tremor that has begun to afflict
her hands, the lines were wobbly.

At some point, we took a break from her bank statements, and as
we sat across from each other at the white kitchen table we gossiped
and traded stories about her friends, my siblings, our families. I talked
about the semester that was about to end—I was teaching the *Iliad*—and

this of course led me to reminisce about the *Odyssey* course; which is how I came to tell her about the last class session, of the moment when my father, gesturing at me, had said, *His mother was beautiful.* Perhaps because of that, she seemed relaxed and humorous, and so I mentioned his strange admission that there are all kinds of things between a husband and a wife that connect them when so much else has dissolved.

Physical things, Daddy even said, I added as my mother and I sipped the tasteless decaffeinated tea. I thought of how my father had so liked a nice big cup of *kawfee.*

"Physical things"? *Please.*

As she looked in the mirror she made a face of horror-movie surprise, widening her eyes so she could put on her eye shadow, she told me a funny story.

I still remember when we were newlyweds, my mother said, there was a book that had just come out, a sex guide for married couples. We all ran out and bought it, Aunt Alice and Aunt Marcia and Aunt Irma and Aunt Mimi and me, and of course we peed in our pants talking about it. You know, in those days everyone wasn't always talking about those things. And this book said, "You must *express yourself* clearly to your husband. You must tell him exactly what *pleases* you."

She giggled.

I remember it had all these sample sentences that you were supposed to use on your husband. "Darling, now I want you to put your hand *here,*" that kind of thing. And—well, can you imagine? *Daddy?*

I didn't say anything. She opened her mouth enormously wide, like that figure in Munch's *The Scream,* while she put on her lipstick.

So one night your father and I were in bed and we started and I took your father's hand and said, *Jay, I want you to move your hand here.* And your father looked at me and said, *Don't tell me what to do!*

I burst out laughing. Mother put a tissue between her lips to blot the lipstick. Then she sighed heavily and said, Oh, your *father.*

Now she could be wistful. But I remembered how she had stood screaming not so many months before, after he had the stroke, as she looked down at his inert figure, the drawn-out cries as throbbing and unrelenting as the lamentations of the women who mourn Hector, the fallen prince of Troy, at the end of the *Iliad*. *Jay, Jay, I love you, I love you, don't go, don't leave me,* she had keened, drawing out the vowels into a singsong wail as old, I suppose, as the race itself. The words, indeed, are almost beside the point; the wild vowels say everything, *ooooo, oohhhhh, eeeeeee.* Homer knew this; simply to say aloud the two Greek words he uses for "throbbing lamentation" in that final scene of his war epic, *adinou goöio,* is to make the sounds of mourning: *ah-dee-nouuuu go-oyyyyy-ohhhh.*

Oh, your father, she said again, as if to herself. On the table she'd piled some papers and things she thought would be useful for my book. One of them I had never seen before: my father's high-school yearbook. My mother's yearbook I'd seen many times; sometimes she would take it out and show us the vampy expression on her face in the yearbook picture (*I was in my Marlene Dietrich phase!*) or read aloud the comical biography she'd written for herself. "Hobby: Spelunking. Career Goal: Taxidermy." But my father's yearbook was new to me. I handled it gingerly as I turned the glossy gray pages. As my mother started clearing away the mirror and the eyebrow pencils and lipsticks, I read aloud the dedications that my father's friends had written sixty-five years before:

"Boy, can you talk—best of luck, Andy Siff"

"To a swell fellow (and head B.S. artist in English) Lots of luck, Seymour Silver"

"To the dapperest boy in English 7-5h, Good Luck, Laurence Schneck"

I looked up at my mother. "Dapperest"? *Daddy?*

She made an incredulous face. Then I went back to the yearbook.

"Hope you build a life of happiness, Jules 'Nunzio' Koenigsberg"

Next to his own yearbook picture my father had signed his name with a message to himself: "Good luck—Jay Mendelsohn"

My mother laughed, but the idea of my father wishing himself good luck made me sad. I could almost see his face, long and tan and youthful, an ironic expression masking who knows what feelings, as he wrote the words. Had he been eager for the future? Afraid?

Suddenly my mother, who'd returned to the table and sat down next to me so she could get a better look at the yearbook, said, That wasn't the high school he was *supposed* to go to, you know.

She sighed and ran her hand, with its bulging blue veins and the knotted joints, over the smooth paper.

I made a quizzical face.

Oh, *you* know the story, she said, a little impatient. He was so smart, your father, and of course he got into Bronx Science. But naturally he didn't go, because of his friend.

She sighed heavily.

I said, What "friend"?

She looked at me. Oh, *you* know, they were always so close! They were best friends!

Who? I said.

My mother rolled her eyes. Gene! Eugene *Miller*! They were best friends since they were little boys, since they were five years old. Daddy adored him. But Eugene didn't get into Bronx Science and Daddy did, and Daddy didn't want to make Eugene feel bad. So he went to DeWitt Clinton, too. But it wasn't his first choice.

My mother looked at my father's teenage handwriting beneath the yearbook picture.

"Good luck—Jay Mendelsohn."

Oh well, she finally said. Who cares about which school he went to? It doesn't *matter* anymore.

I said nothing.

His mother was beautiful, my father said that May day in 2011, the last day of the *Odyssey* seminar. I thought then that this was the only time he had made himself genuinely sympathetic to the students taking Classics 125: The *Odyssey* of Homer: the time he talked about how beautiful my mother had been and about the secrets and the sharing that were, now, the residue of whatever had brought them together in 1948, when they had first met in the Bronx. She was seventeen and he was nineteen, just out of the army—which, as I knew well, he had joined in order to get an *education.*

In the early spring of 2013 Nino was still living in the comfortable, sprawling house where, forty years earlier, we had enjoyed the exotic foods, had delivered the choice guest gifts, the Orrefors and Venini, the expensive jewel-toned liqueurs in their oddly shaped bottles. I had called him a few weeks earlier to say that I wanted to come talk to him about Daddy. I'd interviewed my uncle Howard about his childhood, I told Nino over the phone, and now I wanted to talk to him about when Daddy was a young man, before we were all born.

I got to the tree-shaded house late in the afternoon, expecting to have dinner, spend the night, and leave the next morning; but I ended up staying the weekend. This happens often when you visit Nino and Barbara. Once you're there it's easy to forget that you want to go home, what with the specialty cocktails and the rare vintages, her choice cooking and his expansive reminiscences.

Barbara. Irene, the beautiful, dark-haired Greek, was long gone. For the past twenty-five years there had been Barbara, Jewish and foxy and fun, slim and smartly turned out with a tart, rather theatrical impatience with what she clearly sees as her second husband's foibles, indulgences, neuroses. *Oh, him,* she will say whenever certain subjects come up, Nino's dislike of flying or his waxing overly theoretical about why cucumbers are the perfect garnish for a certain kind of martini. *Him!* she will say, as she brings a burrata or frittata to the table, complaining mildly about this or that detail, since she, like Nino, is a great cook, a lover of the Epicurean pleasures, and of travel, too, and has thus found in this second marriage, as he has done, a measure of *homophrosynê*, a parity of interests and tastes so different from what I think of as the inverted *homophrosynê* of my own parents, whose marriage had somehow survived—or was, perhaps, based on—so many perfectly symmetrical dissonances, his desire to travel, her insistence on staying home, she so *funny* and *outgoing* and *demonstrative*, he so wry and reserved and aloof . . . The martinis that they gave me when I arrived were strong, and Barbara, I noticed, made sure that our glasses were always topped up. "That'll take the pain away!" she announced, raising the faceted pitcher above my glass again and waving away my protesting hand. The glasses were filled and refilled, and the mood quickly became reminiscent.

Nino started talking about how he had first met Daddy, in the early 1950s. It was clear that for my sake, for the sake of his friend's son, he wanted to start by showing how generous my father had been. He took a sip of his cocktail; the pleasure moved visibly over his skin, like a blush. He closed his eyes for a moment and then opened them and, fixing the pale blue irises on me, began to talk.

We met in *unforgettable* circumstances. It was the day I was brought into Grumman for a job interview. Now your father was already working there, and so he was there for the interview. Because I didn't have top-secret clearance, I wasn't allowed to be wandering around the place on my own. So between the sessions of the interview they literally locked me into a room. Now I wasn't prepared for this, I had brought no lunch! Imagine—*me*, hungry!

Here Nino threw up his hands, laughing. Since I knew the stories about the culinary marvels he had grown up with, the feasts of almost mythic proportions that his mother would prepare for him and my parents when they were all young, I got the joke.

So I'm sitting there in this room, he went on, alone and hungry! And then I heard a knock on the door and I opened it and there was your dad, and he says, "You want half my sandwich?"

He clapped his hands in delight at the memory. It was so touching, he went on. It was obvious your dad had noticed everything. So he gives me half his sandwich, and we spent the rest of that little lunch break chatting, and we hit it off. It was sort of like a little magic that happened then and there in that closed room. And when I started working there, I was in his group, and we were inseparable after that.

He looked at me and said, I know your father could seem tough. But he was very soft in a way, very generous. It touched me.

I looked down. Then I cleared my throat and asked Nino something I had never asked my father.

What exactly did you work on all those years together at Grumman?

I reminded Nino, then, that I had never been to my father's office, adding that I'd always been too embarrassed by my inadequacy in mathematics to ask him to explain his work to me, fearful that he would say, as he had said before, *Never mind, you wouldn't understand.*

Nino took a sip of his martini; the slice of cucumber gave it a greenish tinge. There was a gleam in his eye. *Uncertainty!*

I raised a brow and he smiled. In those days, he said, we were working on something called Monte Carlo methods. It's a way of simulating a whole sequence of events where there's uncertainty at every stage. So you simulate it by taking random numbers and using them as you play, say, ten thousand games: the first time the random number tells you to go this way, the second time a random number tells you to go that way. And then, when you do this ten thousand times, the *average* result gives you an indication of what would happen under *real* conditions. Because you're *averaging* over contingencies.

I tried to absorb this for a moment. But why would all this have been so interesting to Grumman? As I said the words I felt the twinge of an old shame; I pictured myself standing at my father's door with my math homework, the figures and equations as meaningless to me as if they'd been Mayan hieroglyphs.

But Nino only laughed. Why? Because we were a defense contractor, an aerospace corporation. You can't go around testing bombs or lunar landing modules to find out what happens when you deploy them. So you do it on paper first.

This was how I learned that my father, with his devotion to *precision* and *logic*, his loathing of anything irrational, his addiction to maps, to websites that would allow him, days in advance of his visiting me in Manhattan, to pinpoint the location of the parking garage closest to my apartment so that he *wouldn't have to wander around in circles like an idiot* when he drove in, had spent much of his working life thinking about uncertainty.

At first I had no clue how to do this stuff, Nino went on, but your dad was patient with me, he taught me. So I let him take me under his wing.

As he said the words "under his wing," Nino's voice wobbled a bit. He said, I think it was a role he enjoyed.

I said nothing. I thought of what Uncle Howard had said, of how alone my father had been in the apartment, Howard off in the war, Bobby hobbling around the neighborhood putting on a tough face, Poppy in Washington working at the Pentagon, Nanny gratefully fleeing uptown to her Rosie the Riveter job, and my ten-year-old father alone with his books, reading, reading, with no one to talk to, no one to share what he was learning *with*.

I let him take me under his wing.

He was a *curious* person, Nino went on. He wouldn't let something slip by without trying to grasp some nugget of truth about it. There was a strong level of skepticism, which might have had to do with his background, with where he grew up. He was willing to question. He was querulous at times. "Why do you *say* that?" he would always say. I don't know if it was because, in order to extract himself from that meagerness that he grew up with, he felt he had to be more alert, more questioning—to not accept what the other kids were accepting. I think he had to be like that to get out of that milieu that he grew up in.

I don't care what everyone else does, we're not like everybody else.

Not that he ever disdained his background, Nino suddenly said. I recall that he had a great respect for his father. He saw his father as— I wouldn't call him a heroic figure, but as admirable, a sturdy, honest person. Not a phony. I think that influenced him a great deal.

I thought of him standing in the hospital in 1975, looking down at his father's shrunken figure.

Your father is your father.

At some point we moved to the kitchen; dinner was ready. *Tafelspitz,*

Nino said in the slightly professorial tone he uses when he talks about food. The most sublime form of pot roast! The basic family meal of the Austro-Hungarian bourgeoisie!

Barbara rolled her eyes. Nino inhaled deeply. After uncorking the "big" Burgundy he'd set aside for the *Tafelspitz,* he grew pensive.

You know, at one point I parted ways with Jay, he said. I went the academic route and he didn't. For a while I was making my career at the university, and your dad was doing what he was doing at Grumman, and we were not seeing each other, except for occasional get-togethers with the families. For a long time our intimacy was not the same as it was before . . .

He reached for his glass. Then he said, It was because of the dissertation.

I put my wineglass down hard enough to set it ringing.

You mean, because you were able to finish yours but he couldn't?

Nino nodded. In 1966 I had left Grumman. Stony Brook University was hiring math professors, but they wouldn't hire anyone without a Ph.D. So I was able to apply for the job. But your dad couldn't. He hadn't gotten the degree.

The room grew quiet. Presently Nino said, So you can see why it was such a great triumph for him when he started teaching at Hofstra University years later. A professor at last!

I thought of the white plastic nameplate on the door of his office at home, our old bedroom door. PROF. JAY MENDELSOHN.

He grew pensive again. I think that professorship, even coming late in life, was a great salve for him—somehow it made up for not having gotten the Ph.D., never having done the dissertation.

I spoke up. Daddy talked pretty openly about not finishing his Ph.D. Honestly, I didn't think it was that big a deal for him. He explained that Mom had gotten pregnant with Andrew—

The blue eyes were inscrutable. Nino shook his head sadly and said, *No.* That is not why he didn't finish.

I stared at him.

He said, We were both *encouraged* by the company to work toward the Ph.D. We were subsidized. Your father was granted the same privileges that I had at the time—they would allow us to take off early in the afternoon to take courses at the Courant Institute at NYU. And your father and I on many occasions would drive together down to Manhattan and he'd take one course and I'd take another. Yes, it's true he was about to start a family and I was still single at the time. But that's not the reason he didn't finish.

I was sitting up straight in my chair, the meat and the wine forgotten. So what do you think the reason was? I finally said.

Nino twirled the thin stem of his glass between his thick fingers. There were two things, I think, he said. First, there was always one little problem with your father. He chafed at being told that in order for him to get this piece of paper he was going to have to write a thesis along the lines of something that had been predetermined as acceptable, and then pass an exam based on *that*. This was the difference between your father and me. Remember, I'd been educated by Jesuits! I'd said to myself, Okay, if that's the rules of the game, I'm going to do that. But no, not your father. And so, although he even went to talk to some of the faculty about possible thesis topics, I think he'd decided not to do it. I always felt bad about that because it put me in an awkward situation.

There was a little silence, and then he said, Maybe it was that he didn't want to set himself up in competition with me. If he didn't do the thesis, didn't finish it, didn't pass the orals, I don't think he would have handled that very well. Because he was like a father figure to me and I was the son, and he had to be smarter.

I was the son. He took me under his wing. He was like a father figure.
I listened and said nothing.
He had to be smarter.
So that was one thing, Nino said at last.
He was silent for a few moments.
And the other was, I always had this feeling that he backed out because he was afraid of failure. I think he had very little reason to be afraid of

failure, but there was always that chance. And it's funny, because, you know, we worked on uncertainty, on *chance*, averaging, random numbers inserted into otherwise identical scenarios played out ten thousand times, on trying to extract some kind of certainty from randomness, and it's interesting actually that what I think he was always afraid of was— chance! Of *not knowing* whether he could succeed. He just did not want to take that risk. Most people would say, "Okay, I tried, I failed, that's the end of it." But your father couldn't handle failure, and so he'd rather not try than risk failing.

My mind was racing. Naturally I was thinking of what Uncle Howard had revealed late the previous year: that Daddy had had a chance to go to West Point but had turned it down, nobody knew why. I was thinking of the times I had come close to quitting graduate school, of giving up on my dissertation, and then my father would say, *You don't want to be haunted by an unwritten dissertation*, and so I went on. All those years he had let us think he hadn't finished because of circumstances beyond his control—because, in a way, of Mother, of us. But now it turned out that the decision had been his. A spasm of anger coursed through me as I thought of how he'd lied to me—to all of us. And then I felt only sadness. He had been afraid, or insecure, or both. I had been afraid and insecure, too. Was there a difference?

Suddenly I flushed with shame and realized what the difference was. Unlike me, my father didn't have a father who pushed him to finish, who wanted him to achieve more than he had, who was willing to have his son beat the Homeric odds and be more than his father had been.

As if reading my mind, Nino said, I always got the feeling that this was a loss in his life, and I think that's why he was very concerned about the success of his children.

Barbara arched an eyebrow. The way my father had driven us all to achieve academic success, his vocal enjoyment of any such achievements on our part, even when he was in the presence of friends whose children were not so academically inclined, were notorious. Barbara and I grinned at each other, but Nino was quiet, ruminating.

I think this is why marks of success were *so* important to him, he went on. An award: that was good! An advanced degree: that was good! It's as if those were a kind of armor. Because emotionally and intellectually, he did not want to be vulnerable. *Vulnerable!* That's the key word about Jay. I suppose he overcompensated by wanting to seem tough, by having this—you know, this strong ethical code. Rigid, even.

Seeing me smile, he grew mellow. Ah, I remember once, we were on a business trip in El Paso—this was in the early sixties, we were young, but of course your father was married by then. After a lavish dinner with our hosts, lots of wine, we got into the hotel elevator to go back up to our rooms, and these two beautiful Mexican girls got in. I suppose they were—well, anyway, they looked us up and down. I turned to your father, and he gave me one of those looks and said, "You do whatever you want. I'm going to bed."

I thought of him saying, *His mother was beautiful—not pretty,* *beautiful*.

I thought of him saying, *There are these things you have with someone, not physical things, but private jokes and memories you gather over time, little things that nobody else knows about.*

I thought of him saying, *When you have those things, they keep you connected long after everything else becomes <u>unrecognizable</u>.*

I said nothing.

Soon after, Barbara spoke up for the first time. At some point the talk had meandered away from Nino's reminiscences of my father to other subjects, mostly about the funny adventures he'd had in Italy while teaching courses at a university there, a time during which his first marriage had fallen apart. But eventually the talk circled back to Daddy and how he'd taken my *Odyssey* seminar a year earlier. Of course Nino had heard about it at the time, from my father. It was in reference to some humorous story about the seminar I'd been telling that Barbara—who, like Mother, had been a public-school teacher and told me that she'd reread the *Odyssey* herself recently—suddenly exclaimed, Of course Jay hated Odysseus! Odysseus was an adventurer, a liar. A risk-taker!

We all laughed. Nino said, A character like Odysseus, getting away with so much all the time, would irritate the *pants* off of him!

It was at that moment that Barbara looked at me and said, slowly, Oh, *I* know what you're doing. I know why you interviewed your uncle. I know why you're here!

I looked at her and said, What am I doing? Why am I here?

Barbara smiled with slow self-satisfaction, like a student who is convinced she has outwitted the teacher. She said, You're doing what Telemachus did.

I laughed, but said nothing.

She pressed me.

And? So? What have you learned?

I started talking.

The last of the *Odyssey*'s recognition scenes takes place in its final book, Book 24. After being reunited with Penelope, Odysseus leaves the palace and goes looking for his father in the countryside outside of town, where the old man has exiled himself. *A son in search of his father.* This is how the *Odyssey* begins, and this is how it ends.

Odysseus finds Laertes tending his orchard, but rather than rushing up to him to "kiss and hug him and tell his tale from start to finish, how he'd returned at last to his native land," he decides, curiously, to test the old man, to "draw him out with stinging words." And so he once again assumes a false identity, introducing himself to Laertes as an old friend of Odysseus—whom, he declares, he'd seen alive and well not more than five years earlier. But the decrepit old king, worn out by grief for the son he is convinced has died, sinks to his knees and, scooping up handfuls of dirt from the ground, rubs it into his hair in abject grief. This sight, in turn, overwhelms Odysseus, who abandons the last of his many lies and, after declaring his true identity to his father, embraces him at long last.

The poem ends not long after, when Laertes, Odysseus, and Telemachus face down a furious crowd of armed men: the fathers of the slain Suitors, come together in an angry mob to seek vengeance for the deaths of their sons. "Ah, what a day for me," Laertes declares as they march out to do battle, "to see my son and grandson vie in courage!" But it is the grandfather, the old man wasted by years, impotent and hopeless, whom the *Odyssey* ennobles in a final moment of magic: as the three generations of men face their enemies, Athena endows Laertes with youthful vigor, and with a mighty cast of his javelin he kills the father of Antinoüs. But this is the battle's only casualty; for Athena and Zeus now connive to bring the poem to an end—just as, fifteen thousand lines earlier, they had connived to set it in motion. After magically wiping the memory of the slain men from the minds of their outraged kin, the two gods force the warring mortals to agree to a peace treaty, whose terms are set by Athena.

Certain commentators and readers, ancient and modern, have disliked this rather stiffly public and civic ending; the epic, they insist, "really" ends at Book 23, with the reunion between Odysseus and Penelope. But to argue this is to forget the way the *Odyssey* begins: with a crisis in Ithaca, a stalemate that has frozen the lives not only of Odysseus' wife and son but of his people, too . . . Still, a final moment of mischief follows the reference to the solemn treaty. In the poem's last two lines Homer describes the goddess of wisdom at the moment she imposes the truce:

> . . . *Pallas Athena, daughter of Zeus who bears the Aegis,*
> *who'd taken on the likeness of Mentor in form and voice.*

And so the *Odyssey* ends with a wink. The disguises and deceits go on.

As if in tacit confirmation of those who have thought that the real climax of the *Odyssey* is the reunion between Penelope and Odysseus, our discussion of that scene during the final meeting of Classics 125: The *Odyssey* of Homer ran over the break and well into the second half of the session. For this reason, we had relatively little time to talk about the encounter between Odysseus and his father and about the controversial end of the poem. The class, like the epic itself, moved more quickly as it reached its end; so many students were talking at once as the hour reached twelve-thirty that my notes from that session are a jumble.

A couple of kids did want to talk about the Odysseus-Laertes scene. Madeline, for instance, said she thought it was probably the most emotionally gratifying of all Odysseus' reunions. Nina was bothered by the hero's capricious needling of his father.

But this seems like complete *torture*, she cried. It was the most vehement response she'd had to anything all semester. I really didn't like that at *all*, she went on. I think it's just Odysseus stuck in the habit of playing his games, but he no longer has any reason at this point to keep his identity a secret. It just felt *off* to me.

Jack had just made an interesting reply to Nina's comment—I think, he said, that testing Laertes was necessary because of who Odysseus is; would Laertes ever believe Odysseus was who he says he is if he *didn't* test everyone?!—when I saw my father pointing at his watch. It was 12:40; we were running late. He had a train to catch.

We were finished. I said a few words about how much I'd enjoyed the seminar, and a few of the kids clapped, a bit self-consciously, and then they stood up and milled around for a little while and then they all left.

I drove my father to the train.

It was only when I was returning home from the station that I realized I hadn't asked the one question I'd really needed an answer to: a question that, unlike too many of my questions, perhaps, wasn't rhetorical, wasn't designed, in some way, to lead them to a thought or an interpretation or a notion that I, or one of my teachers, or one of their teachers, had arrived at through all those years and decades and even centuries of reading, but was a genuine appeal for information, for knowledge, for education. I had been so struck by Madeline's and Nina's outrage over Odysseus' treatment of his father, so intrigued by Jack's notion that distrust is somehow at the core of Odysseus' multifaceted identity, that I'd never had a chance to draw their attention to an anomaly that had struck me often.

As we had so often discussed, the *Odyssey* is a poem in which story-telling in all its forms is celebrated, some of those forms being deceitful and even dishonest, as the stories told by Odysseus himself demonstrate. And yet although he feels no compunction in lying to his men, to his hosts, to his benefactors, to his servants, to his son, to his wife, even to Athena herself, the only falsehood that Odysseus is incapable of narrating all the way to its conclusion is the one he starts to tell Laertes. My question, had I only had a chance to ask it, would have been this: Why is it that, in Homer's eyes, the only truly unimaginable lie is the one that a son might tell to his father?

It was two or three days after this that Froma, my graduate-school mentor, urged me to go on the *Odyssey* cruise.

I'd called her for her birthday. Happy Birthday! I yelled into the phone. She made a dismissive noise. How old are *you* now? she coughed. I told her and she cried, Fifty-*what*?! No wonder I'm old.

Then we started talking, and soon the conversation turned to the semester that had just ended.

So how did it go? she asked. Did he talk a lot in class?

I burst out laughing and told her about some of the tussles we'd had over the course of the semester. *He's not a hero because he cries. He's not a hero because he cheats on his wife. He's not a hero because he gets help from the gods!*

What did the students think of him?

As it happened, I knew with some specificity what the students thought, since, to my surprise, a few of them had e-mailed me after the last class to tell me how much they'd enjoyed having Daddy in the course. I read some of the e-mails aloud to Froma.

Tommy wrote, "You could always tell that he was just as enthusiastic

about reading as we were, and there was a great deal of intellectual curiosity even at his age."

That's sweet! Froma exclaimed.

Jack wrote to say that he thought my father was "quite a happy and
humorous character." "Having your father in class was wonderful,"
he wrote, "he brightened up the room with his presence." Happy and
humorous? I thought when I'd first read the e-mail. Brightened? Who
was he *talking* about?

A note from Blond Tom surprised me for a different reason:

> I had the pleasure of running into your father outside of class. Once
> we were both at the Rhinecliff train station. I was waiting for friends,
> he was waiting to get home. We talked for about an hour about
> the *Odyssey* and life in general. What struck me was how honest,
> engaged, and thoughtful he was. It was a great conversation. Thanks
> for bringing him with you each week.

When I'd first read this, I wondered why my father hadn't mentioned
running into Tom at the train station. In early March—just about when
we were starting on the Apologoi and he announced that he'd decided
to start taking the train up each week rather than driving—I was convinced that it had been because he was afraid of driving and was too
embarrassed to admit it. It had never occurred to me that there might be
another reason for him to want to take the train each week.

I had a note from Madeline.

> I ran into him many times at the Rhinecliff train station; he always
> recognized me and would say hello. We had many discussions about
> the *Odyssey* and class which helped me develop my ideas. He spent a
> whole train ride with one of my good friends, also from Long Island,
> talking about his work as a professor and at Grumman. He was very
> easy to talk to and generally lovely. I'm sure he was very impressed
> with you, even if he didn't always agree with your interpretations!

Brendan wrote:

Your father impressed me one day while we were waiting for the train
by telling me a story about when he studied Latin in high school.
What impressed me was that after all these years he wanted to finish
what he started when he was not that much younger than us. How
many people can say that?

I kept reading and Froma chuckled. Well, he certainly made an
impression, don't you think.

He certainly did, I said. I doubt I'll ever have a class like *that* again.

I tried to sound amused, but I was thinking. All semester long, I'd
been regaling my friends and colleagues with stories about how my
eighty-one-year-old father had decided to go back to college and take my
Odyssey course; but in the end my father really had been a "student," a
word that derives from the Latin noun *studium*, "painstaking application." He'd been applying himself in ways I hadn't dreamed of, and I
hadn't seen a thing.

On the other end of the line, Froma was asking what I was going to
be doing over the summer. I could envision the blue smoke wandering
toward the ceiling of her Princeton office, past the sagging bookshelves,
the macramé wall hangings, the posters from the seventies and eighties
advertising conferences in Paris and Groningen and Berlin and Jerusa-
lem, most of whose participants were now as dead as the Librarians of
Alexandria. There was a metallic rattle in the background, like coins
jingling in a pocket. She was playing with her jewelry, I thought, twining
her latest object around her finger.

Wait! she cried. There is something you have to do! I'm sending you
a link.

I smiled, thinking of all the times over the years that Froma has
pushed me to do things, go places, try to see things in a new, less rigid
way. I thought of something she'd said to me once when I was struggling
to finish my dissertation. I'd come to her office, blocked and despairing

because some big idea I'd been excited about wasn't working out. After I finished, she fixed her eyes on me and said, *Your* problem is that you see everything that doesn't fit your theory as a problem, instead of as an opportunity to enlarge your thinking, to come up with a better theory. You're so fixated on your own ideas that you don't see what's right in front of your face.

I remembered her saying this. And then it hit me. Suddenly I thought, I've done it again—I've been doing it all semester. Again and again, I'd been so intent on having the kids see things my way, so fixated on making sure that the interpretations I had absorbed as a student would be the ones that they took away, too, that I'd seen their resistances, their failures to notice what I wanted them to notice, as a problem, rather than as a solution—as a way to see something I'd never noticed myself. They'd tried to tell me all this, that day when they were so eagerly explaining their ideas about the Apologoi, about how maybe Homer was saying that Odysseus had made his whole story up; but I'd barely listened.

Something Brendan had said that day echoed in my mind. *I wonder if you think we could say it's a story about listening? About how your own perspective affects how you hear things? I mean, the real problem in this story is that from the very start Polyphemus hears what he wants to hear.*

I'd heard what I wanted to hear. And I'd seen what I'd wanted to see, too—and failed to notice, again, what had been right before my eyes. I remember how irritated I'd been with my father at various points during the semester for being aloof from the students, for sitting in his chair off to the left behind my shoulder and referring to Madeline and Nina and Blond Tom with toneless pronouns, *I agree with what she said, I agree with what he said,* and yet all that time he'd been getting to know them, taking the trouble to listen to them. All semester long I'd vainly envisioned myself as some kind of pedagogical Odysseus, leading them on a thrilling adventure through the text, and in the end I'd turned out to be the Cyclops.

As I thought these glum thoughts, Froma cried out, triumph in her voice, I've found it!

Found what? I said. Hold one sec, she said, and then my in-box pinged. I opened her e-mail and clicked on a link. It was a website for a cruise line. "Retracing the *Odyssey*," I read.

You *have* to go, Froma cried; and so I called my father and sent him the link, and to my surprise he called me back and said, Let's *do* it, Dan.

There was one student e-mail about my father's presence in Classics 125: The *Odyssey* of Homer that I didn't share with Froma that day— whether out of my shamed sense of failure or an obscure competitiveness with my father, I still can't say.

The last of the e-mails I received after the semester ended was from Trisha, who would later declare a major in Classics and who distinguished herself in her senior year with a—yes—scathingly brilliant senior thesis about the theme of caves in Homer and later Greek literature, thereby making herself the latest link in a chain of scholars of the *Odyssey* going back to the third century A.D. scholar Porphyry, one of whose treatises is entitled *On the Cave of the Nymphs in the Odyssey*. Her note ended with a phrase that describes, with a terseness and lack of sentimentality I cannot help thinking my father would have admired, the effect that teachers everywhere have always hoped to have on their students:

> He was an incredible man and a wonderful presence in every class. Talking with him was a pleasure. I'll always read the *Odyssey* with him in mind.

You never do know, really, where education will lead; who will be listening and, in certain cases, who will be doing the teaching.

SÊMA

(The Sign)

———◁◦◦▷———

APRIL 6, 2012

"I declare to you that this here is our sign: I do not know
if the bed remains in place, lady, or if by now
some other man has moved it somewhere else . . ."

—*Odyssey*, 23.202–4

The pervasive anxiety that haunts the opening of the *Odyssey*, the seemingly insoluble uncertainty that afflicts the absent hero's son, wife, and household, is symbolized by a memorable if macabre motif: an empty tomb, a missing body. As the epic proceeds, various characters lament the fact (as they see it) that Odysseus, assumed by this point to have died at sea, has not been buried. The missing father, husband, king, has no tomb, no tumulus—the high grave mound the Bronze Age Greeks built to mark the presence of a dead body; no inscription to say who he was and what his deeds were. "If he'd gone down with comrades off in Troy," Telemachus complains in Book 1, "all the Greeks together would have raised a grave mound to him . . . But the tempests have ripped him away, no fame for him!" That the dead might go unburied was a possibility that provoked in the Greeks a special horror, one already evident in the first lines of the *Iliad*, a poem whose own proem expresses revulsion at the thought that some of the heroes who died at Troy ended up as "the pickings of birds and dogs." A pronounced cultural anxiety about unburied bodies is evident in many other Greek myths as well. It is central, for instance, to the story of Oedipus' daughter Antigone, a myth dramatized in Sophocles' tragedy of that name, which was written three hundred years after the Homeric poems were set down:

Antigone, the young princess who, at the cost of her own life, challenges a cruel law that forbids the burial of her brother, a traitor to the state. Interestingly, the play seems to vindicate Antigone's position, since her antagonist, the king who has promulgated the law, eventually gives in and agrees to bury the dead youth himself. This notion that even villains and criminals deserve a decent burial goes back to the *Odyssey* itself. In Book 3, we learn that the murderers of Agamemnon were interred together in a common tomb and given proper funeral rites after being slain by the dead general's vengeful son.

The preoccupation with the rites of burial continues throughout the epic. In Book 11, when Odysseus travels to Hades and encounters the shade of the unfortunate sailor Elpenor, the ghost, as we know, begs him for a funeral:

> *. . . burn me up, together with such armor as was mine,*
> *heap up a grave for me on the gray sea's strand,*
> *so even men to come will know of this unlucky man.*
> *Do all of this, then plant upon my grave the oar*
> *that I plied while still I lived, rowing with my mates.*

As we also know, Odysseus obeys and erects a memorial according to his wishes—a tomb that is, in fact, exactly like the one Odysseus' family wished that *he* might have had, back in Book 1. And a bit later, when the disguised Odysseus takes shelter in Eumaeus' hut, the theme resurfaces. Like some other characters, the loyal swineherd is convinced that his beloved master is long dead, lost at sea, and he repeats, almost verbatim, the sad words we first heard in Book 1: "If he'd gone down with comrades off in Troy, all the Greeks together would have raised a grave mound to him . . . But the tempests have ripped him away, no fame for him!"

Curiously, these same words are repeated once again in the final book of the epic, Book 24, in the course of a conversation between two ghosts, once news of Odysseus' triumph has reached the Land of the Dead. One ghost is Achilles; the other is Agamemnon. Odysseus' success is particularly gratifying to the latter, whose homecoming—murdered at the hands of his adulterous wife and her lover after his triumphal entry into his palace as the conqueror of Troy—represents, as my students came to understand so well, the inverse of Odysseus' secretive return home: covertly, in disguise, to a wife who turns out to have been faithful. The memory of Agamemnon's sad homecoming inspires the ghost of Achilles to repeat the by-now familiar lines: "If only you had found your fated death in the city of the Trojans," the dead Achilles tells the dead Agamemnon, "then all the allied Greeks would have built you a tomb there." Poignantly, Agamemnon replies by describing, at considerable length, the elaborate funeral rites that the Greeks gave to Achilles when *he* died: a scene that the *Iliad* itself, whose narrative ends before the death of Achilles, cannot illustrate for us. For Achilles' benefit, Agamemnon reprises the magnificent obsequies: the wailing of the Greek soldiers, the unnerving cry of his grieving mother, the sea nymph Thetis; the songful lament sung by none other than the nine Muses, the seventeen days of lamentation and the burning of the body on the eighteenth, the golden urn, made by Hephaestus himself, into which his mother placed the cremated bones. "Over them we, the holy host of spear-bearing Argives, then raised a great and noble burial-mound upon a jutting headland."

It is hard not to feel, in this final book of the poem, that in its repeated climactic references to tombs and burials—Agamemnon's lack of one, Achilles' sumptuous funeral—the *Odyssey* is "burying" the *Iliad*: which is to say, providing closure, saying its farewells, both to its predecessor and to itself. Although the *Odyssey* has the broad contours of a comedy—after all, it ends with success, rejoicing, and a wedding of sorts—these oddly frequent references to tombs and burials, with their intimations of finality, endings, completions, have a distinctly melancholy aura.

Indeed, the *Odyssey* goes to great lengths to give us the particulars of Odysseus' own death, although it doesn't occur until long after the action of the poem is over. In a scene set during the same visit to Hades in Book 11 that gives the details of poor Elpenor's death, the seer Teiresias anticipates the end of Odysseus and the end of the poem in the same breath. He tells Odysseus that once he has killed the Suitors he must appease Poseidon, who has been so long angered at him. To do this Odysseus must take an oar, the symbol of his own long hardship and also the symbol of the sea itself, Poseidon's domain, and walk with it inland until he encounters people so ignorant of the sea that they think the oar is a winnowing fan—an object associated with the harvest, with agriculture: with, that is, dry land. There, Teiresias declares, Odysseus must plant the oar in the ground and make sacrifice to Poseidon. Which is to say, Odysseus will bring the sea to where it has never been known before, thereby expanding the renown of Poseidon, the god whom he has offended and whom, in this final act of closure, he now finally appeases. What is so interesting here is that the expiatory monument Odysseus is to erect uncannily resembles the tomb that Elpenor has begged to be given: a mound with an oar stuck on top. This strange monument is, in fact, a kind of "tomb" for Odysseus: for at the very instant the ghost of Teiresias dictates the odd rite that Odysseus is to perform, it also foretells the moment of his death, many years in the future:

> *Far from the sea a gentle death will come*
> *for you, will take you when you're ripe with years,*
> *surrounded by your people: a blessing unto you.*

This extended flash-forward to the hero's end will find a counterpart later in the poem, in the extended flashback to his birth that we get in Book 19, as the story of his scar unfolds. These pairings—the death and the birth, the flash-forward and the flashback—remind you that, however much this lengthy tale may look like a richly detailed account of a single episode in its subject's life, the *Odyssey* is, in fact, a kind of biography, stealthily encompassing the whole of its hero's existence by means of narrative and chronological acrobatics. The death of Elpenor is one such feint, a stand-in for a death we will never experience in the course of the epic; but we nonetheless understand that it is only when the hero himself is dead and buried, mourned and entombed, that the story can end.

The Greek word for "grave" that Elpenor uses when he asks Odysseus to "heap up a grave" for him is *sêma*. The word can mean "grave" or "tomb," but that's only a secondary meaning: the primary meaning is "sign" or "signal," a meaning that survives in the English word "semiotics," which refers to the study of signs and symbols, to the philosophical theory of how meaning itself is generated. As far as the Greeks who built them were concerned, the tombs or *sêmata* (the plural of *sêma*) that have such striking prominence in the *Odyssey* were means of signaling information about their occupants; they were meant to tell tales. In Book 1, for instance, a character laments the fact that, because Odysseus never got a grave mound at Troy, he will have no "fame"—an assertion that suggests the extent to which the tomb is meant to "speak" about its inhabitant. Similarly, in Book 11, Elpenor asserts that his *sêma*, adorned with the oar that symbolizes his life's employment, will provide information about him for generations of the future. And the shrine that Odysseus is commanded to raise to Poseidon, also described in Book 11, is similarly designed to tell a "story"—the story of an enemy of Poseidon who finally makes his peace by introducing the god to men who cannot have known him.

Apart from denoting the various tombs and memorials and monuments associated with Odysseus during his long and strange career, the word *sêma* occurs one other time in the *Odyssey*, although the context is not so gloomy. This is in Book 23, when the outraged Odysseus, snared by Penelope's clever trap, describes in such loving detail the bed that he had built for them, the bed whose tell-tale secret was that it could never be moved. At the conclusion of his impassioned speech, he refers to the secret of the bed as the *sêma*, the "sign," between him and Penelope, the symbol of their immovable bond.

All of which is to say that, in the world of the *Odyssey*, a *sêma* is a story made visible: the monument, the mound, the oar, the bed, all are signals that, for those who know how to read them, tell tales as clearly as does the tale in which these *sêmata* are embedded, the tale the poet himself sings.

Still, it is true that the word most often denotes a grave, which can take the form of a mound or an object (an oar, say) which, in time, becomes a substitute for the invisible body, attracting the eyes of passersby and inviting them to pause and take notice; while the inscription, which is often in verse and which the strangers read once they've stopped to look, tells the story of the life that the body once lived.

My father had his stroke late in January, two months after he'd fallen in the parking lot. By New Year's he had recovered almost entirely from the small fracture in his pelvis caused by the fall; the only glitch had been a small blood clot that developed in his leg just after the holidays, something his doctors had warned us might happen. A couple of weeks after the first of the year he went into the local hospital to have the clot dealt with—a minor procedure; he was out the next day. To prevent another clot they put him on blood thinners, and it was the blood thinners that caused the stroke, the diluted blood leaking through the blood vessels of his brain, the tiny vessels which, the neurosurgeon later told us, all those early years of smoking had made dangerously friable. Essentially, this doctor said as he showed my mother and me a picture of my father's brain that first night, the night I met her in the ER after she'd called 911, after *he couldn't plug in the iPad and I knew something was wrong*, essentially the vessels have the consistency of spun sugar; it doesn't take much to make them crumble away over time. And even as I stood there looking at my father's brain I thought how effective the homely simile was, *as crumbly as spun sugar*. Homer might have thought of it.

As crumbly as spun sugar. I thought of my father all those years ago bragging about how he'd quit smoking cold turkey, of how proud he'd been to have done it the hard way. I looked at the CAT scan and looked at the doctor and said, But my father doesn't smoke. He quit years ago, I think in 1970.

The doctor shook his head. It's a long time, I know, but believe me the damage is already done.

We'd been told from the start that "the damage" was extensive. On the night of the stroke, the young neurosurgeon held up X-rays and MRIs to the light and said things about prefrontal lobes. This, he said, pointing to a dark blotch, is the stroke.

My mother was sitting in a chair next to my father's bed in the neurosurgical ICU, where a number of monitors tracked the rate of Daddy's pulse, his breathing, the chemicals in his blood. It looks like his study, I thought. In her chair, my mother looked smaller, ruffled. She'd tucked her head deep down into her parka, like a bird trying to burrow into its own feathers.

That? she said, pointing with a shaky finger to the Rorschachy stain the surgeon had gestured to. The diamond my grandfather had bought her fifty years before because he thought it suited her better than the ring my father would have been able to buy glittered on a knotty finger as it traced the outline of the blotch: the "bleed." But it looks like it covers his whole head, she said.

The doctor said, That's my point, Mrs. Mendelsohn. It's very extens— it's very big.

My mother suddenly drew herself up. Over the past few years she'd been getting smaller and more curved, but at that moment she seemed half a foot taller. She faced the doctor. I know what "extensive" means, young man. I taught in the New York City public school system. I am a teacher and my husband is a mathematician. My son is a professor. We are not idiots and you do *not* have to use monosyllables with us.

I'm sorry, the doctor said. He was clearly startled.

Don't speak to me like I'm a child, Mother went on. I am just trying to understand what happened to my husband. He was having lunch with his old friends from work, he was fine, and then he couldn't find the door of the restaurant, and then he couldn't plug in his iPad. I don't understand how this could happen.

It was the blood thinners he was on, the doctor said. As you know there was a small blood clot which was caused by the fracture from his fall in—he flipped through some papers on his clipboard—in November.

Yes, my mother said. We were all at Andrew's, that's my oldest son.

We were in California for Thanksgiving. They were only going *shopping*, Jay and Andrew were shopping for Thanksgiving dinner, everyone was on their way. And there was that *fucking* piece of metal—I looked up, startled; I don't think I'd ever heard my mother use the word "fuck" before—sticking up out of the thing in the parking lot where you put the wagons, and Jay tripped over it and he fell down. That's how it began.

Yes, the doctor said, with practiced smoothness. Yes. But we don't need the whole story of that, it's not about the fall anymore, it's about your husband's stroke, which was caused by the blood thinners he was put on last week to deal with the blood clot.

Well, *I* need the story, my mother snapped back. I am trying to make sense of this.

There would be many moments like this over the next three months: the doctors talking down to Mother, Mother snapping back. It's the last of my Assertive Phases, she said later. I laughed. During the seventies, when she was in her early forties—this was when women's lib was in the air, and her conversations with the Gang of Four at our holiday gatherings had taken on a whispered, vaguely conspiratorial note as they talked around the kitchen tables in New Jersey and Long Island and suburban D.C. about Betty Friedan and Gloria Steinem—during the seventies she'd gone through the first of these "phases." M *is for* "mother," *not* "maid"! she would retort when one of us asked her to do something. *Wash your own tennis socks, you know where the washing machine is.* And then, in the eighties, she got involved in local environmental activism, crying into bullhorns at rallies and making leaflets and confronting congressmen with statistics about the groundwater levels of certain toxins, the figures and charts unspooling in red ink across the pages of her yellow legal pads. *Your mother has a very fine mind, and now she's putting it to work,* my father would sometimes say during that particular assertive phase, and it was hard not to miss the note of admiration in his voice. . . . My mother liked to keep the bottles of perfumes she had long since stopped wearing on a shelf in her bathroom cabinet, exquisitely small ampules in crystal or black glass bearing exotic gold labels, SHALIMAR and SUBLIME and ARPÈGE, the liquid inside long since reduced to a brown concentrate visible at the bottom of each bottle, and when you'd open a bottle, as I liked secretly to do when I was growing up, the aroma exploded into the air as powerful as smelling salts, each suddenly recalling some evening from the distant past, Mother in the early 1970s in a green velvet pantsuit, a silver belt low on her hips, going to some fancy bar mitzvah, Mother in the late 1960s kissing me and Andrew good night, leaning down in her Persian-lamb coat with the matching hat, her chestnut hair reddish against the black swirls of the lambskin, off to a dinner party "in the city," Daddy looking at her proudly while he held the door open for her, pretending to be impatient while she tugged her black kid gloves on but enjoying it all. When my father said, *Your mother has a very fine mind and now she's putting it to work*, the aroma of something from the past, something I'd assumed had been emptied out years before, a whiff of something that had been between them long before we were ever born, a respect he had had for her intellect and taste, her energy and humor, her enjoyment of his bristling inquisitiveness and impatience with fools, their love of certain puns, jokes, crosswords, lyrics—this ghost-scent of what their connection to each other had once been rose powerfully into the air; and it occurred to me then, during Mother's years as an environmental organizer, that the enjoyment they seemed to be taking from each other during this period, accompanied by a noticeable relaxation of the atmosphere in the house, was not coincidental.

Now, in the neurosurgical ICU, Mother was asserting herself again. *Well, I need a story.*

She's her father's daughter, it occurred to me then: everything has to be a *story*. And then I thought of the *Odyssey* course. The epic is so filled with stories, not least those told by its hero, tales both true and false, outright lies and "enhanced" versions of things that really did happen; everything that happens, it reminds us, can be a gripping story in the hands of the right storyteller. What is Odysseus, in the end—the hero whose final act of vengeful violence is compared, by means of another memorable simile, to a bard stringing his lyre—but the poet of his own life?

We all need narrative to make sense of the world. The doctor needed his charts; my mother needed a tale to tell that linked Thanksgiving and the misstep in the supermarket parking lot to the blinking screens with their inscrutable blobs and lines glowing green in the darkness, to my father lying there twitching like a doll on a string, a plastic tube, as wide and incongruously bright blue as some item of plumbing, hanging from his half-open mouth, taped into place. Maybe my father—who, as I now know, had grown up so alone, so taciturn—had needed my mother's stories, long ago.

Over the next few days my father lay there, immobile. Then, during the last week of January, he showed signs of awareness: if you called to him loudly he would squeeze his eyes shut to show that he could hear you. For a week that was all he could do. After the news got out, people started coming to see him, and each in turn would sit in the small plastic chair my mother had sat in and would talk loudly to my father and as they talked he'd squeeze his eyes, the way he used to when he was trying to remember something that would prove how sharp he was, a baseball statistic, the year of the Spanish flu epidemic, the name of Franklin Roosevelt's second vice president, of an actress in a B movie. Andrew and Ginny and their kids flew out from California, Matt and Maya and their daughter drove up from D.C., Lily and our boys came from New Jersey, Jennifer and Greg came from Baltimore with their two small sons, Eric came in almost every day from Manhattan. We would take turns sitting in the plastic chair next to the gigantic bed with its tubing and buttons and screens, my father as cramped inside it as an astronaut in a space capsule, and we'd loudly sing Rodgers and Hart songs, ignoring the irritated looks of the staff, sing the lyrics whose fine craftsmanship had so pleased him.

> *Is your figure less than Greek?*
> *Is your mouth a little weak?*
> *When you open it to speak, are you smart?*

But now my father couldn't open his mouth to speak. He could only squeeze his eyes shut so we'd know he was in there, somewhere. Others came, people I didn't know, people from Grumman, people he taught with at Hofstra. Once I came into the ICU early in the morning and a young man was sitting in the chair. Sorry, who are you? I asked, and he looked up and said, My name is Khan. I was your father's student, he was a wonderful mentor for me. On another morning during the first few days of February—a year earlier, in Classics 125: The *Odyssey* of Homer, we'd been discussing the Telemachy—the nurse who was cleaning Daddy said to me, Mr. Mendelsohn was here again this morning, he comes so early! and I said, Which Mr. Mendelsohn? and she smiled apologetically and said she didn't know. Could it be Eric? I wondered as I wandered off to ask at the front desk. Oh, I couldn't say for sure, the woman there said, he's such a nice old gentleman who comes early in the morning and sits with him, he said he takes two buses to get here from Queens, it's over an hour each way.

Uncle Howard.

Nino came with Barbara. *Jay, Jay,* Nino called, grasping my father's hand, you have to get better, there's still so much we have to talk about.

For the next ten days he did seem to improve. Or, as the doctor said, "stabilize," a word we clung to, although we dared not ask what it would mean for the long term: stabilized at *this* level? My brothers and sister and I would hear this word, "stabilize," and we'd shake our heads, not even having to say aloud what we were all thinking: that this is what he had always feared, that rather than linger on this stable but low, low plateau he would rather have us *pull the plug.*

Then, one Monday evening at the end of the first week of February when I was staying at my parents' house, the hospital called in the middle of the night and told us we needed to come in. Your father's condition is deteriorating, the voice at the other end of the line said. I repeated the words to Mother. She was calm: I sensed she had been expecting something like this. We dressed in silence. It was four-fifteen in the morning.

Put on your boots and your scarf and your hat, she said to me in the hallway, as if I were a seven-year-old going on a school trip. As we left she flicked off the light switches one by one, as she had done every night before we went to bed. *Off, off, off, off, and off.* We went out into the cold.

The doctor said, The problem is the swelling of the brain. It's actually swelled so much that the brain has moved.

I looked at him blankly. What do you mean, his brain has moved? How can your brain *move?*

There was something appalling about the idea, repellent. I said, I mean, how can it—it's in your skull, your brain is inside—where would it *go?*

I was babbling. The doctor looked at me patiently. I know it sounds odd, but it can, in fact, shift within the skull.

After a moment my mother looked at him calmly and said, Well, what does that mean? She had brought a yellow pad, and as he talked she wrote things down.

It's not good. The movement, the swelling, are likely to have permanent effects on the brain.

My mother said, What effects? and the doctor said, It's impossible to know right now. But if it worsens, they could be serious, and then we'd be in a situation where you'd have to make a decision.

A decision, my mother said.

A decision, I echoed. We were quiet for a moment, and then I looked at the doctor and said helplessly, My dad is a person who prizes his mind above everything.

My mother didn't say anything. The monitors glowed and bleeped. The space capsule was on its voyage to God knew where. Maybe my father knew, I thought wildly as I looked over at him. Maybe he was actually in there, steering it.

The doctor said, You might want some time with him now, but then you can go home. You'll need some rest for tomorrow. You don't have to decide anything now.

I looked at my mother. I do want some time with him, I said.

She nodded. I'm going to get you a coffee, she said briskly. You still have the drive home and you're exhausted. She marched off with her yellow pad crooked in her arm, like a school principal about to make the rounds of the classrooms. As she passed the nurse's station I heard her saying, Oh, thank you, dear, I know where it is. Can I get *you* a cup?

Then I was alone with my father.

He lay perfectly motionless: the only movement in the room was the jerky progress of the fluids through the IV tubes and the rhythmical wheezing of the breathing machine they'd put him on. Was I imagining it, or had something indeed changed in him? Over the past days he had seemed to be present in his body. It was clear he could hear us, it was clear that—as a kindly nurse had put it one day early on, when I was trying to describe my sense that he hadn't been obliterated by the stroke— "someone was home in there." But now, after his brain had moved, I was no longer so sure. It was as if he were already dead.

I sat there awkwardly, feeling self-conscious. Daddy? I said.

The screens glowed and the graphs pinged.

I looked at the face I knew so well, the sallow oval, the half-moon orbits of the brown eyes deepened and exaggerated now that he'd lost so much weight. As ravaged as it was, it looked curiously innocent and smooth in the half-light, like a sleeping child's. I thought of him as a child, alone in the apartment in the Bronx while his mother and father worked, while Howie was away in the war, while Bobby was trawling the streets on his crutches showing how tough he was. I imagined this solitary child hunched over some book in the empty apartment, hungrily beginning his lifetime of reading; anything to fill the empty space. I examined his face. The furrows in his brow between his eyes were deeply etched—from all that *frowning*, I thought, stifling a grin. I thought of him growling at me, *Don't be such a sissy!* I looked at his face in profile, the prominent cheekbones thrown into high relief by the strange subaqueous light of the monitors, the hooked nose swerving, the tight horizontal of the thin mouth obscenely dragged down by the fat blue breathing tube. I thought of him saying, *It's beautiful, Dan;* and then, *But don't believe that shit about perfect love.* He looked noble, I thought; it was the face of a dead pharaoh laid out on a slab, ready for the embalmers. His hand lay limply at his side, wrapped in tubes and punctured by needles. I thought of this hand holding my own in Calypso's cave. I thought of Ksenia saying, *Your father is a very charming man.* I thought of him saying to me, after the lecture about "Ithaca," something I'd yearned so often to hear from him when I was a boy, and didn't: *You did good, Dan.* I thought of these things, looking at my father on what might be the last night of his life, and thought, Who is this man? and realized that I could never really know the answer, now.

Daddy, I called again. He was still.

And then I thought, I'd never have been able to know the answer anyway. My mind went back to all the things I'd thought I was keeping from my father over the years, and how he'd known all along. Well, why not? He had made me. A father makes his son out of his flesh and out of his mind and then shapes him with his ambitions and dreams, with his cruelties and failures, too. But a son, although he is of his father, cannot know his father totally, because the father precedes him; his father has always already lived so much more than the son has, so that the son can never catch up, can never know everything. No wonder the Greeks thought that few sons are the equals of their fathers; that most fall short, all too few surpass them. It's not about value; it's about knowledge. The father knows the son whole, but the son can never know the father.

I thought, No wonder Odysseus can't lie to Laertes at the end of the poem.

I looked at him again. *Daddy,* I called softly.

Then a nurse came in and turned on the overhead light, and I was suddenly looking at the face not of a king but of a sick old man: a man who, I understood at some primitive level, was no longer present inside his own body, a man whose brain—his mighty brain which had meant everything to him, which had been the means of his escape from his childhood, had put food on the table and paid for his children's lives, had prodded and pushed us and humiliated us, too, which in the end had contained certain secrets that he shared only with the woman he had been with for six decades—had moved.

I looked at him and knew what we would decide, tomorrow.

Soon afterward my mother and I drove home. Look, it's dawn, my mother said calmly. Glimmers of pink streaked the edges of the sky like fingers. I remembered a nurse friend of mine once telling me that this was the time of day when people died. I didn't share this with my mother, but as I drove home I thought, Let him die, let him die. Let it not get to the point where we have to do it.

The next morning, my mother and I drove to the hospital, where Eric was waiting for us; he'd come in on an early train. The doctor and the "termination team" were going to be talking to us at nine. Nothing had to happen *right now,* the doctor had told us on the phone earlier that morning before we left for the hospital. But it would be good to start thinking about it and preparing ourselves. Of course we would want the other family members to be present, if and when the time came.

As I drove, I felt like I was hovering above my own body.

I'd assumed that the meeting would take place in some special room, a hushed paneled office, someplace quiet. But we just gathered outside of my father's room, standing in the hallway as nurses and interns bustled past with clipboards and gurneys. The doctor was there, and a psychologist and an end-of-life specialist. My mother and brother and I stood nodding as they talked, although it was hard to focus on what they were saying. We'd talked to the rest of the family and we knew before we got there what we were going to do. After all, hadn't Daddy always told us, *Just pull the plug, I don't want to end up being wheeled around a nursing home.* We are talking about ending the life of Jay Mendelsohn, I kept saying to myself as we stood in the hallway. We are going to end the life of Jay Mendelsohn.

Suddenly, as the doctor was answering my mother's question about how long "it" would take once they disconnected Daddy—while he talked she was purposefully writing things on her pad, pressing so hard as she wrote that, as I discovered when we got home later that day and flipped through the pad, each page had left a ghost imprint on the page beneath, like a palimpsest; over the past weeks, whenever we had to talk to a doctor or the nursing staff, she'd brandish her notepads and quote from her lists and the nurse, a young redhead, had looked impressed, and listened carefully—suddenly, as the doctor was elaborating on how long "it" would take, the same nurse edged up to our group.

Doctor, she said.

Irritated at the interruption, the doctor held up a finger and kept talking. The words he said rose thinly into the air, impossible to grasp. *We are going to end the life of Jay Mendelsohn,* I kept saying to myself.

Doctor, the redhead said again, clearing her throat.

The neurosurgeon swiveled around smartly. Yes? he said. What *is* it?

The nurse said, Mr. Mendelsohn is awake and seems to be indicating that he'd like a glass of water.

Expect the unexpected.

Both the *Iliad* and the *Odyssey* end with a suddenness that takes some students by surprise. The *Iliad* fulfills its promise to detail the ramifications of Achilles' rage against his commander, Agamemnon, the last of which is the death of the Trojan leader, Hector (who earlier had slain Achilles' beloved companion, Patroclus—an unforeseen consequence of the hero's vindictive withdrawal from battle). In the years I've taught this work, I've found that most students expect it to end with Achilles' vengeful slaying of the man who killed his friend—a high note of satisfying violence. But in fact that poem ends with a lengthy description of Hector's funeral rites, at the end of which comes the modest final line:

And this was the funeral of Hector, tamer of horses.

This quiet note is almost unnervingly undramatic compared with what has preceded it. At the end of the freshman *Iliad* seminar I was teaching a year after Daddy had taken the *Odyssey* course, a student wrote me an indignant e-mail saying, "That's it?"

So, too, the *Odyssey*, the final lines of which are devoted to a flat and undramatic reference to the peace that Athena and Zeus impose on the warring parties on Ithaca, a scene that is capped by the curious detail about Athena's final disguise:

> . . . *having taken on the likeness of Mentor in form and voice.*

When we discussed these lines on the last day of class, Jack had exclaimed, You turn the page expecting more, but there *is* no more!

My father had said, A good book leaves you wanting more.

After that awful week when my father's brain had moved, he slowly improved. Tough Jay was making a comeback, everyone said. I started to send out e-mails every few days to my siblings and in-laws and my parents' neighbors and friends with updates on his improvement. First he opened his eyes; then he got some strength back in his hand, so that he could squeeze back when you held it. After a few weeks they took him off the breathing tube, which meant that he could talk. The first thing he said was, Where is Mother? Is she okay? And indeed the first thing he said for the rest of his life, each time he woke up, was, *Where is Mother? Is she okay?*

On one such occasion one of my brothers was in the room. He turned to me and said, wonderingly, He really loves her.

Between mid-February and the end of the month he got noticeably stronger. The visits from his children and friends were more animated, now that it looked like he'd make it. At the beginning of March, he was moved out of the neurological unit to a rehab unit. There was a TV in the room; he started watching baseball. It was spring. Lily brought the boys one weekend afternoon and we all crammed into the small room to watch a Mets game. I stood against a wall and observed my father watching the ball game with my boys. They were arguing about a call on a play. I thought of Laertes in the one last moment of glory he was so improbably granted on the battlefield, exulting in the fact that he had lived to see the day when he could stand on the field of battle together with his son and grandson. "Ah, what a day for me!" Odysseus' father says.

He got feisty. He wanted his iPad, he said; he was bored watching all that stupid TV. He wondered when he would get home to play his new electronic keyboard. He'd been teaching himself Bach preludes and fugues. They're hard, he said, but that's the *point*. One day I was sitting with him and he swiped with one stiff hand at his jaw and made a face.

Dan, can't you shave me?

He was right: in all this time he hadn't been shaving, of course, and as fine as his beard was, the scruff made him seem seedy. He didn't look like himself.

I asked the nurse if it was okay, and she said, Sure, use the electric razor in his room. And so I sat down in front of my father and cupped his face in my hands and shaved him. He was as pliant as a child getting a haircut. I was trying to remember the last time I had touched his face; years, maybe.

Thanks, Dan, he said, the consonants squashed because of the stroke.

No problem, Daddy. It's nice to see you looking like yourself again.

In the third week of March the rehab people said, Good news! It was time to see if he could start to walk again. I watched as they strapped him into an elaborate harness attached to heavy leg braces. Two burly young attendants held him upright. He took one awkward, robotic step, then sagged, exhausted. Gently the two young men eased him back into the wheelchair. Good job! one of them said to him, the way you'd talk to a toddler. My father looked at me and said, Now I know how my brother Bobby felt his whole life.

Toward the end of March, an article I'd written about our *Odyssey* cruise was published in a travel magazine. I brought a copy to the hospital. When my father first began to improve, to be himself again, the doctor had told us that his vision had very likely been seriously impaired by the stroke. It's likely that half of his field of vision isn't there anymore, the doctor said. I'd tested this one day by holding up in front of my father's face a card on which I'd written, in the black capitals you'd use when teaching a small child to read, BASEBALL. Daddy scrutinized it for a few seconds and then said, in the annunciatory tone of a fourth-grader in a spelling bee, Ball! So on the day I brought the magazine with the *Odyssey* cruise article, I said, You know what? This print is so small, let me read it, and then I sat on the edge of his bed and read the article aloud to him. When I was finished, he looked up and said, nodding, That's just how it was.

Then his eye twitched grotesquely, and I realized he was trying to wink. But I still don't think Odysseus is much of a *hero!* he exclaimed.

During the last few days of March he was improving so dramatically that they decided he could leave the rehab unit and enter a nursing home. It was quite close to the house on Long Island and my mother would be able to drive there easily. It's a *nice* place, my mother kept saying, as if to convince herself, although she knew as well as I did that "nice" wasn't the point. We all knew what my father thought about nursing homes.

Just pull the plug and go have a round of baihhrs!

Things seemed stable. I decided to take a work-related trip abroad that I'd canceled and rescheduled several times since he'd had the stroke. Daddy says it's fine, my mother told me on the phone. It's only a few days. Ginny is flying in from California. Andrew has to work, but she's so good, she'll keep me company, and we'll visit him every day.

Good, I thought with relief. Ginny is clearheaded: her crisp efficiency and level good humor act on my mother like a tonic.

I went on my trip to Copenhagen. I called every day from my hotel. He's doing well in the *home,* my mother said a bit fretfully, although I could imagine what he thought of being in a home. I wheel him around, she said.

Then she said, I think maybe he looks a little depressed.

On the day I was to fly home, my father went back into the hospital. It's some kind of infection he picked up in the *home,* my mother said irritably on the phone when I called from the Copenhagen airport before boarding. They said they didn't notice anything, but I know him and I knew there was something wrong with him. He didn't know who I am, he was talking nonsense. So he had to go back to the hospital, they have to put him on intravenous antibiotics.

I was back at my house on campus fifteen hours later. The next morning I made my way to Long Island and met my mother and Ginny at the hospital. When we got to the room, my father was sleeping fitfully. A nurse was cradling his foot in her hands, and I briefly wondered whether there was something wrong with his legs; then I saw that she was cutting his toenails. There was something touching in the tender way she was performing this homely task. I couldn't take my eyes off his long, slender feet. They were white, as smooth and unmarked as a child's.

The nurse looked up at my mother, then at me. He's in and out, she said. Don't be upset if he doesn't recognize you. These UTIs mess them up in the head, but he's on antibiotics now and he'll be fine soon.

We sat there while he slept. A doctor came in and talked with the nurse, then with us. It's under control, he said cheerfully. He'll be out of here the day after tomorrow.

My father was tough.

Mother and Ginny went to get coffee. When they returned, he had woken up. He moved his lips thirstily and tried to say something, but as hard as I tried to listen, as close as I brought my ear to his lips, I couldn't make anything out. He was so weak that his words were just puffs of air. *Pah pah pah,* it sounded like.

The nurse gently said, He wants to have his mouth swabbed with ice water, I think. She handed me the swab. Do you want to do it?

I said, Yes.

I sat at the edge of the mattress and gave my father water. He smiled weakly. It wasn't for me; it was a private smile, from the sheer pleasure of having his thirst quenched. It was April 5: he'd been fed and hydrated intravenously since January 19, the day he had the stroke. My father hadn't had a drink of water in two and a half months.

He put his tongue out a bit, past his yellowed front teeth. I realized he was trying to say *Thanks*. I said, You're welcome, Daddy. He smiled again and I wondered if he even knew who I was.

Then he started whispering again, agitatedly. I leaned in. The nurse pressed a button, and the bed hummed and buzzed and inched upward.

This way you don't have to lie down to hear him. She smiled.

My father limply patted the bed, as if to thank it for moving. A door, he said, like a child trying his words for the first time. No, Daddy, this is a bed, I said. My eyes met Ginny's across the sheets. We were both thinking the same thing: he was out of it.

Nobody home.

I had to teach the next morning, Friday, so I couldn't stay over on Long Island. I'll be fine with Ginny, my mother said. Ginny looked at me levelly with her green eyes and said, briskly, I'll call you if anything happens.

I called a taxi and went to the train station. I took the train into Manhattan, and then waited for the train back upstate. By the time I got back to the house at the edge of the Bard campus it was after eleven. I realized how tiring it must have been for my father to take all these trains back and forth each week to get to the *Odyssey* seminar.

I trudged upstairs to my study to send out an e-mail with an update on Daddy's condition. As I walked into the room I tossed my book bag onto the daybed where he'd slept every week last spring. It was covered with a linen spread I'd bought in Malta, during the cruise. That was last summer, only nine months ago. A year ago this week we were sitting in a classroom discussing the second half of the *Odyssey*: Odysseus' *nostos*, the theme of *anagnorisis*, his reunions with his child and his wife.

I stood there blankly, looking at the book bag, at the bedspread, at the bed Daddy had built with his own hands. Then I said, aloud, Oh my God.

A *door*, he had said.

I looked at the clock: too late to ring Mother. Tomorrow, first thing, I'd call and tell her.

I was asleep when the phone rang. My iPhone said GINNY.

Hello? I said roughly.

Ginny said, Daniel.

I was half asleep. I looked at the phone. 7:14 A.M. Hi, I coughed. What's up?

In her clear voice Ginny said, It's your father.

Acknowledgments

This book owes a great deal to the support and advice of many friends over many years; they know who they are. I would, however, like to single out a few on whom I leaned especially heavily: first and foremost, as he always is, Stephen Simcock; Bill Blackstone ("DadB"), Lise Funderburg, Patti Hart, Richard Kramer, Donna Masini, Chip McGrath, Nancy Novogrod, Éric Trudel, and of course Jamie Romm and Tanya Marcuse and their wonderful children, who have been my family away from home for so many years now and given me sustenance in so many ways.

Jenny Strauss Clay and Froma Zeitlin continue, as this story makes clear, to teach me, for which I am grateful; I owe Jenny an extra debt of gratitude for her careful vetting of the finished manuscript. (And I fondly remember George Zeitlin, a great adventurer in his own right, with whom Froma and I shared many travels far and wide.) Jake Stortini and Jesse Feldmus and the gang at Murray's in Tivoli provided a delightful haven to write in for many months on end. Bob Gottlieb, who has never stopped living up to the jokey nickname I gave him more than twenty years ago—"Great One!"—made this book better than it would have been, as he has always done for me, through innumerable suggestions and many patient readings.

As for my other Bob, Bob Silvers, he insisted on reading the manuscript even as his health began to fail; in my last conversation with him he deflected all attention from himself, as he always did, eager only to talk about me and my work, which owes so much to his guidance. It grieves me more than I can say that he is not here to read this page.

I owe Lydia Wills a debt of thanks for helping to set in motion the long process of which this book is the end result, and for many other things over the years. Since 2012, Andrew Wylie and Kristina Moore have been as wise and staunch champions as any writer could hope for; their support for and belief in this project through its difficult gestation have meant a very great deal to me indeed. Jennifer Kurdyla at Knopf has been a saint of patience; her shrewd editorial suggestions, as well as help with innumerable practical tasks, have been wonderful to have. Above all there is my editor at Knopf, Robin Desser, to whom our magical *bashert* led me once again after many years. This story could not have been told without her compassion, patience, insight, affection, and above all her brilliant ability to see through to the heart of this book before its author was able to.

At the end, as at the beginning, there is family. I am fantastically lucky to have siblings and siblings-in-law as humane, smart, talented, patient, and humorous as mine are—Andrew Mendelsohn and Virginia Shea; Matt Mendelsohn and Maya Vastardis; Eric Mendelsohn; and Jennifer Mendelsohn and Greg Abel—and this book is in many ways the product of their cooperation and support, to say nothing of their sharp memories. If the reminiscences contained in it are, of necessity, mostly my own—and if they sometimes differ from theirs—it should be remembered that, as my father might put it, this arc is in fact just a small part of a great circle.

To Lily Knezevich I have never stopped being grateful for giving me the chance to have a family of my own. Our boys are the best thing in my life. Thank you, Peter; thank you, Thomas.

Above all I am grateful to my mother, Marlene Jaeger Mendelsohn, whose willingness to share her own memories, not all of them easy, and to allow me to write about them is a greater testament to the *homophrosynê* that joined her and my father over sixty-four years than any book could be.

Permissions Acknowledgments

DANIEL MENDELSOHN is a frequent contributor to *The New Yorker* and *The New York Review of Books*. His books include the international best seller *The Lost: A Search for Six of Six Million*, winner of the National Book Critics Circle Award and many other honors; a memoir, *The Elusive Embrace*, a *New York Times* Notable Book and a *Los Angeles Times* Best Book of the Year; a translation, with commentary, of the complete poems of C. P. Cavafy; and two collections of essays, *How Beautiful It Is and How Easily It Can Be Broken* and *Waiting for the Barbarians*. He teaches literature at Bard College.

A NOTE ON THE TYPE

The text of this book was set in Electra, a typeface designed
by W. A. Dwiggins (1880–1956). This face cannot be classified
as either modern or old style. It is not based on any historical
model, nor does it echo any particular period or style. It avoids
the extreme contrasts between thick and thin elements that
mark most modern faces, and it attempts to give a feeling of
fluidity, power, and speed.

Typeset by Scribe,
Philadelphia, Pennsylvania

Printed and bound by Berryville Graphics,
Berryville, Virginia

Designed by Cassandra J. Pappas